SMILE
Chin Up!

SMILE
Chin Up!

MEMOIRS OF AN
OREGON CHEERLEADER

CORINE LEWIS

DALLAS, TEXAS

Higgins Publishing. All rights reserved. Corine Lewis, **SMILE, *Chin Up*!** *Memoirs of an Oregon Cheerleader*

All rights reserved. No part of this book may be reproduced or transmitted in any form or by any means, electronic or mechanical, including photocopying, recording, or by any information storage and retrieval system, without permission in writing from the copyright owner. The views expressed in this work are solely those of the author and do not necessarily reflect the views of the publisher, and the publisher hereby disclaims any responsibility for them.

THE HOLY BIBLE, NEW INTERNATIONAL VERSION®, NIV® Copyright © 1973, 1978, 1984, 2011 by Biblica, Inc.™ Used by permission. All rights reserved worldwide.

Higgins Publishing supports the rights to free expression and the value of copyright. The purpose of copyright is to encourage writers and artists to produce creative works that enrich our values. The scanning, uploading, and distribution of this book without the express permission of the publisher is a theft of intellectual property. If you would like permission to use material from this book (other than for review purposes), please contact permissions@higginspublishing.com. Thank you for your support of copyright law.

Higgins Publishing | higginspublishing.com - The publisher is not responsible for websites (or their content) that are not owned by the publisher. Higgins Publishing is committed to excellence in the publishing industry. The company reflects the philosophy established by the founder, based on Psalm 68:11, "The Lord gave the word, and great was the company of those who published it."

Library of Congress Control Number: 2024900156 September 2024
p. cm. 484 – Includes Appendix, Glossary, References & Index
Lewis, Corine – SMILE, ***Chin Up***! *Memoirs of an Oregon Cheerleader*

ISBN# 978-1-941580-85-1 (Softcover) * ISBN# 978-1-941580-72-1 (Hardcover)
ISBN# 978-1-941580-83-7 (Audio Book) * ISBN# 978-1-941580-73-8 (E-Book)

BIO032000   BIOGRAPHY & AUTOBIOGRAPHY / Social Activists
BIO026000   BIOGRAPHY & AUTOBIOGRAPHY / Memoirs
BIO016000   BIOGRAPHY & AUTOBIOGRAPHY / Sports

Our books may be purchased in bulk for promotional, educational, fundraising or business use. Please contact your local bookseller or Higgins Publishing Sales Department at, sales@higginspublishing.com.

Cover Photo: Jeremy Bright

First Edition: September 2024 * First International Edition September 2024

Printed in the State or Province indicated on the last page, or dust jacket.

*To my children, Haley and Jaden.
Without your support and encouragement,
I could not have written this book.
Thank you to my Lord and Savior Jesus Christ
for giving me the strength to endure.*

SMILE
Chin Up!

March 1990: **SMILE,** ***Chin Up**! Look them in the eye.*
Exude energy and grace, no one will know.
Little did I know, this would be my personal mantra
for the next thirty years of my life.

Author's Note

SMILE, *Chin Up!* reflects my perspective and best recollections of the people and events that helped shape my journey. Throughout the book, I have changed the names of specific individuals to protect their identity and the privacy of their families. I have changed the identity of some of the less forgiving characters because the book is not about retribution but empowerment. I only look back in order to go forward with strength and determination.

This memoir is intended to be a "hope to" and not a "how to" book.

I was raped as a teenager and later underwent a decade of domestic abuse. I am a survivor, one who refused to remain a victim. I have chosen to speak out at this moment in hopes of encouraging other survivors and those who want to drive out the scourge of violence against women. My goal is to give hope, inspiration, and courage; to help other survivors stay safe, feel empowered, and transform their lives.

Throughout the book, I offer some suggestions and words of wisdom, but I am not a trained psychologist or psychiatrist, teacher or preacher; I am simply a survivor, a single mom, a woman who cares about other survivors and other mothers. I hope my storybook resonates with people of goodwill everywhere and serves as a powerful motivator for change.

In the Battle of Okinawa, U.S. Private Desmond Doss lowered seventy-five injured men down the side of a four-hundred-foot cliff and single-handedly saved their lives. After securing each man, Private Doss would say out loud, "Lord, help me get one more." Doss repeated this plea seventy-five times, and seventy-five times he secured a man, including three injured Japanese soldiers. This is the reason I wrote this book. I figured that if Private Desmond Doss can single-handedly save seventy-five lives in the midst of a combat zone, I too can fight to save victims of abuse, one life at a time. "Lord, help me get one more."

Contents

Author's Note ix
Prologue 15
Part One Cheerleading Is My Life 19
   Chapter One *My New Normal* 21
   Chapter Two *Friday Night Lights* 25
   Chapter Three *The Hula Bowl* 31
   Chapter Four *Making the Grade* 37
   Chapter Five *Battle of the Bands* 41
   Chapter Six *Sexual Assault and My New Normal* 45
   Chapter Seven *Lightning Strikes Twice* 51
   Chapter Eight *It Hurt so Bad* 57
   Chapter Nine *Masters of Impunity* 61
   Chapter Ten *Rip City* 65
Part Two Surviving Abuse 69
   Chapter Eleven *The Moment of Truth* 71
   Chapter Twelve *Mice* 75
   Chapter Thirteen *Crossing the Rubicon* 79
   Chapter Fourteen *Trial of the Century* 81
   Chapter Fifteen *We are Family* 85
   Chapter Sixteen *Married to the Enemy* 87
   Chapter Seventeen *Wine and Roses* 91
   Chapter Eighteen *Forever a Queen* 97

Chapter Nineteen *The Aftermath* 103

Chapter Twenty *Down but Not Out* 107

Chapter Twenty-One *The Face of Evil* 111

Chapter Twenty-Two *Bringing Down the House* 115

Chapter Twenty-Three *The Lady Doth Protest Too Much.* 119

Chapter Twenty-Four *A Little Reminiscing* 123

Chapter Twenty-Five *At Home with the Taliba*n 127

Part Three Renavigating **133**

Chapter Twenty-Six *On the Road Again* 135

Chapter Twenty-Seven *A Sordid Affair* 143

Chapter Twenty-Eight *Gotham's Reckoning* 149

Chapter Twenty-Nine *Showtime at the Apollo* 159

Chapter Thirty *Let the Church Say Amen* 165

Chapter Thirty-One *Wakeup Call* 171

Chapter Thirty-Two *Pandora's Box* 181

Chapter Thirty-Three *Cheerleaders are Heroes Too!* 187

Chapter Thirty-Four *The Making of an Oregon Cheerleader* 191

Chapter Thirty-Five *The Night Stalker* 199

Part Four The Awakening **209**

Chapter Thirty-Six *Déjà vu* 211

Chapter Thirty-Seven *Red Flags and Risk Factors* 225

Chapter Thirty-Eight *I'm Just not that Cool!* 233

Chapter Thirty-Nine *My First Love* 241

Chapter Forty *Preseason* 249

Chapter Forty-One *Rule of Thumb* 259

Chapter Forty-Two *Destination Weddings* 265

Chapter Forty-Three *I Broke the Internet?* 271

Part Five Empowerment **275**
   Chapter Forty-Four *Fly the Friendly Skies* 277
   Chapter Forty-Five *The Sound of Music* 285
   Chapter Forty-Six *The Tower of Babel* 293
   Chapter Forty-Seven *Moonshot to Asia* 301
   Chapter Forty-Eight *The Lassiter Effect* 305
   Chapter Forty-Nine *Strangers in the Night* 309
   Chapter Fifty *Spotters Up* 315
   Chapter Fifty-One *An Intervention* 325
   Chapter Fifty-Two *On Bended Knee* 329
   Chapter Fifty-Three *The Wedding Crashers* 337
   Chapter Fifty-Four *My Friend's Enemy is My Friend* 345

Part Six *Finding My Purpose* **349**
   Chapter Fifty-Five *The Unvirtuous Cycle of Abuse* 351
   Chapter Fifty-Six *Sex Education* 357
   Chapter Fifty-Seven *What Men Can Do* 361
   Chapter Fifty-Eight *Uncle Sam Wants You!* 365
   Chapter Fifty-Nine *I've Got Your Back* 371
   Chapter Sixty *Romeo and Juliet* 375
   Chapter Sixty-One *Finding My Purpose* 379
   Chapter Sixty-Two *The CL Way* 383
   Chapter Sixty-Three *Audrie and Daisy* 387
   Chapter Sixty-Four *Roll the Credits* 391

Epilogue **395**
Acknowledgments **437**
Appendix **443**
Glossary **445**

About The Author	453
More from the Author	455
References	459
Index	469

Prologue

As the saying goes, everyone needs someone. If God only blesses you with one good friend, you are truly blessed indeed. Becca has been that special someone in my life. When I told her I was writing a book, she was eager to contribute her thoughts and perspective on our relationship. The letter below is her thoughts.

To the readers of this memoir:
I first met Corine at a University of Oregon football game, where I volunteered with my dad for his 20-30 club in Eugene, Oregon. Active 20-30 International is an international organization that encourages community involvement and helps develop leadership skills in younger adults. As a dancer from birth, I was captivated by Corine's cheerleading squad; the choreography precision; the intricate dance moves; unique, creative, profound. Her style was absolutely adorable, or as the kids say, "fire." Her choice of music was electric; the energy was infectious. From that moment on, I was intrigued, my quest to become a University of Oregon Cheerleader was unwavering.

My first year at the University of Oregon, I enrolled into the family and human services program, where I worked with abused women and children, as well as an assistant parole officer working closely with domestic violence abusers. Outside of class, I spent most of my waking hours with the cheerleading squad and my two coaches, Corine and her mom Laraine. As the months passed, Corine and I developed a close bond. She became my older sister, and Laraine became my mother away from home. Laraine was not your typical head coach. She was the Mama Duck. She had an eagle's eye, if ever there was one. Nothing got past her. She led our cheerleading team like a special forces unit but always professional, always loving. I had the utmost respect for her as both a head coach and a squadron leader. Similarly, my relationship with Corine grew from cheerleader and coach into little sister big sister.

Corine was the assistant coach and choreographer. She was lightning in a bottle, known for her intricate dance moves, choreography, charisma, and outgoing personality. She was well known within the community, not only for her talent but as a mentor and role model to the hundreds of cheerleaders who passed through over the years. Corine displayed poise and inner beauty; she could light up a room with her sparkling blue eyes. If that didn't get your attention, Corine was absolutely hilarious. She had a great sense of humor and an entrepreneurial, can-do spirit. She pushed us to be the best that we could be, always offering words of encouragement, always harassing us out of an early morning sleep. Corine and Laraine made cheerleading fun. They were my coaches but also my extended family.

From my curriculum at Oregon, work with abused women and children at "Women's Space," a non-profit that provides a safe space for victims of domestic violence, and as an assistant to a city of Eugene parole officer focused on domestic violence abusers, I became intimately familiar with the signs of domestic violence and child abuse. I started to notice some signs in Corine and her four-year-old daughter Haley. This once completely responsible, electric coach and choreographer started showing up late for meetings and practices, and she became remarkably clumsy. The bruises were always the result of a slip and fall or running into a wall. Mentally, she wasn't herself.

Of course, Corine tried to cover her bruises with makeup. However, all the signs were there and the symptoms obvious. Her demeanor changed from being incredibly bubbly and confident to being deeply introverted and repressed. Corine was less confident, fallen. I knew in my gut this was not the result of slip and falls but of something more sinister. When I inquired about her husband, she was always evasive, steering the conversation in another direction. At times, I could see the fear on her face. I remember her husband showed up on one occasion, and I saw a complete change in this once confident, vibrant, outgoing, brilliant woman. She was a shell of herself, someone unrecognizable. Her demeanor completely changed, becoming scared, childlike. She stepped out of her leadership role into a position of submission, even questioning her own *coaching abilities. There was a nervousness about her in his presence. There were always excuses about his demeanor and rudeness, in the hope of avoiding a conflict in front of the cheer squad.*

I began to confront her about my observations. At first, she denied everything; she refused to talk or would change the subject. However, sometime later, she completely opened up and shared with me what was truly going on at home. Because of my experience and work, I felt a special obligation. It was painful to hear, painful to witness. I remember the complete transformation, the fear, the insecurity. I also remember her five-year-old daughter telling me how Daddy yells at Mommy, and how she felt scared when that happened. Unfortunately, one of the byproducts of domestic violence is to create a mentally and emotionally unstable environment for children. I observed this in Haley, a sweet and loving child.

I am so very proud of Corine for her strength, her renewal, and her ability to face her fears and push beyond victimhood. Corine is a survivor, but much more than that; she's an overcomer. She has taken the time to share her journey in order to help millions of other women and families deal with the emotional stains of physical and mental abuse. The good news is there's a way to unlock the code of abuse. You must realize that your abuser has no power over your freedom or future or God-given potential. I am deeply proud to call Corine a mentor, friend, and sister. I love her with all my heart. She didn't write this book for herself but for women everywhere who want to stand up but may be questioning whether they are good enough, strong enough, beautiful, or worthy.

The answer is YES YOU ARE!

Sincerely,

Rebecca Mora

Part One
Cheerleading Is My Life

Chapter One
My New Normal

Our squad got back to the hotel, and we started making plans to eat and hang out. Cheerleaders bunked two to a room. On the road, I always roomed with the same girl, Erin. She was my ride or die, more like a sister than a teammate. We always had fun. Erin was a year older. She knew everyone, and people loved her. After we had our team dinner, I decided to lay low and stay in the room. I was bummed out; my boyfriend was gone. Erin decided to hang out with the other cheerleaders and athletes. She didn't intend to stay long, so I flipped the bolt lock on the door and said, "See you later, girlfriend."

The door was slightly ajar, resting on the bolt lock. I got ready for bed, turned on the television, and turned off the lights. After about thirty minutes, there was a knock at the door. I said, "Come in," and in an instant, a six foot seven two-hundred-and-ninety-pound basketball player walks in with a bottle of Old English. I didn't know him personally, but I knew that he was one of the players in the tournament. He asked to use the bathroom and I mumbled something like, "Okay." I could hear people laughing and talking outside, so I didn't suspect anything.

A couple minutes later, the guy came out, and we exchanged niceties. I asked him to take the key to my roommate and watched him grab it off the credenza. As he went toward the door, a wall obstructed my view. I heard the door open and shut, then I turned off the television and began to turn over.

Suddenly, I felt a huge weight on my body. It was pitch black, and I struggled to breathe. It took me a moment to realize what was happening. The guy landed on top of me like a huge sandbag. I tried to yell, but nothing came out. I could barely breathe. He was so heavy, bearing down against my hundred and five-pound frame. I remember the smell of beer on his breath. His mouth was parked against my cheek. His knees pinned between my legs. His hands restrained my arms overhead. The deep grumble of his voice and slurred speech still play in my mind. "Stop fighting me, you know you want this." "Come on, relax, I won't tell anyone." He let up to reposition himself, and I tried to scream, but still, nothing came out. I had no voice. I was so afraid. It was like a bad dream. I was desperate, gasping for air, trying to catch my breath.

I had on my boyfriend's button-down shirt and a pair of underwear. The perpetrator ripped off my shirt; I could hear the buttons fly. He ripped off my panties, and I was terrified. He grabbed my face, forcefully squeezing my jaw. He tried to kiss me, but I refused. He became more agitated and forceful. The smell of beer rang in my nose, and he placed his hand over my mouth and pressed my head deep into the mattress. I was trying to grab his wrist and pull his hand away, but the more I fought the harder he pressed. He began kissing me, and I felt so defeated, so scared, tears rolling down my cheeks. The taste of beer reverberated in my mouth. It was repulsive. To this day, I hate beer. He ramped up the tension, started cursing and calling me names, making it clear that he was going to have his way with me or someone was going to get hurt. All I could think of was who could help me.

Suddenly, he began the sexual assault. It was violent and ferocious! The more I resisted, the more violent he became. He threw me around like a rag doll, then pinned me down in different positions; his elbows and knees digging into my flesh. He was so violent and aggressive. He raped me for what seemed like forever, forcing me to endure the pain. Rape is a war crime, and anybody who's ever been raped knows why. Once he was finished, I got up

CHAPTER ONE: MY NEW NORMAL

and went to the bathroom. He stood right behind me, and for the first time, I saw his face. I was standing there naked, eye makeup running down my face. I had welts and dark red marks all over my body. As he got dressed, he laughed and taunted me. He was proud of himself, as if he'd scored the winning basket. I heard a loud knock on the door. My roommate was trying to get in.

Before I opened the door, he warned me, "Who are they going to believe, you or an NBA prospect?" In that moment, he took away all of my power. He took my innocence and a part of my soul. Right then, my life would be forever changed. I went from being a vivacious, super diehard cheerleader to a disillusioned teenaged victim. As I opened the door, Erin saw the look on my face. She looked at him with piercing eyes. I think she knew. She was stunned and confused. My attacker walked out like the prince of darkness. Erin hesitantly said, "Bye, Mark." That was the first time I heard his name. They had been friends since high school. If she hadn't said his name, I might never have known.

The following morning, I looked in the mirror and didn't recognize the person I saw. My arms and legs were bruised everywhere. My face was badly bruised around the jawline. My eyes were puffy from crying. I remember getting in the shower and feeling the sting of the soap. The trauma caused tears and abrasions in my intimate parts. Drying off was its own ordeal. The towel felt like sandpaper.

I got glammed up for the game as normal, but this was a new normal.

Chapter Two
Friday Night Lights

I grew up in Centralia, Washington in the 1970s. It was like living in the movie *Footloose*; peaceful, homogenous, idyllic, classic small-town Americana. My parents began dating in their teens. They got engaged after Mom's senior prom and were married right after her high school graduation. In 1964, my dad landed the quarterback position at Central Washington University as a freshman. My brother Rick was born a few years later. They lived in Ellensburg Washington until Dad graduated with his degree in teaching. After a brief stint as the head football coach at Elma High School, Dad became the head football coach at my parents' alma mater, Centralia High School (CHS) in Centralia Washington. Dad doubled as head coach and a teacher, while my mom became the head cheerleading and dance coach and doubled as a teacher's assistant. I was born a few years later in 1971.

My family was unique in that my paternal and maternal grandparents were the best of friends. They did almost everything together, well beyond normal family functions. I was fortunate to grow up in Centralia where both sides of my family were well known and respected. It was a world filled with love and happiness. I grew up accompanied by all of my aunts, uncles, grandparents, and even great-grandparents. My maternal cousins were more like my siblings. In fact, by the time I attended kindergarten, we all lived on the same street: Bengal Court. The street was named after the Centralia "Tigers." The whole town was rabid fans.

We had our own version of "Friday Night Lights." My grandpa, JC Gibson, my mom's dad, owned a real estate development company. He wanted everyone together and set aside the requisite lots for our families to build on. So, there we were, in the mid-1970s, all on Bengal Court, snuggled together like a clan of tigers huddled in cold weather… and they say that football is king in Texas.

From time memorial, my brother Rick was my hero and protector. He took me everywhere and always made sure I was included, even when his cool friends were at the house. He was always loving, kind, and above all hilarious! Rick would make every situation fun, whether we were traveling as a family or lounging around the television. A big part of my character was shaped by watching my big brother. Rick was also a hard worker and a bit of an overachiever. Things seemed to come easy for him, but later I realized he just didn't accept failure as an option. He was a stellar athlete in multiple sports, had a 4.0 grade point average, and was elected student body president of Willamette High School. Later, Rick became the starting quarterback at Southern Oregon State College and earned his master's degree in communications. His senior year, Rick was voted league MVP. I prided myself on being his little sister. For us, family and football were everything.

My childhood was a fairytale. We had a white picket fence, and every Friday night was a spectacle. We played to win. Dad was Billy Bob Thornton, and I was Morgan Farris.

World Expo 86: In 1986, I was a freshman at Willamette High School. Although I was immersed in dance and cheerleading, I was also fascinated with drums. One of my idols growing up was the legendary percussionist Sheila E. I started playing the drums in sixth grade while attending Cascade Middle School and played through high school graduation. I used to practice in the garage,

Chapter Two: Friday Night Lights

playing everything—Prince, Morris Day and the Time, and Sheila E, at least as much as the family could stand. I would blast the music and drum various cadences, all the time pretending that I was Sheila E. I believed that if you could dream it, you could achieve it! The irony is that I never met my idol, but many years later my daughter Haley did! Haley became a cheerleader for the San Francisco Forty-Niners. One day, she accompanied her roommate to Oakland to see her aunt. It turned out that her aunt was Sheila E! I nearly jumped out of my skin.

We had an amazing marching band at WHS, but it was the drumline that stole the show! My drum leaders, Eric Jones and Darbey Bud, were insanely talented and could play every percussion instrument to perfection. I was in awe of them both. They were shy, extremely soft spoken, and often misunderstood because of their hard rock style and appearance. But they were the motivational force behind the drumline and the epitome of never judge a book by its cover. Under their tutelage, I grew as a drummer by leaps and bounds. These guys gave me the best years of my percussionist life. One day, during band rehearsal, we were informed that we would be playing at Expo 86 in Vancouver, British Columbia. Expo 86 was the world's fair. The theme that year was, "Transportation and Communication." The motto was, "World in motion-World in touch." Over twenty-two million people attended the Expo from May through October. It was a big deal for us to travel to Vancouver for the weekend, especially with the prospect of playing for the Prince and Princess of Wales. I was ecstatic!

This was my first trip to Canada but certainly not the last. Throughout my life, I have been fortunate to perform as a cheerleader in Edmonton, travel for television production and business ventures throughout the Maritimes and enjoy the splendor of Canada's beauty as a flight attendant. I love Canadians, and I look forward to visiting their magnificent country again.

On this occasion, the entire WHS band traveled by charter bus from Eugene to Vancouver. There was a huge mix of personalities in the band, from all different walks of life, so it never felt cliquish. Most of us didn't associate with one another outside of band, but there was an unspoken understanding: in Vancouver, the Willamette Marching Band would represent the city of Eugene, the state of Oregon, and the USA with style and class.

During the day of our performance, we lived up to our pledge, mostly, with one bit of a surprise. We spent an hour dying the hair of our two most notorious drummers. We used all the colors of the rainbow. These guys looked fierce, and a little scary, like Kiss or Mötley Crüe, without the drugs and sex. The band director saw them and was furious. But we performed sensationally and knocked the ball out of the park. We truly represented. Excellence tends to calm the nerves of an irate band director. And things went from good to great when the Prince and Princess of Wales showed up and made the whole experience more memorable. It was a remarkable opportunity. Chalk up another for the coach's daughter!

Flashback: In May 1983, Diane Downs shot and killed her daughter and wounded her two other children on a secluded road outside of Springfield, which is just outside Eugene. Initially, Diane blamed the death on a carjacker, leading to a composite sketch of the supposed killer. I remember seeing his menacing face in the Register Guard newspaper. The vision stayed in my mind. The supposed killer was still at large, making the situation all the more frightening. This went on for nine months, until Diane Downs was convicted by one of her surviving children; they told the authorities the gruesome story, and Diane was sentenced to life in prison, plus fifty years. She successfully escaped prison in 1987 and was recaptured. There was a book and made for TV movie about Diane Downs entitled "Small Sacrifices."

I relate this story to make several points: first, domestic violence is not new. It's not related to any political party or public policy issue. It's a scourge that affects every part of the country and every social class. Secondly, as a country, there is a huge stigma attached to mental health. This keeps people from seeking the help that they need, which all too often results in tragedy. Third, Springfield is just a stone's throw away from Eugene. The story was huge and hit really close to home. It had a big impact on the community. Little did I know at the time, but I would have my own struggle with domestic violence down the road.

Chapter Three
The Hula Bowl

God gives each of us a portfolio of gifts. And when He was handing out the gift of dance choreography, I was near the front of the line. From the time I was in kindergarten, I was singing and dancing. I would see a musical on television such as *The Wizard of Oz* or *Guys and Dolls* and try to mimic the routines. I studied performers and dancers of all genres. I loved the *Solid Gold Dancers* and watched variety shows like *Donnie and Marie* or *Carol Burnett* every chance I got. I was hooked, sprung, addicted; however, you want to say it, I loved to dance.

In 1976, I remember walking into the football stadium at Centralia High School with pom poms in hand. It was just a typical day at the track: cheerleading practice with Mom's high school squad. I watched as the big girls practiced their moves on the track, while my dad rallied his football team on the field. How cliché: my mother the head coach of the cheerleading and dance teams; my dad the head coach of the football team. "Hello, Mrs. Cleaver. Hello, Mr. Cleaver." Idyllic! If I close my eyes, I can still hear the sound of coaches yelling, blowing their whistles, and metal cleats in the locker room. This was my life. Starting practice with my mom and her cheerleading squad and ending the day with Dad in the coach's office. I was always in tow, at practice sessions, games, or pep rallies. Aside from that, my parents had me in dance classes of every sort: tap, jazz, and ballet. I couldn't get enough. I loved learning new steps and performing new routines. Lessons, practice sessions, dance recitals, oh my.

In addition to dance, I was on a *Pop Warner Cheerleading Squad* for the Lumberman football team. My big brother Rick was the quarterback. Like father like son. Like mother like daughter.

My road to cheerleader began at age five. My love for football started even earlier.

One night, my dream came true. I was six years old, and a tiny Tigerette. I got my first big break when I had the opportunity to perform at the halftime of a basketball game with the CHS varsity cheerleading squad. The gym was packed, and all eyes were on us. We nailed the routine, and the crowd went wild. I felt a certain tingling down my spine, and, at that moment, I knew exactly who I wanted to be—a dancer, a performer, an entertainer. I felt a passion like never before.

In 1981, my family moved to Eugene, Oregon. My dad got a teaching position and became the head football coach at Willamette High School (WHS), and my mom became a teacher's assistant and the head cheerleading and dance coach. I was in fifth grade.

Eugene was the big city, and home of the University of Oregon Ducks. The city has a natural beauty and is known for offering great outdoor recreational sports, especially cycling, water sports, and running trails. In the 80s and 90s, virtually all aspects of social life in Eugene seemed to center around the University of Oregon. The city was affectionately known as "Track City U.S.A.," or "NIKE Town."

Everyone supported the Oregon Ducks, regardless of their alma mater, the alma mater of their kids, or whatever else was going on. Hayward Field, the home of John Belushi's Animal House, was the main attraction. The University was famous for its track and field athletes, producing such world class phenoms as Steve Prefontaine, Mary Decker Slaney, and Albero Salizar. The

Chapter Three: The Hula Bowl

team was headed by legendary Coach Bill Bowerman, one of the cofounders of Nike Corporation, along with Phil Knight. As the story is told, Coach Bowerman matted a rubber sole to a waffle iron in his garage and created a special purpose, lightweight, running shoe. Coach Bowerman gave the shoe to Prefontaine, who then won the Olympic trails. Sometime later, Nike Corporation was formed, and the rest, as they say, is history.

Eugene felt easy, low key. I lived in a nice area, near the high school, in a typical middle class, three-bedroom home. I can't ever really remember experiencing fear or concern for my safety. Life was fairly drama free, although there were those two little incidents…

… At school, most of my teachers said that I talked too much, and my grades reflected it. As an aside, I've met a lot of strong female leaders over the years, and almost all of them had the same problem. Hmm? I wonder what that's about. In any event, my talking got so bad that my dad promised to buy me a bike if I put a lid on it. I did, and he did. Then, one day, I was getting ice cream from Garibaldi's parlor with my brother. We stepped out of the shop, and my Mongoose dirt bike was gone. Stolen! I was so mad; I was fighting mad. I couldn't see straight for days. I can't remember whether Rick was crying along with me or laughing in my face. He had never seen me so mad. Sixty pounds of pure fury. Madder than Harley Quinn out on a stroll. After that, I went to back to talking too much…

…On another occasion, during my senior year in high school, I had a beautiful red Fiero with a banging sound system. It was a Sony, "the one and only." The sound system had a detachable face. The quality was amazing, and I did my best singing in that car. Unfortunately, it was short lived. One day, I came out of the house and my beautiful red Fiero had been broken into; the stereo system was stolen, right in front of our house, in our driveway. Again, I was so mad that I wanted to "Will Smith" somebody.

Other than that, Eugene was easy, breezy. After school, I would walk across the field from Malabon Elementary to Willamette High School, where I would meet my mom in the main gym as she started practice with the cheerleading squad. One day at practice, Mom gave me news that would forever solidify my path in the world of cheer and dance. She told me that I was going to choreograph the WHS dance routine at the state competition! Are you kidding me? Am I dreaming? I was only ten, but an unexpected sensation tingled down my spine. Choreography ran in my veins; it was part of my DNA. I didn't think twice about my age. It made perfect sense. My body breathed eight counts and formations. This was exactly what I was made for.

Nevertheless, it was a big "frickin'" deal. It was my first big break at choreographing live bodies in live competition. Yes, I'll do it. Mom and I held dance practice in the gym five days a week. Reveille was six-thirty a.m. I taught the routine; Mom did the coaching. At the state competition, we played some Pat Benatar, Blondie, and Queen's "Another One Bites the Dust." We did a little sassy, jazzy, high-energy routine and nailed it. Willamette High brought the house down; the crowd went crazy. And we won state. This was the first of many dance and cheer state titles that we would win together.

My senior year in high school, 1989, life was a bit surreal. Dad was my Health and Physical Education teacher, Mom was my head cheerleading coach, and Rick was in his senior year of college and the starting quarterback on the football team. Not much had changed over the last thirteen years. I started cheerleading practice right after school and ended my night on the football field with

Chapter Three: The Hula Bowl

Dad. You could always find me in the locker room, weight room, or coach's office. "Where's Corine"? Just look for her dad.

It was my final year as the team captain of the multi-year reigning state championship cheerleading team. The experience of collaborating with my mother was a different type of special. In the three preceding years, I had made the high school dance team as a freshman, became captain of the Junior Varsity squad my sophomore year, and was voted captain of the Varsity squad my junior and senior years. With numerous trophies and state champion titles on the shelves, it was time to level up. I was honored to be selected as a member of the Hula Bowl All-Stars squad in Honolulu. The team was coached by Jerry Whaley, the University of Hawaii head cheerleading coach. A hundred of the best cheerleaders from all around the country performed in this prestigious bowl game. The game was nationally televised, and we were the halftime entertainment, along with The Beach Boys. During the week, I was so excited, all I could think about was what comes next. What could I do to elevate myself and my cheerleading career?

I remember watching the University of Hawaii cheerleading squad, thinking, *That could be me on one of those pyramids. That could be me doing elite stunts and dancing on the sidelines.* Then, like a dream come true, I felt a tap on my shoulder. I turned around to find Jerry Whaley. He popped the question, "How would you like to be an instructor for my summer camps?" It was like a proposal for marriage. Are you kidding me? Is this really happening? I blurted out a resounding YES without even taking a breath. Weeks later, I would find myself teaching high school and collegiate cheerleading camps for power cheerleading. I got the coaching bug, and at seventeen, it was the beginning of my professional instructing career.

High school graduation was approaching, and I had to make some important decisions. Following my heart was the easy part. I was determined to be a division 1 collegiate cheerleader.

I remember the day like it was yesterday, walking out of my bedroom and down the hall toward the living room. Dad was in his chair and Mom was sitting in front of the fireplace. I blurted it out loud, as I always do, "I need to tell you guys something."

Dad muted the remote and Mom said, "What's up?"

I took one big breath and announced, "I'm trying out for the Oregon Rally Squad." That's what the Ducks called the cheerleading squad back in the day.

There was a brief silence, then my dad in his coaching voice said, "Good for you!"

I don't know why I expected to hear something different. The goal was huge. No freshman had ever made the squad. But the sky was the limit in my family. I had the tryout packet in hand and fifteen years of preparation.

Within a few weeks, my biggest challenge awaited.

Chapter Four
Making the Grade

In April of 1989, two weeks before my eighteenth birthday, I pulled up to Macarthur Court at the University of Oregon. I parked my red Fiero and put my game face on. It was day one of cheerleading tryouts. I remember looking out the window and seeing all these beautiful girls talking and laughing. They were in groups of two or three, moving together like a military procession, all on a mission. It was the first time I felt out of place. For the first time in years, I wasn't the leader. I was a rookie, out trying to earn my stripes. For a moment, I panicked. I felt so alone. I seriously thought about starting the car and going home. But I pulled down the visor and looked at myself in the mirror, remembering all the reasons why I belonged: preparation, state championships, passion, and talent.

I walked into the arena, and everything seemed so massive. The doors, hallways, concession stands, even the "Pit," the nickname of the basketball floor. Girls in groups were pinning numbers on each other at a long registration table, and out of nowhere, I was greeted by a breathtakingly beautiful woman with long blonde hair down to her waist. She smiled and said, "Welcome, Corine!" My heart started fluttering. It was Kasey Brooks! She was a former Oregon cheerleader and one of the Ducks' cheerleading coaches. Kasey was a legend. She had been judging me for years at all of the high school competitions. The fact that she remembered my name was a shot of pure adrenalin. At that moment, I came alive, and I got myself ready. Bring it on, pom pom girls! It was showtime! It was about to get cracking!

The first round of tryouts involved learning a tough dance routine. We had about twenty minutes to practice, then we had to perform. The first round of cuts were made, and I advanced to round two.

Day two of tryouts was my favorite. It involved an interview with the panel of judges followed by your own choreographed routine. I remember sitting across from the judges and, to my surprise, the head football coach, Rich Brooks, was sitting directly in front of me! The head cheerleading coach, Mike Maulding, asked the first question. I was in awe of the panel. The best of the best, and I had their undivided attention. I felt great after the interview, and I was ready to show off my routine. *Boom! Bang! Bong!* I nailed the routine, and the judges were all smiles.

All the auditions were conducted, the cuts were made, and after another harrowing day, I advanced to round three.

Day three was the toughest test I had ever encountered in cheerleading. We had to learn a grueling, extremely advanced dance routine with only an hour to practice. Then, they called it a day and we had to return the next day for finals.

Most of the other contestants were either sorority girls or knew one other from campus. I was the only incoming freshman left in the competition, and I didn't know anyone. I had to go home and practice alone.

The other contestants all got together the next morning for one last practice. The pressure felt overwhelming, and I found myself in uncharted waters. I had no choice but to pull it together.

On the day of finals, I felt cautiously optimistic. The performances occurred in random order. After tryouts were complete, the judges went behind closed doors to deliberate and select the 1989-90 University of Oregon Rally Squad. Seconds

Chapter Four: Making the Grade

seemed like minutes; minutes seemed like hours. Then, finally, after an hour of waiting, Mike Maulding and Kasey Brooks re-entered the gym with paper in hand. "If we call your number, then you made the squad." That's all I remember hearing; it was as if time had stopped. There would be eight numbers called for the girls and four for the guys. A few numbers in, and I got the call. I couldn't believe what I heard.

I was a University of Oregon cheerleader!

I felt like the number one pick in the NFL draft. I was so excited. I felt larger than life.

Later, I was told that I was the first incoming freshman to ever make the squad. What I wasn't told was that in eleven short months, my life would change again… forever.

Chapter Five
Battle of the Bands

December 1989 closed out the year with a game called the "Civil War." The University of Oregon versus Oregon State. It was always the last conference game of the football season. The clock was ticking down. Finally, the time read zero. The game was over. The University of Oregon won 30-21. Which meant that the Ducks were going to the Independence Bowl! The crowd went crazy! It was the first time in years that the Ducks football team had a winning season. It was the first bowl game we were going to appear in since 1963. A twenty-six-year drought. That was like a hundred Mohave desserts. I couldn't wait. We were Bowl-bound to Shreveport, Louisiana.

We arrived in Shreveport like the Laker Girls, looking to spend money. This was going to be our town for the week. We were so excited. I can't think of a single moment I wasn't laughing or smiling. We performed to perfection at every event, but the one that stood out most was the battle of the bands. That year we were playing against Tulsa. The battle of the bands featured a pre-game competition between each team's marching band and cheerleaders. The cheerleading style in the Pacific 10 Conference was categorically different than cheerleading in the rest of country. Most of the collegiate squads at the time were extremely conservative, with bows and ponytails in their hair. We were collegiate too, but our flare was all Dallas Cowboys. We were glamorous, our routines were sharp and sassy—pure entertainment. Part "Moulin Rouge" part "Pussycat Dolls."

We faced off reminiscent of the movie *You Got Served*. The two teams were about twenty feet apart. Hundreds of fans encircled the squads to watch and show allegiance.

Tulsa started first.

Their band was fabulous, and the cheerleaders were tossed in the air like a circus act. The Tulsa fans went wild, and truth be told, we were impressed, too!

We were next.

Our band was phenomenal, and our drum line would make your jaw drop. The lead drummer clicked his drumsticks, the band major raised his hands, then our captain, Stephanie, yelled, "Five, six, seven, eight!" And it was on! Our band belted out the song "All right now" by the English rock band Free.

> Whoa-oh-oh-oh-woah
> There she stood in the street
> Smilin' from her head to her feet;
>
> I said, "Hey, what is this?
> Now maybe, baby,
> Maybe she's in need of a kiss."
>
> I said, "Hey, what's your name?
> Maybe we can see things the same.
>
> "Now don't you wait, or hesitate.
> Let's move before they raise the parking rate."
>
> All right now, baby, it's a-all right now.
> All right now, baby, it's a-all right now.

Chapter Five: Battle of the Bands

The dancers performed a sexy dance routine, while the stunters were thrown sky-high in the air. We performed with smiles on our faces, hair flipping from side to side, with occasional winks to the crowd. We were showstoppers, the crème de la crème. Tulsa started their next song, but their fans started clapping for us. They were taking pictures and shooting videos.

Needless to say, we won the battle, bigly!

Later that evening, we all sat down for dinner Louisiana style! Walter Cronkite was the host and keynote speaker. He was a fascinating man. As we were eating and listening to Walter speak, several of us kept commenting on how good the food was. The funny thing was no one knew exactly what we were eating! Was it chicken? Was it turkey? They wouldn't serve duck, now, would they? Walter kept talking, and we kept eating. Finally, we finished, licking our lips and fingers.

Suddenly, Walter said, "So, what do you think of this Louisiana cooking? I bet it's the first time most of you have eaten Gator!" I almost puked. I reached for a flask but remembered I didn't drink. It goes without saying, that was the first and the last time I have ever eaten Gator.

The weather on game day was absolutely bone chilling. It was the coldest cold day I had ever felt in my life. We were truly miserable on the sidelines. It was so cold we could hardly think, let alone cheer. But, like always, we soldiered on. We jumped out to a big lead over Tulsa and held on for dear life to win 27-24. That was an incredible ending to an unforgettable season.

Chapter Six
Sexual Assault and My New Normal

March of 1990 rolled around, warming the air with promise of spring in the new decade. Because the squads were smaller then, cheerleaders were able to travel to almost every game, football and basketball. The Ducks were on a roll in the '89-90 season. Our men's basketball team was thriving, and the crowds were amped up. It was always a full house at Mac Court.

On game day, the Pit would come to life. Fans would stand all game long, from the floor level to the nosebleed seats. The place was electric. I felt the excitement every time I took the floor. I was always the happiest at practice or games. For me, college was a perfect fit.

The news got even better. I went to practice that week, and Coach Maulding gave us the great news, "We're leaving for the PAC-10 tournament." We would be heading to Tucson, Arizona for the men's basketball conference playoffs.

Yes! Amazing! A week in sunny Arizona with my teammates and... boyfriend.

I had been dating a basketball player at USC for three months. Despite the distance between Los Angeles and Eugene, we had the best relationship. He was originally from North Carolina but got a scholarship to play basketball for Southern Cal. I can remember my dad shaking his head every time our home phone bill arrived. We didn't have cell phones back then, so the long-distance calls were a few hundred dollars a month. My boyfriend's bill was no different. We would talk for hours. He was one of the most honest and incredible people I had ever met.

When I think back to that time in my life, it amazes me to recall how much love and support I had. My parents attended every home game and major event. My cousins, aunts, uncles, and grandparents were always cheering me on and attended as many games as possible. We had such a close family. My cousins were more like siblings. Sometimes I hear other people talk and realize just how unbelievably special my family is.

When we traveled, we traveled like the queen of Egypt. So, travel days were always a process. We gathered everything known to man: the mascot's suit, megaphones, banners, pom poms, game signs… and makeup! Always lots of makeup! We were required to uphold the Oregon tradition whenever we were representing the athletic department. We weren't just a team; we were a brand, walking logos. Although, we generally traveled in our cheerleading sweatsuits, our hair and makeup were always done to perfection. Everything was a Hollywood production.

Once we landed in Tucson, it became a whirlwind. The pace quickened. I remember getting to the arena and watching all the teams, bands, and cheerleaders coming and going. The schedule was tight, so everyone was given a specific time to practice.

It wasn't long before we loaded up the buses and headed to our hotel. When we arrived, my jaw dropped. The hotel was fabulous. It was open and elegant, and all the rooms were close to a swimming pool and lounge. All the pools had waterfalls, and each was connected to a hot tub and bar. We were traveling in high style.

Chapter Six: Sexual Assault and My New Normal

As the men's PAC-10 tournament got underway, it was bittersweet for me. Oregon was advancing but USC lost early, so my boyfriend was preparing to go back to Los Angeles. I walked outside the arena after the game and stood by USC's charter bus. I was terribly sad; I loved him so. He was absolutely the kindest and sweetest man. He loved me and treated me like a princess. He would have done anything for me. We said our reluctant goodbyes, and my boyfriend boarded the bus.

Our squad got back to the hotel, and we started making plans to eat and hang out. Cheerleaders bunked two to a room, and I always roomed with the same girl on the road, Erin. She was my ride or die, more like a sister than a teammate. We always had fun. Erin was a year older. She knew everyone. People loved her. After we had our team dinner, I decided to lay low and stay in the room. I was bummed out; my boyfriend was gone. Erin decided to hang out with the other cheerleaders and athletes. She didn't intend to stay long, so I flipped the bolt lock on the door and said, "See you later, girlfriend."

The experience that followed scarred me, broke pieces of me on the inside. Reshaped the person I was. It became a marking in the calendar—the 'before' and 'after.' And while I struggled to hold those pieces together, life went on around me, the whole world unaware that an important piece of my soul had died that night.

So, I did what I was good at.

I got ready for the game as normal, Oregon glam.

But this was a new normal. It was early. There wasn't much talking as the squad loaded the bus. We needed to set our routines on the floor and get warmed up. I kept on my sweatsuit for as long as possible, hoping no one would notice.

The band started playing all the traditional tunes; it was about that time. I told myself, "**SMILE, *Chin Up*!**" Dance your heart out, no one will know.

There wasn't much to our uniforms. Our tops were sleeveless; our skirts were about an inch below our gluteus maximus. We were the University of Oregon cheerleaders; we had a reputation to uphold. We were undeniably the best squad in the PAC-10 conference. We were more than cheerleaders; we were a spectacle, showtime entertainment.

I had worked at a tanning salon for several years in high school and always had a gorgeous tan. That, plus great makeup, helped disguise most of the bruises.

But nothing could hide the shame I felt inside.

My stunt partner noticed something was a little off. I guess when you spend countless hours throwing someone up in the air, you get to know them fairly well. He asked me on several occasions if I was okay. I gave him a big smile and said everything was fine. He didn't press the issue, and I was performing well. Ostensibly, I was fine, but I was dying inside.

I tried to get through the rest of that trip without breaking down. I held it together until I got home to Eugene. The first thing I did was call my best friend from high school. He was my confidant, my most trusted friend. I could tell him anything. We met at his house, and I told him everything. I showed him my bruises, and he begged me to report it. I just couldn't do it. I was so afraid to embarrass my family. I was so scared by what he'd said. I had big dreams for my future, and all I could think about was what might happen if it became public.

My friend took me to a counselor at Lane Community College. He sat by my side and supported me through it all. They both encouraged me to report the assault. It was many years before the "Me Too Movement," and I became just another statistic, another victim who didn't have the courage or wherewithal to stand up for herself.

Chapter Six: Sexual Assault and My New Normal

My life was never the same after that tournament. I struggled mentally and emotionally. The weight of gravity felt ten times normal. I finished out basketball season, then I took time off from college. I needed to step back and get myself together. In hindsight, I wish I would have had a candid conversation with my roommate or even my parents about the rape. I think things could have been very different if I'd only had the courage to ask for help. Instead, I bottled up the nightmare inside.

There is no right or wrong answer after someone has been assaulted. There is no set of directions to follow or a list of boxes to check that will make it all go away. Everyone handles stress, trauma, and grief differently. I chose not to come forward publicly for thirty years, and I owe no one an explanation. However, my choices as a young woman were based on inexperience, fear, embarrassment, and uncertainty. Times are very different today, and for that I'm grateful. A huge reason for writing this book is to let others know that their choices can be better than mine. There is help available. And I hope this book offers some insight, encouragement, and a few tools to other women undergoing such trauma.

Chapter Seven
Lightning Strikes Twice

After high school graduation, and before attending University of Oregon, I was hired as a cheerleading instructor for Universal Cheerleaders Association (UCA). UCA was the biggest and most highly respected cheerleading company in the country. During that summer, I traveled all over the US, teaching at both high school and college cheerleading camps. I was in my element—coaching, instructing, and leading incredible groups of cheerleaders and dancers.

I returned to UCA after the rape. I think pouring myself into this work kept me going over the next four years. Ultimately, I became one of the many lead instructors across the country. Some of my best travel and cheerleading moments occurred during those summers and with those amazing people, but then, I made the difficult decision to step away.

It was 1991, and I was in Eugene visiting my parents. I was in the kitchen grubbing some food when the phone rang. I picked up and on the other line was a good friend from high school. We'd also worked together at the tanning salon. She didn't sound right. I could tell something was wrong, and she struggled to get the words out. I started to feel a sense of panic.

Then it came. "Lisa, she's dead; she was murdered."

A thousand questions raced through my mind as my friend began to tell the story. Lisa was visiting a friend in Charbonneau, Oregon, a suburb of Portland. She was brutally murdered by a sixteen-year-old boy who tried to rape her, but when that failed, he resorted to violence and stabbed her repeatedly.

It was a gruesome crime, and a gut punch to my soul. My heart sank. I listened as long as I could, then ran to the sink and threw up. I could hardly hold it together. I began crying hysterically; I thought I was going to faint. Lisa Flormoe was one of my closest friends. I was going to be a bridesmaid in her upcoming wedding. She was only twenty-two and absolutely one of a kind.

A few days later, a friend named Cheryl called. Cheryl owned a tanning salon and was my former boss. Lisa, Cheryl, and I were as thick as thieves. We were the fabulous trio, like Charlie's Angels. I looked up to Cheryl and will never forget the advice she gave me, "Slow down. I love you, but please slow down." It felt like a premonition.

The funny thing was, I had never told her about my rape. I think in some small way, maybe the advice was really coming from Lisa.

Afterward, for months, I had intertwining nightmares about Lisa's murder and my rape. One night at my apartment in Beaverton, I was awakened out of a dead sleep. I had a vision of Lisa standing at the foot of my bed. I was terrified at first, then overcome with peace. I opened my eyes and there she was, as radiant as ever. She smiled at me and nodded with assurance. I could have reached out and touched her. It lasted less than a minute, but I believe it was real.

I don't know why she came, but I consider her my guardian angel. Subsequently, during the difficult days, I always knew that Lisa was with me.

I had been fourteen and a sophomore in high school when I first met Lisa. She hired me to work the front desk at the Tanning Hut salon. I remember the first time I saw her. She was standing behind the counter of the salon checking in clients. Lisa was

Chapter Seven: Lightning Strikes Twice

literally the most beautiful girl I had ever seen. She looked like a Hollywood actress and exuded a level of confidence well beyond the norm. I didn't know it at the time, but she had graduated from high school early and worked as a buyer for a high-end boutique. She was barely eighteen years old and already making boss moves. It was rare in the eighties to be so young, let alone a woman, and excelling at such a rapid rate. Lisa dressed like a fashion model, always runway ready. She was the total package: brains, beauty, and class.

Over a two-year period, I became increasingly close to Lisa and her fiancé Brian. He came to the salon just about every day to tan and see his girl. They were the perfect couple, the epitome of Ken & Barbie. Brian was tall, dark, handsome, and extremely successful. He was several years older than Lisa, but she was mature for her age. They were extremely supportive and strongly encouraged me to pursue my dreams in cheerleading and dance. If there were two people whose advice I valued and heeded, it was definitely Brian and Lisa. I remember being so excited when Lisa asked me to be one of her bridesmaids. To the best of my recollection, they were planning a winter wedding. It was going to be something special, a fairytale wedding, the social event of the year!

Not long after their engagement, the horrendous tragedy occurred. Lisa's death rocked all of our worlds. I became desperately heartbroken. Brian was a tortured soul. He had been on the phone with Lisa as the attack occurred and heard every moment of the brutal encounter. Todd Davilla attempted to rape her, and when Lisa resisted and began to overpower him, he pulled out a boy scout knife and began stabbing her viciously and repeatedly. Finally, Todd sliced across Lisa's neck and nearly decapitated her. Brian was a witness to the terror and screams. He cried out for help, and it was Brian who called the authorities, then raced two hours down Interstate Five to reach the love of his life. By then, he was too late.

Lisa's murder became national news. It was televised on "A Current Affair" and reported by Maurie Povich.

Even seeing the story on television wasn't enough to process Lisa's death. Her memory never goes away for me or her family. Todd Davilla was sentenced to fifty-years in an Oregon State Penitentiary. In 2017, a Clackamas County judge upheld the sentencing due to the heinous nature of the crime. However, under a new policy signed into law by Governor Kate Brown, Todd became eligible for early release as a previously convicted minor. Kate Brown is a terrific governor, but I sent her a strongly worded letter of disapproval of the decision.

January 7, 2022

Dear Governor Brown,

My name is Corine Lewis, I voted for you and have been a strong supporter of your agenda as governor. As a woman and leader, you have been a tremendous role model to millions and represent a positive example of woman's empowerment.

I am an Oregonian through and through. I was reared in Eugene; attended the University of Oregon; was a proud member of the University of Oregon cheerleading squad; and later served as the coach and choreographer for 15 years. I spent 13 years in Portland and was a member of the Portland Trailblazer dancers. During my tenure at the University of Oregon, I was also crowned Mrs. Oregon International. I have taken great pride in my community service throughout our beautiful state and have devoted much of my life to

Chapter Seven: Lightning Strikes Twice

raising awareness for noteworthy causes, including sexual and domestic violence against women.

I am a victim of both, a sexual assault and domestic violence. I spent decades fighting my trauma behind closed doors. Currently, I am completing a memoir which discusses my journey and is scheduled for release later this year. The good news is that I survived. I am one of the fortunate ones. I decided to write the book to serve as a powerful motivator to victims of sexual assault and violence worldwide and hope that it serves as a ballast for change. And this is the purpose of my letter, to ask you to reconsider a recent decision to release previously convicted juveniles who were tried as adults; at least in one case.

Governor Brown, I found this announcement alarming, in part because it's personal. My best friend Lisa Flormoe was murdered in 1991 by Todd Davilla, who at the time was 16. It was a brutal, heinous crime. He attempted to rape her, and when that failed, stabbed Lisa over and over with a knife, nearly decapitating her. Lisa was a vibrant 22-year-old. She was in the midst of planning to wed the love of her life. We were all broken in ways that's hard to fathom. It was so sudden and so ghastly.

Lisa's family has shown up to every parole hearing for decades, and each time, the parole board has denied Mr. Davilla parole because of a shockingly unabashed lack of remorse. To my knowledge, he has never expressed remorse for the crime or to the family. In fact, in 2017, the presiding judge sentenced Todd to an additional 50 years in prison because of his lack of empathy and remorse.

I implore you to please reconsider your position, at least in this particular case. I know you are a champion for justice and are trying to do the right thing, but there is an exception to every rule. In this case, I ask that you make Todd Davilla this exception. It would be a disservice to the state and to your legacy as a phenomenal role model.

Thank you for your consideration, and I would be more than happy to speak to you directly if that would be helpful.

Respectfully,
Corine Lewis

I don't know if the Governor received it, but, as of this writing, Todd Davilla has not been released.

As I struggled to process the death of a great friend, little did I know that there was a storm cloud brewing in my own life.

Chapter Eight
It Hurt so Bad

It was 1991, and I had barely been able to process my assault in Arizona, and now I was trying to absorb the tragedy of Lisa's death. I was at a crossroad. I needed to make a decision. I didn't want to stay in Eugene, but I wasn't ready for Los Angeles. Dancing was the only thing that seemed to motivate me. I felt the most alive and free when I was performing, and I was phenomenal, if I did say so myself!

Somehow, I found the strength and courage to move forward.

It was hard, but I decided to move to Portland and try out for the cheerleading squad for the NBA Portland Trailblazers!

After a couple days of intense tryouts, I would find my name on the Team roster. I was back! I was a professional cheerleader! Being a member of the "Blazer Dancers" would go down as one of the happiest periods in my life. It went far beyond dancing and performing, far beyond the glitz and glamor. It was the relationships that were formed and the family of sisterhood that would carry on throughout my life.

It was better than special; it was everything.

The women who entered my life at that time had no idea what I had gone through, or how much I grew because of them. I took a little piece of wonderful from every dancer on the team. As a result, I became a better dancer and a better person to boot.

As time rolled on, I continued dating my boyfriend at USC. I wasn't forthcoming about my assault, though he could tell something was wrong, but I didn't let him in. Instead, I was short with him, difficult. We still loved each other, but I started slowly pushing him away. I couldn't have asked for a better person in my life, but the guilt and shame were so deep. I couldn't stand not telling him the truth, and I hated that I couldn't be vulnerable with him.

He flew out to games to support me. He did everything right, and my conscience was eating me alive. I knew logically that the rape wasn't my fault, but the trauma was absolutely unbearable. Somehow, I didn't feel like I deserved him, so I did the inevitable thing, the only thing I knew to do, and broke off the relationship. The truth was, after I walked away, I started shoving my assault down as deep as possible, and there began a toxic new normal.

I had a couple different roommates while I was in Portland. We began having girls' nights out, and I loved it. It felt great to be social again.

I had gone on a few dates but nothing serious. Then, one day at a gas station, I ran into a well-known professional athlete, let's call him Clay Randall. Clay recognized me and said hello. We talked for a while and exchanged numbers. I wasn't home thirty minutes and Clay was calling. We talked for hours that night and several nights after. We began going to lunch, then eventually dinner. It was the first time since my breakup that I was really crushing on someone.

We started spending a lot of time together and decided to be exclusive. Clay's brother and sister came to Portland to stay with him. I got to know them, and they eventually accepted me.

Clay was such a fun and genuine guy. Over the course of the year, an issue arose because cheerleaders weren't supposed to date players. It was against the rules, a complete "no, no!" It was becoming increasingly difficult to hide because Clay wanted to take me to various functions. I remember one night he was so excited, because he knew how much I loved football and he surprised me with tickets to the Super Bowl! The Buffalo Bills were playing the New York Giants in Super Bowl XXV in Tampa, Florida.

Chapter Eight: It Hurt so Bad

Clay was from New York, so he was beyond excited. Finally, it was an opportunity for us to be public, just a normal couple.

We had a unique relationship, it was natural and genuine, and we loved being together. With him, I began forgetting my demons and just living again.

We were both in the middle of the NBA season, and I had a required appearance to attend, but I was a huge football fan and watched the Super Bowl every year with my dad. I was ecstatic to fly to Tampa with Clay, but I couldn't get out of my obligation with the team. I had to decline the trip. I was sick about it, but I was committed to the team and my career. I realized that I was breaking a major rule by dating Clay, but I guess hypocrisy is easier when you're young and in love. At this point, Clay was thoroughly frustrated. After the weekend, he asked me to quit so we could be together. I told him maybe he should get a different job so I could continue dancing. Yeah, that went over like a load of hot lava. We were both serious and both stubborn and neither was willing to give an inch. After many discussions, we eventually decided to dial it back and become friends. No hard feelings. I stayed strong; I was surprised. But however well intentioned, and for whatever reason it occurs, breaking up is hard to do. I think someone wrote a song about it. And once life gets in the way, it makes it nearly impossible to maintain such friendships over time, particularly in the world of sports where life is played at light speed given all the travel, players coming and going, pressure to perform, and media attention.

I spent my entire life as a cheerleader at every level and as a Division One coach. I have been immersed in athletics from birth. I understand that rules are in place for a reason, but now, with more than forty years in the world of college and professional sports, please indulge me just a moment. The no dating rule for cheerleaders and professional athletes is absurd! Cheerleaders are not in the players' chain of command any more than a software engineer is to the accountant. Cheerleaders are no more susceptible to malicious influence than a maître d' is to a parking attendant. We are all adults, and no other profession proposes such absolute restrictions... as far as I know.

To tell professional men and women who are more than 90% college educated, provide millions of dollars of philanthropic support to their communities, and are exposed to unprecedented media scrutiny that they are insufficiently capable of choosing who they want to date is almost un-American. It's like telling them that they don't possess the same relationship skills as the average factory worker, truck driver, software engineer, plumber, carpenter, pipe fitter, longshoreman, military personal, or fast-food cook. Given the divorce rates among doctors, lawyers, bankers, university faculty, airline pilots, and others, I'm not sure this policy is rooted in fact. So, on behalf of cheerleaders, I will just say that it's almost impossible not to develop friendships with athletes. You work at the same venue, tread the same game trails, and drink from the same watering holes. My understanding is that back in the day, some disgruntled wives got upset because their philandering husbands were cheating with a few cheerleaders. The wives started a petition to prevent such fraternizing. Then, one by one, team by team, a non-contact policy was put in place. But the problem is the policy presupposes that cheating husbands are only drawn to professional cheerleaders and not to female trainers, public relations executives, hotel staff, broadcasters, sports writers, cocktail waitresses, real estate agents, actresses, and others.

The point is, ladies, if you have an unfaithful husband, that's just who they are.

Losing Clay hurt; it hurt really bad.

Okay, I'm done now. I'll put my soapbox away and we can return to regular programming.

Chapter Nine
Masters of Impunity

The year was 1992, and, like every other game, I pulled into the Portland Coliseum parking lot, grabbed my pom poms, threw my bag over my shoulder, and ran to the back side of the arena. I flashed a smile at the security guards and scooted down the hall to our locker room.

It's always a hurry up and wait situation once we get on the floor.

This particular game pitted the Trailblazers against the Lakers. I was always super excited when the Lakers came to town because the crowd got extra hyped. Something about beating LA made our day, week, and month.

I remember how cold it was in the arena that night. It took a while to get warm. Our coach, Dee Dee, yelled out starting formations, and we folded into place. In addition to us, the players were having a shoot around, the sound guys were testing the music and sound bites, the camera crews were setting up the cameras, and media people were getting settled at the broadcast tables.

For some reason, we were spending more time than usual on pre-game. We got through the first two routines and had some lag time. I was getting overheated and decided to peel off a layer of clothing. We danced hard, so there were always little piles of clothes laying around the perimeter of the court.

My starting position was right in front of the sports commentators, just to the side of the Blazers' bench. The players were dribbling and taking shots. It was hard not to notice, because they were constantly retrieving balls in our area. Dee Dee told us to set the routine and dance full out.

Our routines were intense, so I took off another layer of clothing and tied it around my waist. At this point, like all the other dancers, I was down to a sports bra and leggings. Then, out of nowhere, I hear, "F— yeah, baby, take it off." There was a lot of background noise with everything going on, yet everyone looked to the media table. Dee Dee turned completely around in disbelief. Standing there looking directly at me was the color commentator for NBC. Crass, arrogant, and unashamed. As if the first comment wasn't enough, he blurted out, "Show me your t—ts!"

Dee Dee immediately confronted him. Before she could say anything, players from both of the teams got in his face. They were irate. One of the Lakers walked up to me and said, "That was some bulls—t, you're about to get paid."

I wasn't even sure what he meant until one of the other dancers said, "Yes, you need to sue him!"

Now, I ask you, where's the policy against NBA commentators? I was so shocked and embarrassed. I couldn't believe a grown man, let alone a professional analyst, could be so crass. I felt victimized once again, this time verbally, but assaulted, nevertheless. I tried to let it go, but the blatantness caused me to sink even deeper. I was called into the Trailblazer office later that week. They wanted to assure me that the situation would be handled and that I need not take any further action.

Later, I learned that a veteran player stood up for me and really wanted something done. He didn't know me personally but we're both from Eugene. I guess he had that thing called chivalry, or maybe he was just old school. Before, I had appreciated all of his basketball accomplishments, but after that, I became a fan for life. I was told by a friend in the organization that the commentator had a history of sexually harassing dancers around the NBA. I don't know how he got away with it. Fortunately, things are changing, but in the early 90s, it was "boys will be boys." As of this writing, I'm still waiting for an apology. Come on, y'all!

Chapter Ten
Rip City

Notwithstanding the above, my time as a Blazer dancer was genuinely the best experience in my cheerleading career. I was finally on my own. Moving to Portland allowed me to mature, but finding my way around the City of Roses was no picnic, especially for someone from a small college town. In the early nineties, we didn't have GPS or Google maps. It was old school. You wrote the directions on a piece of paper and allowed yourself enough time to get lost. It took me several weeks, but I finally got over the hump.

One of my favorite moments with the Trailblazer dancers was performing in the 1992 NBA Finals against the Chicago Bulls and the renowned Michael Jordan. Everyone else in America may have wanted to "be like Mike," but in Portland, he was public enemy number one!

Rip City, as the basketball arena was called, was rocking. The crowd was in full force. Clyde "the glide" Drexler and the rest of our beloved Blazers had clawed their way to a sixth game. The fourth quarter was sizzling. We were up at the start of the fourth quarter, but it was Michael Jordan's world. We lost a close one, 97-93.

It was my first season (1991-1992) as a Blazer dancer and probably the most memorable. In that same year, I also performed in the pre-Olympic qualifying tournament for the USA Men's Olympic basketball team nicknamed "The Dream Team." It was the first time an American Olympic Basketball team included professional players from the NBA.

"The Dream Team" included some of the greatest players in basketball history: Michael Jordan, Magic Johnson, Larry Bird, Charles Barley, Patrick Ewing, Scottie Pippen and more. Journalists described "The Dream Team" as the greatest collection of basketball athletes ever assembled. The tournament took place at the Portland Coliseum. Coming off an incredible season, our own Clyde Drexler was selected as a member of the team, so we had an even greater sense of pride.

One of my teammates was Jill Layport, a veteran cheerleader for Oregon State University and their former head cheerleading coach. Jill and I were still in close contact with our former cheerleading squads. We had an idea and decided to invite the male stunters from both squads to join us. It was the first time the Blazer dancers ever mixed dancing and partner stunting. Jill and I were both in our prime, and the stunters and other dancers were elite. We performed at the halftime show of one of the games! The energy was electric. Our performance was through the roof. The fans loved it. So much so, the Trailblazers invited the stunters back again and again and eventually created a full-time stunt team. Jill and I can proudly say we put the Blazer Stunt Team on the map!

As an aside, earlier in the regular season, I had a fluke incident with Larry Byrd. The Blazer dancers always sat under the basket on both ends of the court. I was sitting on the sidelines, and Larry was inbounding the ball. He took a step back and accidentally stepped on my foot. There was no way he could have known that my leg was extended, and no way I could have known that he would step back. I remember the moment it happened. My foot was crushed. It was like being stepped on by a grizzly bear. I instantly pulled back and Larry turned and immediately apologized, right in the middle of the play.

That wasn't surprising because Larry Bird was such a class act. However, what did surprise me was that he remembered the

Chapter Ten: Rip City

incident when we played later that season and came over during warmups and asked about someone's foot. One of the other dancers pointed at me. He flashed a great big smile and inquired, "Were you alright?" Of course, I shrugged it off. But truth be told, I had a painful foot fracture! It wasn't career ending, but the rehab was a b—! Needless to say, I was a huge fan of Larry Bird and, if I had to suffer a foot fracture, at least it was done by a legend!

There are so many amazing stories and memories as a Blazer dancer, it's hard to pick just one, but a particular fact I cherish from that time in my life are the bonds and friendships that I made with the other dancers. To share a common bond and a mutual passion with an elite group of people, under pressure to perform, is really quite special. For me, that was my time with the Trailblazers. Every woman in the sisterhood of Blazer dancers was unique and magnificent in their own way. It was such an honor and privilege to be a part of their lives and to share such a tremendous experience.

Part Two
Surviving Abuse

Chapter Eleven
The Moment of Truth

It was 1993, and Clint Eastwood's *Unforgiven* won the Oscar for best picture and Steven Spielberg released *Jurassic Park*. These should have been omens, but I was still in Portland and riding high.

One night, after one of our games, a group of the Blazer dancers and some mutual friends decided to hang out at a club called Champions, located at the top of the Marriott in downtown Portland. I remember walking in and seeing several former Oregon Duck football players at the bar. Although I hadn't seen them since college, we instantly recognized one another and exchanged hugs and pleasantries. I introduced my girls to some of the guys, including one named Johnny "Flash" Taylor. Sometime later, Flash approached me and said another former Duck player wanted to meet me. I didn't know Devin at Oregon, but I agreed. Devin and I had an instant connection. We talked a bit, then ended up on the dance floor, where we stayed for a couple of hours.

The dancers and former players were all paired up but stayed together as a group. We had so much fun, and I began feeling like my old self again. The bartenders gave last call, and it was time to leave. I wasn't a drinker back then. In fact, I could count on two hands the number of times I drank alcohol. As a result, on girls' night out, I was always the designated driver, which continued through age forty.

Devin asked for my telephone number, and I gladly agreed. He lived in Eugene, as did most of the guys. We said our goodbyes and went our separate ways.

A couple days later, Devin called with an invite. He was having a small get together the following weekend. We had been talking on the phone, so I was super excited. We were building a real connection. I invited Jill to join me, and we drove the two hundred miles from Beaverton to Eugene. The get together was great, and we had an absolute blast. There was a lot of laughing, dancing, joking, and showing off. Jill and I were the only girls, but we felt absolutely safe. After that weekend, Devin and I decided to become a couple. It didn't take long before I found myself falling in love. He was so attentive and so charming. I believed I had finally found my Mr. Right!

Several months later, Devin and I were on our way to Los Angeles to meet his family. We were driving over the Grapevine mountains headed for sunny southern California. He was singing and I was singing, we serenaded one another the whole way. Devin had a beautiful voice, stage ready, and I wasn't bad either. We joked, sang, and rapped to all our favorite artists. The look on his face was priceless when I sang all the lyrics to a song by "NWA." For a moment, I think I took his breath away.

We had been driving for about twelve hours, nearing our destination, and I put on some lipstick and a little makeup. We were both excited and I wanted to make a good impression.

Devin turned off the radio and began to tell me a story about two unlikely lovers. A guy from So-Cal and a girl from Eugene. We were rolling down the mountain when he pulled out a ring and asked me to be his wife. I couldn't believe what was happening! I was shocked and surprised. Everything was happening so fast.

I said, "Yes," with excitement. My voice was shaky as I tried to hold back the tears. "I will marry you!" I put the beautiful ring on my finger, feeling fully loved and perfectly complete.

Chapter Eleven: The Moment of Truth

We were getting close to his parents' house, and Devin wanted his family to meet his fiancé, not his girlfriend. He thought it would be a better look.

As I reflect back, it was a classic predatory move. Build trust by any means necessary.

When we arrived in Los Angeles, I wasn't sure what to expect. I didn't know much about Los Angeles beyond cheerleading camps, visits to theme parks, and trips to USC and UCLA games. The only other references I had were *Baywatch* and "Boyz N The Hood."

When we pulled up to the house, we were greeted by his dad and brother. They were all smiles and showered me with hugs. After some time, I realized that I hadn't met Devin's mother. I asked whether she was home, and everyone hesitated. It didn't take long to figure out that she wasn't interested in meeting me.

Devin's mom was in her bedroom. As I walked down the hall, I vaguely heard Devin say something about not holding my breath. I got to the room and knocked on the door. She invited me in. She was sitting on the bed studying her Bible, preparing a lesson for Sunday service. She didn't say a word, so I sat down next to her and introduced myself as Devin's fiancé. She shook my hand and welcomed me. Within minutes, I laid across the bed and we had a wonderful conversation. If memory serves me right, we talked for over an hour before Devin came to break it up.

From that first meeting, Devin's mom always treated me with respect. We developed a genuine bond. Her heart was open, and through all the trials and tribulations to come, she treated me as a daughter.

I was in So-Cal for two weeks, learning to cook soul food from scratch and building a solid relationship with his family. I loved them, and when I left, I felt they genuinely loved me too.

Chapter Twelve
Mice

In 1994, the government convicted Aldrich Ames, one of the most notorious double agents in CIA history, of spying for the Russians and causing the death of a number of CIA assets. In the world of espionage, there is a mnemonic called "MICE" (money, ideology, coercion, and ego), which explains the principal reasons why people betray their country. MICE is also a useful mnemonic to explain why some people tend to betray their spouses.

At this point, our life had become unexpectedly complicated. I had been admitted to Emanuel Hospital three months early due to preterm complications. I was going into labor at twenty-four weeks and had to be bedridden. I spent Halloween, Thanksgiving, Christmas, and New Year's in bed. At thirty-five weeks, I was transferred to Good Samaritan Hospital, where I delivered my beautiful daughter Haley Nicole two weeks later.

I remember bringing Haley home to our apartment and having this overwhelming feeling of joy, but I had been gone for three months and felt a little out of place. I had picked out everything for the nursery from the hospital catalogs. My parents made sure to set it up just the way I wanted. It was surreal. At twenty-three, I was a wife and mother. My life went from performing in front of thousands of cheering fans to changing diapers around the clock, recovering from a C-Section and sleep deprivation.

Devin had started a new job as a drug and alcohol counselor for juveniles. He was trying to get adjusted to his new normal as well.

It wasn't an easy transition, and I immediately noticed a change. Devin seemed easily agitated and short tempered. Little things began to set him off. When I tried to talk about it, he became even more agitated. The situation became increasingly uncomfortable. I started to walk on eggshells.

Devin was hot and cold; his yelling became unpredictable. I kept thinking it was just the stress of a new job and a new baby, things would get better. But deep down inside, I knew something was wrong, I didn't know just how wrong. That, I would soon discover. And when I did, it changed every ounce of my being.

Devin counseled juveniles and young adults with drug and alcohol addictions. I soon found out that he was being accused of sexual misconduct with one of his clients. I was questioned by a detective about intimate details. It was terrifying, heartbreaking, confusing, and frustrating all at the same time. The detective asked me to describe my apartment; the furniture; the setup in every room; and Devin's body parts. The victim had given the detective a detailed description of each. As I answered questions, the detective took notes, and meticulously compared my responses to the victim's. I was irate! I thought the woman was lying. I couldn't believe she was attacking my husband. Regardless of the environment at home, I couldn't imagine Devin would be involved in something like this.

They couldn't prove the sexual misconduct, but the victim did, in fact, describe every room of our apartment. Later, she admitted that the sex was mutual and, because they were both consenting adults, there would be no charges filed. Of course, Devin emphatically denied everything. And of course, he ended up losing his job.

Soon afterward, he got a job at a residential treatment facility owned by some close family friends of ours in Beaverton. Within short order, Devin was accused of similar behavior under similar circumstances. Once again, it cost him his job. The pattern was repeating: the same bad behavior, accusations, loss of job. The betrayal was unbelievable. Twice in under two years. The stress and emotional anguish were through the roof. In retrospect, when I look back at our dating process, I clearly missed a number of red flags and anti-social behavior. His controlling style and demeanor; the obsession over my whereabouts; the personal insecurity; the excuses for not making the NFL; the gentle critique of my family and friends. They were all part of a grooming process; a slow process of isolation, control, and dependency; a process to keep me dependent and reliant on him. Devin got into my head. The only opinion that counted was his. I was young and naïve, but more importantly, I had never been mistreated. I had never experienced the rage, the verbal abuse, and the cheating. But I was also a competitive person and determined to make things work. I didn't get married to get divorced. I would do anything to save my marriage. Plus, I loved him.

Chapter Thirteen
Crossing the Rubicon

In May 1994, Jackie Kennedy Onassis, the former First Lady of the United States, died of cancer. The entire country was in morning.

A month later, my five-month-old daughter was struggling with severe stomach pain. Devin and I made an appointment to see her pediatrician. During our visit, the pediatrician said she was constipated and needed help using the bathroom. He gave us a prescription and suggested that we mix her baby formula with prune juice. I wrote down his suggestion, and Devin and I went to the grocery store. I was holding Haley in my arms as we strolled down the baby section, and I grabbed a bottle of prune juice. Devin protested. He said, "He said apple juice."

I looked at him and said, "No, he said prune juice." Before I could explain, Devin hit me in the head so hard that I dropped to the floor.

I was on the ground holding my five-month-old. Had I turned an inch, he could have killed her. I managed to pick myself up, clinging to Haley even tighter. I was absolutely stunned and in shock. I was so embarrassed and hurt that I couldn't look at him. I remember grabbing the prune juice off the floor and grabbling an apple juice as well. I was fighting back tears with every ounce of strength I had. We walked up to the cashier, and I couldn't even look up. When we got in the car, Devin started making threats and disparaging remarks under his breath. I didn't say a word.

Once we got home, I changed Haley and fed her. I got her to sleep and put away the groceries. Devin came out of the bedroom yelling about what had transpired. He blamed me for pushing his buttons. I tried to explain what I had written on the paper. The more I talked the more upset he became. I saw a look in his eyes; I hadn't seen that level of rage before, ever.

Out of nowhere, he grabbed me and threw me on the floor. He hit me again when I got up. It was a true beatdown.

That was the first day he hit me. It was the first time he crossed the Rubicon. That's how it began; that's how I became victimized once again.

A week passed, and I tried to put it behind me. I made excuses for Devin's behavior in order to justify the abuse, and for staying. I was determined to make things right. I made sure that the apartment was immaculate every day. Not one ounce of clutter. No undone laundry, and not a dirty dish anywhere. I had dinner on the table the moment he walked in. Everything was in its perfect place. I vacuumed the carpet so that all the lines flowed in the same direction; exactly the way he liked it. Every night before bed, I ironed his clothes, set them aside, and picked out a tie and perfectly matching pair of socks. I took care of my husband in every way. I respected that he was working hard so that I could be home with Haley. I figured the fewer reasons I gave him to be angry, the better the chances that I wouldn't get hit.

The next couple weeks were touch and go, but a pattern began to develop. Devin would walk in; I would greet him with a smile and a hug, then hang on for dear life. I never knew what to expect. I was so stressed out that I was down to 102 pounds six months postpartum.

During this time, I thought about Jackie Kennedy; her class and grace; her style; how she held her head up high. I tried to emulate those qualities but fell woefully short.

Chapter Fourteen
Trial of the Century

It was mid-June 1994, and Devin was leaving for work. On his way out, he asked me to get my car washed. I had just gotten a job at Gold's Gym teaching dance and aerobics. It was the perfect fit because the gym had a childcare room and Haley would be able to play and get some socialization.

Between juggling my new job, keeping my baby on schedule, and maintaining the perfect home, time was at a premium. When I got in the car, it started pouring down rain. We didn't have money to burn, so I elected to defer washing the car until the following day. When Devin got home, he zeroed in immediately and asked why I didn't get the car washed. I told him that it had rained, and I would have it washed tomorrow. He flew into a rage and started yelling, then grabbed me by my hair and dragged me to the window. He started calling me all kinds of stupid, an ignorant, worthless b——. He dragged me by the hair into the kitchen and told me to get dinner on the table. I was fearful and upset, but I knew to keep my mouth shut. Unlike with my father, there was no promise of a Mongoose bike.

I couldn't comprehend the rage. Devin was totally out of control, like a man possessed.

I woke up the next morning and made a pot of coffee. I turned on the news and saw a picture of Nicole Brown Simpson. The headline said, "The ex-wife of O.J Simpson was brutally murdered." The story indicated that she and a friend were stabbed to death outside her Brentwood home. I was captivated by the story, partly because she reminded me of Lisa and partly because I was sensitive to assault. Once I learned that she had been a victim of domestic violence, had biracial kids in an interracial marriage with a former football player, I felt connected to her story in a deep way.

Like most Americans, the O.J. Simpson trial would become all-consuming for the next year of my life. The media called it, "The Trial of the Century."

In July 1994, we moved to a new apartment in Beaverton. It was a beautiful complex, and we had close friends in the building. I was hoping that if we spent time with them, I wouldn't have to be so isolated. Sometimes, I would go for weeks without seeing friends. They were a young interracial couple like us. They also had a son, who was close to Haley's age. Devin was increasingly verbally abusive. His threats and demeaning comments were constant and overwhelming. He accused me of the craziest things. It was fake news before fake news. His mind ran wild with conspiracies, and the accusations were absolutely ludicrous.

Devin was obsessed with my former boyfriend Clay because he played in the NBA. Devin had been a standout defensive back at Oregon but hadn't made it to the NFL and was jealous of other professional athletes that I knew. Several of his close friends made it to the league and had many years of success. Devin always carried a chip on his shoulder, and, strangely enough, I also think he harbored jealousy toward me as well; the fact that I made it to the pinnacle of my profession. Devin would come to many of my games and brag to all his friends. I was an Oregon cheerleader and a Blazer dancer. In public, this fed his ego but behind closed doors he hated all the adulation that I received.

Before Devin and I were engaged, he'd played in the Arena Football League for the Sacramento Attack. The Trailblazers were

Chapter Fourteen: Trial of the Century

on the road, so I had the weekend off, and Jill and I decided to take a road trip to Sacramento to watch the game. We sang and laughed the entire way, just happy to be away from the Oregon cold. The night that we arrived, Devin had a game. So, we got settled in and then headed to Arco Arena. It was the first time I had been to an arena football game. The rules were different, but it didn't take long to get the gist. We had a great time, and Devin played well. We returned to the complex and were ready to party. There were several other girls and some family members there, and Jill ended up connecting with Devin's roommate from Arkansas, Chris. His uncle was former heavyweight champion of the world George Foreman. Chris was such a nice guy. There was always a smile on his face, and he was respectful beyond measure. Jill and Chris stayed in contact and later began dating.

About three weeks later, Devin and Chris showed up at our apartment in Portland. They had a few days off, and I was happy to see them. Later that night, there was a loud knock at the door. We didn't hear it at first, and the visitors came around and tapped on my bedroom window. Chris opened the door and saw Clay Randell and James Kennedy standing front and center. My jaw dropped, and I was super nervous. I got out of bed, put on my sweats, stepped outside, and shut the door. Clay was his usual happy, smiling self. It had been a few months since we broke up and had spoken.

It was snowing outside and freezing cold, so I jumped in Clay's car. The three of us were making small talk when, suddenly, Devin approached and knocked on the car window. Clay rolled the window down, and things escalated quickly. Words grew heated; it became an east coast, west coast thing. Suddenly, Devin pulled out a gun and Clay did likewise. I was so scared. In an instant, a misunderstanding had become an existential threat. I didn't even know that Devin had a gun.

Chris came out and talked him off the ledge. Somehow, cooler heads prevailed, and Devin returned inside. I was truly shaken, and a bit embarrassed. I tried to explain the situation, but it wasn't necessary. Clay and James were laughing like mad. This wasn't their first rodeo. In their minds, no harm, no foul. We talked for a while, and they left without incident.

This was a clear warning sign. A blinking red light. Devin never bothered to get my perspective before escalating things to an almost deadly level. Why didn't I see it? Why didn't I get off the ride then? Why did I ignore my instincts? I guess I was young, dumb, and in love. Maybe I mistook jealousy for chivalry. Maybe I felt some culpability. Maybe I should never have gotten into the car.

If I had to do it all over again, I would certainly handle the situation differently.

Little did I know that this incident would be a constant theme throughout our marriage. And little did I know that this wouldn't be the last time I saw Devin's gun.

Chapter Fifteen
We are Family

In January 1995, the History Channel was launched. Six months earlier, I got some great news that would allow me to make a little history as well. My mom was hired as the head cheerleading coach at the University of Oregon and asked me to come aboard as an assistant. Once again, we were getting the band back together. The dynamic duo would be back in action, only this time at the Division 1 collegiate level. Lest you think there was something nefarious, my mother had a long history of success. She served as the head cheerleading and dance Coach at Willamette High School from 1981 to 1993, earning multiple State Titles in the All Girl and Co-Ed Cheerleading Divisions. Mom also took the dance team to numerous competitions, where she won additional local and state championships. She had remade those programs in her own image, with the help of some amazing assistant coaches. I was once asked to describe her coaching style, which was a lot like her parenting style. I summed it up in two words: "Don't play."

Mom had an impeccable reputation throughout the state. After receiving a call from the outgoing cheerleading coach, Kim Barger, she came in for the interview and was hired on the spot. Mom became the head coach of the University of Oregon cheerleaders, where she served until 2010. She and I had been a dynamic duo for decades, so I was super excited. I was just coming off my time as a Portland Trailblazer dancer and was about to be a new mother! We talked on the phone endlessly, Mom in Eugene and me in Portland, about building the best cheerleading program in the country. In order to make that happen, we consulted our mentor, former Oregon head coach, Mike Maulding. Mom put together an unbelievable program, and we took things to new heights. With her expertise in running programs and my strength in choreography, we would prove to be untouchable. But the most important thing we did was bringing on the best assistant coaches in the country. This was Mom's secret sauce. Year after year, we were able to recruit and retain the best of the best assistants. Mom became a legend at Oregon thanks to them. That first season was fantastic. Under the leadership of football Coach Rich Brooks, the Oregon Ducks found themselves headed for the Rose Bowl in Pasadena! We had the time of our lives. There is nothing like the Rose Bowl—the tradition, the pageantry, the parade. Our squad was amazing, and we stole the show everywhere we went.

It was fun for the whole family as well. Devin and my dad attended almost every function, with my daughter Haley in tow. Haley was eleven days shy of her first birthday, and she survived all the festivities, adoring fans, and the game itself. The Ducks lost, but the Oregon contingent was awesome, and we were extremely proud of our team and coaches.

After that, Coach Brooks retired. He was a great man, I went to two bowl games under his leadership, one as an Oregon cheerleader and now as a coach and choreographer.

It was a fantastic week. Devin and Dad had a close relationship and laughed and cracked jokes relentlessly. Devin was truly a guy's guy. Most people loved him. My family had absolutely no idea what was happening inside our marriage and inside our home. They had no idea what I was going through. Sometimes, the face of pain wears many masks.

Chapter Sixteen

Married to the Enemy

On March 31, 1995, I was driving from the gym in Beaverton, listening to FM Z100, when I heard the devastating news about singer-songwriter Selena. She was murdered, shot in Corpus Christi, Texas. I was heartbroken. Selena was only twenty-three and one of the most talented young artists of our time. Besides her wonderful music, this caught my attention because we were the exact same age, born less than a week apart. Selena was shot by her manager-friend over a financial dispute. The manager was under suspicion of embezzlement and acted in desperation. As I think about it, the mnemonic MICE (money, ideology, coercion, and ego) explains many different kinds of betrayal under a variety of circumstances.

But this was another day, May 14th, Mother's Day. I woke up excited because this was my special day! I dressed Haley like a little princess in anticipation of my parents arriving later. I assumed that Devin would make breakfast for me, so I got some coffee and sat next to my husband. After some time, Devin asked when I was going to make breakfast. I started smiling and giggling, thinking he was joking. But the look on his face said otherwise. My heart sank as I realized that he didn't give a crap about Mother's Day. I was highly aggravated. I didn't ask for much, but I did expect a "Happy Mother's Day' greeting, a smile, and some grub. When that didn't happen, I jumped in the car and drove to McDonalds.

I came back with pancakes, sausages, eggs, and hashbrowns. I put the plates and silverware on the table. Haley was taking her morning nap, so I sat down and started eating.

Devin walked over, grabbed my arm, and dragged me into the living room. He slapped me across the face and told me I was an ungrateful b—.

I didn't shed a tear. In that moment, I genuinely hated him. I stood silent, and he slapped me again. My lip began to bleed, but I didn't move a muscle. He put his hands around my throat and began choking me, shoving me backward, and I stumbled into a cabinet. Things started falling off the shelves, and Devin shoved me backward into the wall, pressing hard on my neck, squeezing my throat. I was beginning to pass out. I tried to break his grip, but I wasn't strong enough.

The noise woke up Haley and she started crying. Her distress startled Devin just long enough for me to loosen his grip, and I slid down the wall to the floor, Haley screaming non-stop. I began coughing uncontrollably, trying to catch my breath, and started crawling down the hallway toward her on hands and knees. Suddenly, Devin kicked me as hard as he could and broke my tailbone. It gave renewed meaning to the phase, "I got my butt kicked." I let out a horrendous scream. I was in absolute agony and rolled into the fetal position, screaming and sobbing. There was a loud banging at the door, Haley was crying her eyes out, and I was on the floor in excruciating pain.

Devin stood over me, refusing to answer the door, a man possessed. I wasn't his wife; I was his enemy. Finally, he picked up Haley and put a binky in her mouth. The person at the door eventually left. I dragged myself into the bedroom and shut the door. It took some time to collect myself, but I managed to call my mom and tell her that I wasn't feeling well. There was no way I could have them come to visit under these circumstances.

I waited a few days, but I knew my tailbone was broken. I had fractured it once before in a cheerleading accident. I knew from

Chapter Sixteen: Married to the Enemy

that experience exactly what was wrong. There's not much you can do for a broken tailbone but wait it out.

I knew what I had to do. I put a smile on my face, made up an elaborate explanation, and moved on.

One thing a victim of domestic violence learns early is how to mask trauma. In my case, a broken tailbone, broken ribs, black eyes, even a concussion. I can't speak for other victims, but, for better or worse, I had a high tolerance for pain. I was mentally tough and had a "just do it" philosophy. I had the mentality of a triathlete fighting through the last few miles of pain. I went to great lengths to hide my injuries over the years just to save face. I did more acting than Julia Roberts.

The fear of failure is a powerful intoxicant. It sometimes leads to irrational, dysfunctional, self-defeating behavior. I didn't realize it at the time, but every bridge doesn't have to be crossed. Sometimes, a battle is best won in retreat. Unfortunately, I was young, naïve, hopeful, and secretive, the combination of which can get you hurt. Badly.

In 1989, the cheerleading squad had been practicing in the lower level of McArthur Court at the university of Oregon. The floor was predominantly concrete. We were working on the new three-high pyramid routine. Partner stunting had really taken off, and we were anxious to incorporate a new routine. Normally, we operated with the utmost safety, but this was the rare exception. My teammates made several attempts to pitch me to the top of the pyramid; we got closer and closer with each toss. Then, after several attempts, it happened! I was launched straight to the top! Everyone was excited. We did it! However, what we hadn't done was figure out how to safely dismount. I sat there at the top of the pyramid as my stunt partner held me above his head, while standing on the shoulders of two other guys. This was a precarious situation.

Our captain began shouting out instructions. We all listened intently. The cadence began, "One, two." Suddenly, I felt a dip in the pyramid, and the formation began to collapse. Before I knew it, I had hit the floor, butt first. Unfortunately, my stunt partner got tangled up with the other guys in the dismount, and there was no one there to catch me.

Within minutes, I lost all feeling in my lower extremities. As soon as I hit the floor, I screamed in agony. I couldn't catch my breath and had the wind knocked out of me. An ambulance was called, and I was rushed to Sacred Heart Hospital.

I was in shock. My body was completely numb. But for some strange reason, I was emotionally calm.

We arrived at the hospital, and I was put on a stretcher and wheeled to the ER. From there, time stood still. Later, as legend has it, my brother Rick showed up to the hospital demanding answers. Supposedly, he found my stunt partner and punched him in the face. With that, Rick was my hero forever. The story lived on for many years, until Thanksgiving Day of 2021. That's when the ugly truth emerged, and I discovered that the story had been greatly embellished. I was heartbroken because the telling had seemed so real. Rick never took my wellbeing for granted, except when I was forced to walk around campus with a "donut" for about a month. I can't tell you how many constipation jokes I'd endured, and Rick had been one of the main ringleaders.

Chapter Seventeen
Wine and Roses

I had been traveling back and forth to Eugene for months. Three or four days a week, I would put Haley in the car and make the two-hour trek to practice. I couldn't wait to get there. It was my safe place. I felt complete doing choreography and coaching. We were running the squad like a special forces unit. My girls were athletic, disciplined, creative, and hard working. In short, they were sensational. The stunt guys were approaching elite level status. We were only two years in and already the gold standard in college.

I started staying a couple days a week in Eugene to take a break from the toxicity of home. I even talked to my parents about moving back. I needed to be closer to the day-to-day activities of the squad. We had two teams now, one for men's games and one for women. We were covering all major events. I mentioned the idea to Devin of moving back to Eugene and he was surprisingly receptive. I hoped a change of venue would do us good.

It was still 1995, and Devin had been working at his current job for some time. His hours were unpredictable, and he was gone for long stretches of the day. I still made sure the apartment was immaculate and that dinner was ready when he came through the door. This job seemed to put him in a better mood, and I enjoyed the extra free time alone.

A girlfriend of mine, Angela, lived in the same complex, and our kids would play together. Sometimes we confided in one another, finding strength in our mutual ordeals. We shared our hopes and fears. It was Valentine's Day, and Angela stopped by with her son to keep me company. I had gone all out. I made a terrific dinner, set a beautiful table, and had on a sexy red dress.

I made all of Devin's favorites: greens, mac n cheese, sweet corn, fried chicken, corn bread, and peach cobbler. I had gotten him a card and was expecting him around five-thirty p.m.

But as the hours ticked by, I was so hurt and disappointed. I hadn't heard from him. Finally, he arrived around a quarter to eight. Haley was already down for the night, and Devin barged through the door with a bottle of wine and a bouquet of long-stemmed red roses in hand. "Happy Valentine's Day, wife," he yelled. I walked up to him and hugged him tight around his waist. I had instantly forgotten my anger, and we enjoyed a romantic evening together.

The next morning, I got up early to go to the gym and decided to take Devin's car so that I could have it washed after my workout. I was making an effort to keep the good vibes rolling. I ran his BMW through the soft cloth wash and got out to vacuum. I had his interior looking spotless, then opened the trunk and grabbed the vacuum hose. For a moment, I stood motionless, in disbelief. There was a nauseous pit in my stomach. My heart was racing. I was staring at a blanket, used picnic items, a wine gift bag, cellophane wrapping, and a Valentine's Day card addressed to "My Love." I opened the envelope and began to read the card. It was a letter to my husband from someone expressing her love. At the end of the letter, she added, "I hope you love the roses and enjoy the bottle of wine, think about me."

Devin had arrived two hours late on Valentine's Day with roses and a bottle of wine bought by his side chick.

Now the consistent late nights and excuses made sense.

Chapter Seventeen: Wine and Roses

This was a body blow. He had moved the goal post again, and I was a mess. I had missed all the red flags. Devin had me completely out of my comfort zone. His incessant lies and manipulation and the verbal assaults and physical abuse; it was psychological warfare. The kind of thing that spy services do to break down terrorists. Entice them with lies, gifts, and illusions of grandeur. Then, when the target discovers the plot, they resort to threats, intimidation, coercion, and violence.

Devin had broken me down. I was afraid to defend myself for fear of the unknown. He had dulled my instincts to a point where I didn't notice the extra-marital affair. The new normal had become vulgar and immoral. How could I have not seen the problem?

I walked in the apartment acting as though I hadn't a care in the world, got Haley dressed and fed, showered, and got ready for the day. I knew he would be leaving for work soon and would discover that I had detailed his car.

Devin walked out the door saying his typical goodbye, see ya later, yada, yada, yada. About thirty minutes later, he returned to find me packing. I was planning to take Haley and go stay with my parents. Truthfully, I was in a state of shock. Devin walked up behind me and wrapped his arms around my body. He pulled me in tight, put his chin on my shoulder and began with the doublespeak.

"You did a great job on my car, I was surprised." I was filled with confusion. I genuinely hated him, and at the same time, I longed for affection. I remained quiet, and he fed me the "Okidoke," saying, "It's not what you think. She's someone from my past, and I just met up with her."

I told him that I was taking the baby and leaving. I pulled away and continued packing. Devin grabbed my arm, squeezing it hard,

"You're not going anywhere," he said. The look on his face was different, more menacing, yet there was an arrogance to his demeanor. He felt a power over me. But I'd had enough. I told him that I wouldn't live with the cheating and the constant lies. He squeezed harder and pulled me close. He grabbed me by my neck and looked in my eyes. He said, "I won't talk to her anymore, and if you try to leave me, I will kill you."

That was the first time he threatened my life. He told me not to bring it up again, and I didn't.

Throughout our time in Portland, most of our friends had been people we knew from the University of Oregon. We hadn't gotten together often, but when we did it was just like old times.

I can remember one occasion when our closest friend, Flash, ventured down from Olympia, Washington. Flash was Haley's Godfather, along with my brother Rick. That night, we'd been hanging out, and Devin was being his usual self. Flash didn't like the way he was talking to me and told him to stop. Flash had my undivided attention. He was updating us on his love life. He was like a brother to us. I was sitting on Devin's lap, when he went into a rage and threw me to the floor.

Flash jumped off the couch, grabbed Devin, and dog-walked him across the room, threw Devin against the door, and held him by his shirt. Flash gave him a stern warning, saying, "If I ever see you lay hands on her again, you won't remember it." It was the first time anyone had defended me. As mad as Flash was, he'd remained calm enough to say goodbye to me and Haley. He hadn't said a word to Devin, but got in his car and drove back to Olympia.

A few weeks later, some our friends from the University stopped by. They had no idea what had just transpired before they arrived. I had been punched repeatedly in the back of the head and

Chapter Seventeen: Wine and Roses

told to "shut the f— up." Recently, I learned that they suspected that something hadn't been right, but without a cry for help, people are reluctant to get involved. I'm sure that many others suspected foul play over the years but were also reluctant to reach out. I didn't help matters, either. Instead of sending out an S.O.S., I learned to navigate the violence. I learned how to put on a smile and disguise the pain. Sometimes, silence is golden, and sometimes it's just a lead balloon.

Chapter Eighteen
Forever a Queen

During the 1991-1992 season, one of my Blazer dancer teammates, Kelly Jones, served as Mrs. Oregon. The Mrs. Oregon International Pageant is the premiere pageant for married women in Oregon. Kelly told me about all the fun events, public appearances, and philanthropy work involved. It sounded like a first-class organization. I attended the final competition and watched Kelly relinquish the crown to the new queen. Later, after a lot of thought, I decided to run for Mrs. Oregon in 1996.

I wanted to get up on that stage and show Devin that I wasn't the stupid, worthless b— that he thought I was. I wasn't someone he could hold down and repress. I wanted to show him that I knew exactly who I was. I made up my mind and applied for the city title. I was selected as Mrs. West Eugene, but I only told my parents. I wanted to surprise the rest of the family at our Christmas party. I knew that once I made the announcement, Devin would have no choice but to support me.

No one knew the pain I was suffering. There was no evidence of mental anguish behind my smile, so they couldn't see the despair in my soul from the abuse.

Before our Christmas gift opening, I made an announcement. In un-Jackie Kennedy fashion, I blurted out that I was running for Mrs. Oregon in April. Everyone was excited and hit me with a flurry of questions. My mom had the biggest smile. My cousins, as always, gave me the thumbs up. Everyone was really excited. Even my cool, calm, collected dad had to bust a smile. There was so much to do and only three months to prepare. I was fortunate to be physically fit because of my background. Even so, I hired Shane Kessler, one of our closest friends, to be my personal trainer. Shane was an Oregon alum and played football with Devin. He was one of the most instrumental people in my life, bringing positivity and encouragement at a time when I was just struggling to survive.

I first met Shane at a get together at Devin's apartment. Most of the athletes lived in the same complex just a few blocks from Autzen Stadium. I remember thinking how confident he was. There were plenty of guys with big egos, but Shane, with his bright blonde hair and baby blue eyes, had an extremely charismatic personality and a smile that would light up a room. Joke after joke and wisecrack after wisecrack, Shane had us all laughing to tears. He was the guy everyone was drawn to. His personality was magnetic. Today, he's exactly the same. Shane was married to an equally awesome woman, Laurel. She was a track star at the University of Oregon and, afterward, became an incredibly successful businesswoman in Portland.

By the time we got started, my bruises had healed, but the abuse persisted. It was an unbelievably emotional time. In order to compete on stage, I had to pull myself together. I had to believe in myself. I had to rise above the psychological warfare. When a lie is repeated enough times, sometimes it takes root inside. But I wasn't worthless; I wasn't a piece of s—! I trained hard, and working with Shane helped transform my confidence. He prepared my body, but more importantly, he prepared my mind. When I walked on that stage, I knew I was ready. I was the Hebrew Lazarus. Shane had rescued me and brought me back to life. I can't give enough credit for how he helped me.

Finally, it was pageant week. The experience of running for Mrs. Oregon was full of mixed emotions. On the one hand, I was

Chapter Eighteen: Forever a Queen

competitive by nature and wanted to win, and on the other hand, I had something much larger to prove.

DeeDee Brant was the pageant director. She was a former Mrs. Oregon and a real boss! There were twenty-four contestants in the pageant, and all were beautiful, poised, talented, and amazing. I loved them all and built significant friendships around the state. Each year, I loved watching the Miss USA, Miss America, and Miss Universe pageants, but when it came to competing, I was a complete novice. I wasn't sure what to expect, but from the beginning, I found the pageant to be empowering and self-affirming. The humanitarian work conducted by the organization was a major positive as well.

The pageant consisted of three specific segments: 25% for evening gown, 25% for physical fitness, and 50% for the interview. All the contestants performed in a production number to "Lady in Red" and were serenaded by a wonderful local artist named Dan Henson. God rest his soul.

I absolutely loved my production outfit! I wore red high heels to die for and a red Marilyn Monroe type dress. All the ladies looked fabulous. The audience was pumped and showed their full appreciation.

The most challenging part of the competition was the interview segment. There were multiple judges at separate tables. Each contestant went round-robin style to the individual judges for a private interview. I had donned a beautiful red designer suit, the power color, and black stiletto pumps. I felt fabulous, wearing dazzling jewelry and my contestant sash.

The interviews were intense. Each judge had their own specific questions. They really wanted to get to know us, what we stood for and what we represented.

There were too many questions to remember, but I do remember one particular question from Shelley Kurtz, a local news anchor for KVAL TV. Shelley asked me about my dreams. I remember the warm smile on her face and thinking what a layup this should be. Before being married, before all the "active measures," my dream would have been to perform in a dance company worldwide, or tour around the globe as a backup dancer for Janet Jackson. Now, I was just dreaming of peace and normalcy, for survival. The answer I gave was something to the effect of, "To teach dance around the world and inspire young women to pursue their hearts' desires." At the time, that dream seemed so far way, so out of touch with my current reality.

For the evening gown portion, I wore a stunning Periwinkle gown with a slit up the leg. It was embossed with diamond-colored crystals and fit me like a glove. I accessorized with stunning diamonds on my ears and wrist and glass stiletto pumps. For the physical fitness segment, we were asked to wear aerobic wear. I wore a fun, form fitting tank top bodysuit, Lycra shorts, and tennis shoes. I was in tremendous shape and felt fabulous! Then, there was an elaborate production number choreographed by Kelly, after which our husbands were invited on stage.

Devin escorted me. I remember the look on his face when he saw my evening gown. I hadn't seen that look in a very long time. He was wearing a black tuxedo, and we looked fabulous.

After all the rounds were completed and we were perfectly placed on stage. The Master of Ceremony, Jon Michaels, in his radio voice, began reading the results, "And the third runner up is… and the second runner up is… and the first runner up… and the 1996 Mrs. Oregon International and new reigning queen is… Mrs. West Eugene."

I couldn't believe my ears! I didn't hear a thing after that! The crowd was screaming; my cheerleading squad, family members, and numerous friends leading the charge.

CHAPTER EIGHTEEN: FOREVER A QUEEN

It was a magical moment. Devin wrapped me in his arms and told me how proud he was. He said it over and over and over, smiling the whole time. They placed the crown on my head and put on my new banner. I was even draped in a full-length mink coat. I took my walk across the stage, waving and thanking everyone. Later that night, DeeDee told me that I also won a new car. It was all so surreal.

There was an after party for the former queens, contestants, pageant staff, and husbands. We were eating and drinking champagne, when out of nowhere, Devin got down on one knee, grabbed my hand, and professed his love. He said, "I was forever his queen."

So many thoughts were running through my head, I wanted so much to believe it. I put a smile on my face and said, "I love you too, babe."

Chapter Nineteen
The Aftermath

As the weeks went by, I was feeling wonderfully confident. I was working hard in the gym and teaching classes. I signed with a booking agency and began juggling the statewide promotions and public appearances.

One weekend, I was invited to Seaside Oregon for the Miss Oregon America Pageant. Dee Dee invited other former queens as well. We always had fun together and developed such strong bonds. That same weekend, I was asked to judge the finals for the Miss Hawaiian Tropics contest. I couldn't be there, so I asked Devin to step in. My friend Erica Winger drove up from Eugene to babysit Haley. Erica was a high school cheerleader at my alma mater, and her mom Brenda was the coach. I did the choreography for their State and National competitions, and our families were really close. Erica was like a little sister.

She arrived at the apartment and relieved Devin of baby duty. I spoke to her a couple times to check on Haley, and I also heard from Devin. He planned to get home around two-thirty in the morning. I told them that I would be home in the morning, and when I arrived, Haley was happily playing with her toys, and Devin was hungover, watching television in bed. I asked about Erica, and Devin said that she got up early and drove home. I didn't think much of it.

A few days later, I was in Eugene for cheerleading practice at WHS. I was choreographing routines during the summer, and Erica was assisting as well. She had just graduated high school and was about to attend Oregon State University. Erica pulled me aside and told me what had transpired the night she babysat. She told me that Devin came home drunk and tried to force himself on top of her. She told me how he tried to convince her that it would be okay and that I wouldn't find out. She was unbelievably shaken. Erica explained how she had to move Haley into the bedroom and lock the door. She hardly slept that night and left at the crack of dawn.

The incident weighed heavily on her mind.

I was sickened.

Erica was uncomfortable telling the story but felt obligated. We went back to my parents' house after practice to talk. They were away for the weekend, so we were free to talk. I'm not sure how I found the courage, but I decided to confide in her. Little by little, I began to reveal everything that I had endured. I started to pour my story out like rainwater. I couldn't stop. I barely took a breath. By the time I finished, Erica knew everything, the complete unvarnished truth about all the physical and verbal abuse. That was a lot to put on a teenage girl, even if we were as close as sisters. She was already upset by what Devin did to her, but to hear this, she could hardly take it!

After what seemed like hours, Erica jumped in her car and went home to shower. About an hour later, she returned with reinforcements. Erica was so overwhelmed that she got her mother Brenda involved. Brenda was one tough cookie and considered me to be like a daughter. She meant business; she was like Miranda Priestly in The Devil Wears Prada. Brenda wanted answers, and she wanted them fast! I was shocked by their arrival and, truthfully, a little ticked. After all, who really wants to be outed, especially when they're living a lie, and a dangerous one at that. I remember the look on Brenda's face as I confirmed the stories one by one.

Chapter Nineteen: The Aftermath

The various injuries and ailments that I'd had over the years. It all began to add up. Brenda composed herself and gathered her thoughts. The only sane solution was for me to immediately press charges against Devin for assault and battery. I absolutely had to hold Devin accountable. Brenda was as worried about the psychological repercussions on Haley as she was for me. She was a teacher and school administrator and knew firsthand the ravages of abuse. Brenda and Erica pleaded with me to turn him in. They begged me to stay in Eugene. I listened to their plea, but I was Mrs. Oregon, I was a cheerleading coach at the University of Oregon, and I was a pillar in the community. There was no way I could come forward.

Beyond trying to protect my public persona and reputation, without a shadow of doubt, I felt that Devin would follow through on his threats and kill me. I was terrified, caught in the paradox of fear, a deer in the headlights. Feeling afraid yet too afraid to act.

I could see the car crash coming, but, once again, I refused to move. It was all that Brenda could do to keep from beating me herself. I told her everything, yet I forbade her to speak, even to my parents, with whom she was extremely close. I agreed to tell her immediately if things got worse, and I promised to seek counseling and consider getting a divorce. I was like the drug addict asking for one last fix.

I promised the world; but deep down inside, I had no intention of doing either of those things.

Chapter Twenty
Down but Not Out

I remember walking into the hotel in Tyler Texas and seeing the wonderful decorations and the welcome signs for the 1996 Mrs. International Contestants. I was overwhelmed.

I checked in, got my welcome gift, and picked up a highly detailed schedule of events. I made it to my suite and was greeted by the sweetest smile imaginable. My roommate was Mrs. Kansas; she was sensational. We instantly hit it off and became inseparable. The pageant included contestants from all fifty states and from around the world. We were paired two to a room. Our husbands had their own rooms, along with family members and friends. I was blessed to have in attendance my mom, mother-in-law, Erica, Brenda, and friend Libby from the Mrs. Oregon Pageant. DeeDee was by my side when not in director meetings.

It was a week full of surprises. We had to learn a huge production number for the event and made a number of appearances, including at the Kentucky Derby.

The night before the finals, I was in Devin's room when he received a distress call from his sister. She was extremely distraught because her husband had badly beat her and tried to kill her. Devin was apoplectic, and rightfully so. He hung up the phone and talked about it. I tried to show empathy. He said that she didn't deserve that. I looked at him and said, "I'm someone's sister and daughter, too." Instantly, he went into a rage. He grabbed me by the throat and shoved me backward, then grabbed my hair and dragged me to the bed. He punched me with a closed fist repeatedly in the back of my head. When I tried to get away, he threw me around until I fell to the ground. I tried to get up, and he punched me again, right next to my ear. I laid there for a minute as he yelled profanities. I was dizzy and nauseous. I just wanted to leave.

Finally, I stood, regained my balance, grabbed my purse, and walked out. There were people in the hallway, but I could hardly focus. I made my way to the elevator and back to my room. I took off my makeup, brushed my teeth, and laid in bed. My roommate wasn't back yet, and I didn't want anyone to see me. I had a pounding headache, and I was sick to my stomach. I closed my eyes and talked to myself, determined to go out on that stage once again.

The next day, I made the finals. I was wearing a stunning evening gown, and I looked flawless. I put on a big smile and walked out, proudly representing the beautiful state of Oregon. The ringing in my ears was so bad from the beating that I couldn't hear half of what the MC was saying. My marriage meant nothing to me at that point. I was competing for all the battered wives and victims of domestic violence everywhere. The smile on my face wasn't about my vows. It was about all the children who witnessed domestic violence at home. It was for every woman who had ever been sexually assaulted or raped. Entering the competition was never really about me, it was about all the lives I wanted to represent.

What I began to realize was that courage is not the absence of fear, courage is being able to act in spite of your fears. I placed eleventh, but I competed, I showed up with courage, and, given all I had endured to get there, I felt like a winner.

Chapter Twenty: Down but Not Out

The next day, my family and posse boarded the plane to fly back to Eugene. Devin and I didn't make eye contact. Actions speak louder than words, and given his actions the previous night, there was nothing more to say.

Chapter Twenty-One
The Face of Evil

It had taken some time, but it finally happened. In 1997, we moved back to Eugene.

The plan was to live at my parents' house for about six months, then buy a house. My parents had just built a beautiful home and had plenty of space.

Haley was thrilled. While Mom and I were still coaching at Oregon, we continued to do side gigs for statewide and national competitions. I was just about on the tail end of my reign as Mrs. Oregon. I got hired as the admissions director for ABC Kids and Teens Modeling and Talent Agency. Devin got an administrative position at the University of Oregon, so, career wise, we were both happy. Mom and I continued to build an amazing squad, taking the program to new heights.

One day, I was in the kitchen making breakfast. Haley was playing with her toys, and Devin was on the couch, reading the newspaper. It was a great morning; we were enjoying family time. Out of the blue, Devin asked, "Babe, what was the name of the basketball player who raped you?" I stopped for a moment, turned around, and gave him the name. Devin began reading out loud. I was numb. As it turned out, my attacker was a repeat offender. Several women had come out against him. Tears began rolling down my cheeks. I felt a bit guilty for not coming forward. Perhaps if I had done so, I could have prevented their trauma. My mind was cluttered with what ifs.

The story was broken by a remarkable reporter at the Oregonian. I contacted him and we spoke at length on several occasions. There was a part of me that had a huge sense of relief. Both because my attacker was caught and because I felt validated. I knew it wasn't my fault, but even so, the shame you carry feels like a ton of bricks. I found out from my source that my attacker apparently impersonated different NBA players in order to entice women. Later, he suffered from schizophrenia and was living in a mental institution. I broke down when I heard the news. Two wrongs don't make a right. And I don't take pleasure in other people's misfortune.

Despite the fact we were staying in my parents' house, I still endured abuse. Most days it was verbal unless we were alone. Devin coached football with my dad and brother at WHS. He was the defensive coordinator and, according to Dad, one heck of a coach. My family still had no knowledge of my abuse, although they did notice how he spoke to me from time to time. My dad wasn't pleased and always let Devin know it.

After football season ended, my parents took a week-long vacation to Hawaii. We were at the house, and Devin had some of his boys over. They were playing cards at the dining room table. As usual, they were cracking jokes and laughing, while I was playing the good hostess; cooking food and making drinks. Devin's friends always treated me like one of the gang. One of Devin's friends had a stacked hand. He was excited and asked me to take a look. I peeked at his cards and started laughing. It was a sure winner.

Then I walked into the kitchen and brought out some snacks. When I returned and looked over, Devin was giving me the evil eye. I started rubbing his shoulders, trying to massage his ego. I peeked at his hand and tried to be encouraging. Devin lost, and the guys harassed him to no end. One of the guys started calling my name. It was all good fun, but I could feel the tension mounting; my heart started racing. Regardless of how I responded, it would

Chapter Twenty-One: The Face of Evil

be wrong. I knew the look in his eyes. I had seen it all too often. I kissed Devin on the cheek and said, "You're always the winner to me."

Afterward, I went in the back to check on Haley, who was sound asleep. I waited a few minutes and went into the kitchen to clean up. I walked fast with my head down so that I didn't make eye contact. I heard laughter, trash talk, and the sound of the dominos crashing on the table. Their indoor voices were like game day voices. I knew they would be staying longer now that the competition had switched to dominoes. I peeked around the corner and said "Babe, do you need anything else? I'm going to bed." He looked right through me and shook his head. I walked over and gave him a kiss. I said, "I love you, goodnight." Of course, he was mute. Sulking inside. Now came the moment of truth; do I say goodnight to the guys or not?

I was d—med if I did, and d—med if I didn't. I quickly said goodnight to his guests. All the while hoping I had picked the right response. It went something like, "We always appreciate you spending family time, thank you for being here. Goodnight." They all stood and gave me a hug. I turned sideways to avoid any misunderstanding. I absolutely dreaded every hug; I knew each one would cost me.

I walked into the bedroom and went straight to bed, no television, no reading, no talking on the phone. Just darkness, alone with my thoughts. After an hour or so, the guys started leaving. Finally, I heard the television go off, then the bathroom toilet flushed, and the bedroom door opened. I laid in bed like a frozen corpse. I had purposely pulled the comforter over my face, but the hallway light was still on, so I knew he was there, watching me. Silence is absolutely deafening when you're terrified. Suddenly, Devin ripped off the covers, grabbed me by the hair, and dragged me down the hallway, through the kitchen, and into the living room. He backhanded me across the face, and I fell back on the couch. I stood up and tried to plead my case. I hadn't done anything. His face was transformed. I didn't recognize him. He looked like the embodiment of evil; he literally looked insane. Devin began yelling every type of obscenity, "B— a— wh— and combinations of the same. He said, "You're going to embarrass me like that! I ought to kill yo a— dead. F—ing wh—!" He punched me in the head, then started taking body shots.

Haley came down the hall, holding her stuffed bunny rabbit and crying. I begged Devin to stop. He sat Haley on the couch and told her, "Your mommy deserves to die." I was sobbing uncontrollably. I tried to grab her to protect her, but Devin put me in a vice grip. I fought as hard as I could, but I couldn't break the hold. Somehow, in the struggle, he cracked my ribs with his elbow. We both heard it. I let out a piercing scream. Devin stepped back with a wry smile and said, "That's what you get, you can't turn a wh— into a housewife."

He started chuckling, as if he'd just made a touchdown-saving tackle. I grabbed Haley and held her tight. We sat in the rocking chair for hours. I prayed for God to intervene. I begged for the nightmare to end. The abuse was so severe, I was beginning to believe everything he said.

But I didn't get married to get divorced. I felt that if I just worked harder, I could make the marriage work. I was twenty-six; Haley was two and a half. I grew up in a happy, loving family, and I wanted that for her.

Despite the pain and trauma, I found a way to block it out of my mind. I told myself that "good conquers evil." And I believe that, eventually, in the long run. But in the short run, we have to live day-to-day, and in those moments, sunshine can be a distant memory.

Chapter Twenty-Two
Bringing Down the House

Spring had come, and we finally moved into our beautiful new house. It was my dream home, two blocks from my parents' house and close to my grandparents. Devin and I were excited to have our first house together, and it was everything we wanted. We were getting along really well for a few weeks; he even came home with the cutest American Eskimo puppy for Haley. She named him Tito, and he became a great addition to the family.

My reign as Mrs. Oregon was coming to an end. It was pageant night and time to crown a new queen. I would soon be one of the "Has Beens." That was the name of the group of former reigning queens. They were the most fun, supportive, loving, and genuine group of women. I admired them all. The pageant was held at the prestigious Hult Center for Performing Arts in Eugene. I choreographed the production that year, and Devin and I sang "Endless Love" by Lionel Ritchie and Diana Ross. We walked out on stage from opposite sides. Devin began singing, "My love, there's only you in my life, the only thing that's right." His voice reverberated throughout the hall, and he sounded like an angel. Devin had an absolutely incredible singing voice.

Next, it was my turn, "My first love, your every breath that I take, your every step I make." I belted out those lyrics as we joined together at center stage. He looked into my eyes, and at that moment, he was the guy I met at Champions Night Club years earlier. He was the man who asked me to be his wife while driving through the grapevine mountains. He was the man I fell deeply in love with. We continued in harmony, "And I, I want to share all my love with you, no one else will do." We harmonized together like Peaches and Herb, or Sonny and Cher. We sang to each other's souls, and for that moment, our love was real. When we finished, there wasn't a dry eye in the place. We received a standing ovation. Haley ran on stage with roses. She was dressed like a Disney princess and said, "I love you, Mommy." The entire night was magical; a memory I will always cherish.

At the time, I was working at the ABC Talent Agency. One day, I was sitting in my office and received a phone call from a producer on the *Judge Judy* show. She asked for me by name. I was a little surprised, but I assumed it was talent related. She proceeded to tell me there was a lawsuit against my husband from his girlfriend for unpaid tires on his BMW. It made my blood boil. She informed me that the woman purchased four new tires for his car and, after several failed attempts to reach him, has filed a small claims suit.

This suit was filed in Washington County, just outside of Portland. Once I caught my breath and picked my jaw off the floor, I asked her what does *Judge Judy* have to do with the claim? She educated me on the business of the show. They looked for cases that they found interesting and offered financial incentives to both sides. I was becoming unhinged, absolutely furious! I kept my cool on the phone but wondered why they'd contacted me? According to the producer, Devin had refused to take their call or answer the complaint. As a result, the claimant searched online and gave the producer my contact information. They knew how to get a party started, so, in turn, they gave me her contact information.

I hung up the phone and called the woman immediately. The claimant told me everything: the intimate details of their sex life; the fancy dates out on the town; the special afternoon getaways; and about how we were going through a divorce. A divorce? Oh,

Chapter Twenty-Two: Bringing Down the House

h— no! But the irony was, she was the same salesperson who sold us my wedding band. Apparently, when Devin came back to pick it up, he'd asked for her phone number, and it had all started from there. How scandalous is that? I guess if you lay down with dogs, you're going to get fleas.

After we hung up, I called Devin and summoned him to my office.

The agency director and booking agent weren't in the office at the time. I was completely alone, pacing back and forth. I heard Devin come through the front door, and I sat down behind my desk. He knew from the look on my face that he was not there to eat ice cream. He sat down and said, "What's up?"

I went straight for the jugular: "I hear you have some new tires that haven't been paid for?" He didn't expect that. But as usual, he started to lie. I cut him off mid-sentence. I told him that I had spoken to the producer. I had everything written down, including the dollar amount owed, the location, and type of tires purchased, when they were put on the car, and the name of the purchaser on the receipt. I even had the case number and the location of the case filing. He knew he was caught, but sociopaths don't relent. They don't say I'm sorry. They don't sit and reflect. They don't consider the consequences; they just plow ahead. So, like any good narcissist, Devin began spinning an elaborate tale about how he had gotten over on some chick that worked at the tire shop. He said that he didn't really know her, but the opportunity just presented itself. Devin didn't realize that I had spoken to the girl at this point.

Just then, my coworkers returned from lunch. I heard them talking but I didn't care. In fact, their presence empowered me. I stood up and gave Devin all the gory details about the dates on the town, the intimate sexual interludes, the spontaneous afternoon getaway. He was in unfamiliar territory, caught with his pants down, schooled by a gimp.

But you don't get to be an "old G" by being weak in the knees. Devin kept at it, spinning like a top. He was relentless; the lies kept coming. Sociopaths don't quit, you have to take them to the ground and handcuff them. By now, I had realized that Devin was a master manipulator. He tried to convince me that he never intended to take the relationship that far; he said he never had feelings for her and that's the reason he never returned her calls. Again, I wanted to believe. He knew just what to say. He leaned in to kiss me, and I slapped him as hard as I could and told him to leave. He stood up and said, "I'm going to give you that one."

But total defeat is never an option. Devin pushed me against the wall and ominously said, "You won't ever bring this up again, and if you ever try to leave me, I will kill you." Devin walked out my office door and passed the agency director like the invisible man. My office had a full-length glass window, so my coworkers saw everything. Once Devin was gone, I broke down crying. I told them the whole story. They were totally supportive, and I wanted to tell them about the domestic violence. I wanted to be vulnerable; I wanted to let them in, but I just couldn't do it. Not at that moment. But, in the end, it didn't really matter. They knew.

Chapter Twenty-Three
The Lady Doth Protest Too Much

Not long after the confrontation, I decided to make a career change. I started working for a title and escrow company called American Title Group. Little did I know, that the move would result in some of the most profound business relationships of my life.

I started out learning the industry as a front desk receptionist. Later, I became the marketing manager, then the assistant vice president. It was thirteen wonderful years.

The owner was a man named Curtis Irving. Curtis also owned several other related businesses and proved to be one of my most important mentors. No matter the circumstance, Curtis was always there, a pillar of strength. He taught me the art of sales and marketing. He taught me how to understand value and worth. Most importantly, Curtis taught me how to stand up for myself yet never look down on anyone. Curtis once said, "Bring me the solution, and I will help you defeat the problem." I didn't understand it then, but he was trying to encourage me to think, to be deliberate in my actions. He knew exactly how to motivate me.

Eventually, I would find my strength and understand completely.

After we moved back to Eugene, I reconnected with many of my friends. Thirteen years had passed, but it only felt like weeks. One place I loved was the tanning salon where I had worked for many years. Cheryl had expanded and leased out the vacant space next door. She'd turned "The Tanning Hut" into a full-service salon and spa. It was fun to see my former colleagues and, of course, secure all my beauty needs. I would walk through the door, make the rounds, and give hugs to all the girls.

The one face I missed was Lisa's. It didn't matter that over a decade had passed since her death. Those of us who knew her always knew something was missing.

I used the tanning beds several days a week and got my nails done every two weeks. Trying to keep my naturally brown hair blonde was a process, so the Tanning Hut was like a second home. I usually had my nails done by either Jenny, Tanya, or Coquette. They were the best in the city. Because my schedule was so unpredictable, I frequently had to take whoever was available. Everyone sat close together, so the gossip was always shared.

It was an extremely rough patch in my marriage, and the rumor mill was in full effect. One of the nail techs, Michelle, went out clubbing on the weekends and had personal friendships with many of the athletes at Oregon. Michelle and I started getting to know each other fairly well. She would fill me in on the latest gossip, with a fair degree of creditability. Increasingly, I became more comfortable talking about some of the problems at home, particularly the cheating. I never discussed the physical abuse, but the salon made me feel safe. One day at practice, I broke a nail, and it was bleeding underneath. When I left practice, I went straight to the salon.

Michelle saw the pain I was in and quickly squeezed me in. She started asking questions about Devin, then told me how he came on to a teller at the bank. They exchanged numbers and went out to eat. Eugene could be a small place when you're the topic of conversation. Apparently, they saw each other a few times before the bank teller discovered that Devin was married.

I was so embarrassed. I was sick of the infidelity and began loathing him. The room was full of customers, so Michelle and I started talking quietly. I opened up to her; allowing myself to be

Chapter Twenty-Three: The Lady Doth Protest Too Much

vulnerable. I needed to vent. She was so easy to talk to and always found a way to make me laugh.

On another day, I returned to the salon to buy a bathing suit for an upcoming trip to Los Angeles. Cheryl ordered all the best swimwear, jewelry, vacation attire, and accessories, and she gave me the employee discount even though I hadn't worked there in years. The dressing room had fabulous lighting and three full-length mirrors, so a girl could see herself from every angle. Some of the other girls were sharing their opinions and by the time I finished, I was fully outfitted from head to toe. I walked to the front desk to pay and was pulled aside by Michelle. She asked a few questions about the specifics of my trip, but I didn't think much of it. Looking back, however, I can clearly see the seeds of deception. I finished paying and headed home to pack.

A couple of weeks later, I had an appointment at the salon. I sat down at the nail desk and listened to the girls laughing and telling stories. It had a little bit of a circus atmosphere. I drew Michelle again that day, and she started telling me about various things in her life. Then, out of nowhere, she popped the question, "So, how's the sex life at home?" It didn't happen often, but I was speechless. She was always blunt and had absolutely no filter. It wasn't uncommon for her to say off the wall things, but this came out of left field, and it was personal. We hadn't even been talking about sex. I heard one of the other techs say, "Geeze, Girl!" followed by multiple people laughing.

I smiled, looked her in the eye, and told her, "It's tense at home, let's just keep it at that." I had already confided in her. She knew that I wasn't happy. And up to this point, she had always been encouraging.

Not long after I confided in her, I found out that Michelle had spent the night with Devin while I was away. Now it all made sense, the interest in my itinerary and sex life. I was in disbelief; I felt completely betrayed.

Money, ideology, coercion, and ego. How does a person regale you with wild stories week after week, look you in the eye, profess their friendship, all the while they're shagging your husband? Un-frickin'-believable!

And to add insult to injury, I had tipped this chick handsomely, so this one was ego! A mutual friend spilled the tea. It was hard, but she made me realize that everyone who smiles to your face is not your friend. This seemed so elementary, but it was another hard lesson.

There's a difference between being loose and being a slut. Michelle was both, and we never spoke again.

Yet, there was a silver lining. Something inside me began to change. I always believed that respect begets respect. Do unto others as you would have them do unto you. It was instilled in me from birth. How could such a simple concept be such an extraordinary request? I tried to see the best in everyone until proven otherwise. I judged people based on my personal experience, not from social media, gossip, or the opinions of others. Maybe I was naive. Despite what I had endured, I tried to give people the benefit of the doubt. But now, because of this betrayal, I became much more cynical. I embraced the motto; "If I trust you a little bit, that is a lot."

Chapter Twenty-Four
A Little Reminiscing

I was young when I first met Devin. He groomed me like a sterling pony. I had no idea what was happening. I mistook control for concern, "love bombing" for love, and excuses for empathy. Devin said he wanted my undivided attention. It made me feel special, like he really cared. Had I been older or more sophisticated, I might have recognized the red flags. The grooming and courtship stage of a relationship can be infectious; it can have your head spinning. This is all the more reason to pay attention to your instincts and listen to those inner voices.

One day, Devin and I stopped by a youth football camp held by NFL great Anthony Newman. There were hundreds of boys waiting to be coached. Anthony had asked several other NFL players there, volunteering their time, giving something back. Alongside the football camp was a cheerleading camp ran by Anthony's wife Teri Newman, who was a cheerleader for the Los Angeles Rams. I had known Anthony for five years. He played defensive back for University of Oregon, although we actually met at the Hula-Bowl in Honolulu. Anthony was the "golden boy" for Oregon. He was one of the first homegrown athletes to make it to the NFL, where he played fourteen years.

As we walked up, Anthony gave us a huge smile. He called Teri over and introduced us. She was so gracious. Teri flashed me her famous smile, gave me a hug, said that she hoped to see me again, and went back to work. A couple of the football coaches were looking on.

Devin pulled me close and positioned me behind him. I thought it was a little strange, so I tugged on his jacket and quietly asked if something was wrong? He looked me in the eye and said, "You don't need to be talking to any of these guys." I didn't remember talking to anyone, but if so, what should it have mattered? I stayed silent the rest of the visit. It bothered me. Yet he was holding my hand, and I felt a warm embrace. He didn't seem mad, just protective. Looking back, he was just teaching me how to behave in his presence: seen but not heard. Looking good but under wraps. Devin was showing me who called the shots.

Sometimes, when I think about the abuse I endured, I almost get dizzy. It was a roller-coaster, with dramatic twists and turns. I never knew what was coming next. Simple things like pulling up to a stoplight became an ongoing ordeal. I had to look at Devin or straight ahead. I couldn't risk being accused of having a wandering eye. How ironic. Shopping at the mall was similarly treacherous. In the store, I kept my head down and focused on the task at hand. Between stores, full speed ahead. Devin didn't want me stopping to chat, even with old friends. If he initiated the pause or saw a friend, that was completely different. Control was the common denominator. It was the only way that any of this made sense.

By the time the indoctrination was complete, I wasn't sure whether Tuesday followed Monday or vice versa. He had me so brainwashed, I couldn't see straight. I couldn't see the red flags. My instincts were dulled, my sixth sense dimmed. From the start, I was mesmerized by Devin's charisma, and my silence only emboldened him.

With strong-willed, controlling types of people, you either establish proper boundaries or you get run over. I was roadkill before I knew it, walking on eggshells, afraid of committing the smallest offense. I self-censored and became my own worst critic.

Chapter Twenty-Four: A Little Reminiscing

Before Devin ever abused me physically, he had infected my mind. I lost all confidence. There were days when I was so mentally exhausted, I just couldn't keep up.

Was all this Devin's fault? No! I made mistakes, too. A great historian, I think it was Fredrick Douglass, once said something like "Show me how much injustice a man will allow, and I will show you exactly how much injustice the man will endure." As such, I take full responsibility for my inaction. I was weak when I could have been stronger. Nevertheless, I didn't beat myself. I didn't encourage my spouse to cheat. I didn't engage in psychological warfare and try to strip myself of my dignity and self-respect.

Why don't victims leave?

That question is as old as Methuselah.

Some of the psychologists say that it's because of a "trauma bond" or the "Stockholm Syndrome." The specifics are above my pay grade, but I know that millions of women find themselves in this situation.

My goal is to help, and later in the book, I offer up some tools.

Chapter Twenty-Five
At Home with the Taliban

In June of 1997, Timothy McVeigh was convicted on fifteen counts of murder for the 1995 Oklahoma City bombing. At the time, it was the deadliest act of terrorism in United States history before 9/11. The bombing resulted in the death of 168 people, including many women and children. McVeigh was a Gulf War veteran and, reportedly, betrayed the country because of differences over American foreign policy and the government's handling of a 1993 incident in Waco, Texas.

In writing this book, I began to see a strong linkage between the behavior of terrorists and abusers. In many ways, they seem to operate on the same basis of extreme grievance, anger, self-righteousness, and conspiracy. In other words—based on ideology and ego.

In our fight against terror, we hunted down Al-Qaeda with brutal efficiency and held them accountable. Now, I'm not suggesting that we use the same tactics at home, but having the same sense of urgency in the fight against domestic abuse would be very helpful.

By this time, we had settled into our house, which had a circular driveway on a corner lot. Standing in the living room, you could see every house on the block. We were facing a beautiful park, where Haley loved to play.

One day, coming home from practice and pulling into the driveway, the garage door was open, and Devin had his car parked out front. When I walked into the house, he was pacing in the living room and visibly upset. Out of nowhere, he began yelling and screaming about something I had done. I didn't have a clue what he was talking about. Most everything he accused me of was fabricated. I lived my life devoted to my family. The last thing I wanted was conflict with him.

Privately, Devin hated the fact that I had the respect of his friends and that they would openly check him on occasion. There were two tiers of friends: acquaintances and those he genuinely thought of as family. I knew the difference. The fact that Devin and I both worked at the University caused tension regarding some of my relationships. He seemed especially irked that I was well liked throughout the athletic department.

On this particular day, Devin was ranting about some conversation I'd had. Like always, he was embellishing and creating imaginary conspiracies to make some obscure point. He worked himself into a frenzy. It was gibberish, garbage, manic, a ridiculous web of lies. I couldn't believe it. I was being berated and falsely accused of cheating by a serial adulterer and pathological liar. It was so frustrating; it was like dealing with the Taliban.

Things were escalating quickly. He became almost manic; his temper turning violent. I knew I needed to get away. As I turned around, he yanked me by my hair and started screaming in my face. Tears were falling down my cheeks, and I cupped my hand around the back of my neck, I thought I had whiplash.

He said, "B—, that didn't hurt!"

When I replied, "That's a lie," he took a step forward and punched me straight in the face.

Devin was 245 pounds, and he hit me like a grown man. I was knocked to the ground. I grabbed my eye, crying, rocking back and forth, shocked, and afraid.

He walked away, and I got up and went to the bedroom. I blew my nose and washed off the mascara streaming down my

Chapter Twenty-Five: At Home with the Taliban

face. Within minutes, I lost sight in my right eye. My face swelled up to the size of a grapefruit. My eye was swollen shut. I panicked and started yelling, "No! No! No!" I had to pick up Haley from my parents, and I looked insane.

Devin came to look, and his face went blank. He was worried, not about me but about potential trouble for himself.

Before I knew it, I was scrambling to cover up his dastardly deed. How sad! How disgraceful! I was working to gaslight myself. But before you are too hard on me, I had a purpose. Picking up Haley wasn't my only obstacle. I had a marketing presentation at Coldwell Banker the following morning and a men's basketball game at Mac Court. It was one thing to have a sick day, and it was quite another to explain a black eye.

Devin picked Haley up from my parents' house. She came through the door and immediately pointed to my eye. I told her, "Mommy got an owie." She seemed to accept it, and I went about the night's business as usual. I didn't want Haley to feel the stress. Devin sat next to me on the couch, holding a bag of ice. He gently placed it on my eye, cuddled me, and said, "I'm so sorry, it won't happen again." It was the first time he ever apologized. I don't know if he was truly remorseful or just concerned about the repercussions.

After calling in sick for the third day in a row, my boss Jeremy came to the house. I've never known anyone who could read people quite like Jeremy. He was a genius in real estate, but more importantly, he respected everyone and always treated people fairly. Jeremy got along well with Devin but was always suspicious. He sensed something in Devin that didn't feel right. When I came to the door and he saw my face, Jeremy wasn't surprised, but he was furious and wanted some answers. Suspicion was rampant within the office. Jeremy wouldn't let it go and pressed me. I felt cornered, like a rat caught in a trap. I had to pony up. I had been thinking about leaving for some time but was finally ready to pull the trigger. Jeremy encouraged me to work with a greater sense of urgency. I knew he was right but still needed some time.

That night I called one of our closest friends, Hansen. He was the only family friend who really knew the situation. Hanson was a funny guy, a natural, the type of guy who would have you rolling on the ground laughing. He was loyal to the core. I needed someone I could trust and rely on. He had my best interest at heart.

The next morning, Hanson stopped by the house and saw my face. He was struggling not to beat Devin's a—. I put him in a horrible position, but I wasn't prepared to take meaningful action. I look back on how unfair that was. He was Devin's best friend and a former roommate. They had a brotherhood from football and a genuine bond. Hanson and I were close as well, and my whole family loved him. A year later, he would find himself in the middle of our criminal trial.

Years before, I had been working hard between the title company and coaching at the university. I would drop Haley off at Allison Park Christian Center for preschool, then get into the office by eight-thirty. The marketing team was on the hunt for Red October, constantly scouring the landscape for new business. Almost daily, we made sales presentations somewhere and to someone. I loved pitching business and closing deals. We would walk into a bank or real estate developer's office like a group of Navy Seals. We dazzled them with smiles and service and consistently brought home the bacon. There was lots of competition, so we had to hustle hard.

From the hustle and bustle of sales marketing, I would transition into the grit and grind of cheerleading. Both take a lot of energy to be successful. Despite the battles at home, cheerleading was always my safe place. I would put on a smile and

Chapter Twenty-Five: At Home with the Taliban

walk into the gym with the spirit of Grace Kelly and the confidence of the Sundance Kid. I felt alive. I was in my element, soaking up my passion. Whether at practice or games, cheerleading was my peace. For me, there's nothing like the bond between coaches and their cheerleaders. It's a precious bond and a timeless door that never closes.

When you build a program for fifteen years, you develop many meaningful friendships. Some of the football coaches on staff when I was a cheerleader in 1989 were still on staff when I stepped away from coaching in 2010. And because of the bond Devin had with many of the football players from California, they became almost like extended family. We gave them a place to hang out and relax. I would cook soul food dinners; guys would play cards or watch games; we even threw an NFL Draft party for one of the guys. Devin used to refer to us as Bonnie and Clyde. He would tell people how we were a power couple.

To our Duck family, we were untouchable, but in the confines of our home, we were a facade. With all of the violence and abuse, we were much more like the Taliban than Ben and J. Lo.

Part Three
Renavigating

Chapter Twenty-Six
On the Road Again

Like mother, like daughter, I have always been considered an intense coach. I guess the apple doesn't fall far from the tree. I expect extremely hard work and dedication from every member of the team. I don't expect perfection, especially at the risk of a cheerleader's health, but I definitely push the envelope on game time performances.

Being a cheerleader at the University of Oregon meant meeting a certain standard, rising to a particular level. We had tradition, a brand, an expectation. Being a member of the squad wasn't a designation; it was a way of life. There was no room for excuses and even less for bad attitudes and a lack of effort.

Throughout my tenure, the one thing that always remained true was my commitment to help any member of my team. As long as they were transparent and honest, I had their backs no matter what they were going through. Unfortunately, I didn't have to hold myself to the same standard.

The combination of my desire to make my teams the best and my team members' desire to be the best proved to be a winning formula year after year. I was completely crazy about all of them. They weren't cheerleaders; they were extended family. I genuinely loved them regardless of any moments of contention. Like the famous Philly two-guard, Allen Iverson, I believe strongly in game time performance. However, my coaching style greatly centered around practice, practice, practice, and more practice in order to enjoy the benefit of performing.

It was spring of 1997, and as usual, I parked my car at the University's Casanova Center. I grabbed my luggage and Oregon cheerleading bag. Talking to myself out loud, I was scrambling to gather my things. We were heading to Ames Iowa for the women's NCAA basketball tournament. I was taking a large squad of cheerleaders with me, so there was much to consider.

While I was walking toward the team bus, I was taking deep breaths and fighting back tears. I knew that within a few minutes I would have to put a smile on my face despite the emotional torment I had just undergone. I worked harder at masking my abuse than anything else in my life. It amazes me I had the energy to accomplish anything being married to Devin.

Intent on making my way to the bus, suddenly, I looked up and saw my favorite group of pranksters directly walking my way. They were always up to something. I could consistently count on one of these three to make me laugh and relieve the weight of the world. Becca, Frankie, and Bob; the three Amigos! They looked out for me in more ways than one.

They didn't know what I had been through an hour before, but Becca looked me in the eye and asked, "You want to sit by me?" Becca didn't have to ask; she already knew something was wrong. She had my back without saying a word.

We got to the Eugene airport and began the tedious task of toting luggage and checking in. I barely remember the flight to Iowa. I spent hours replaying the fight in my mind.

I had been packing for the trip when the dark clouds appeared. Devin started going ballistic. He was on the rampage and called me a f—ing wh—. He was going off the deep end. He accused me of talking to someone and having an affair. Was this not the pot calling the kettle black? I was so sick of his mouth.

Chapter Twenty-Six: On the Road Again

I yelled at the top of my lungs, "You are crazy! Stop making things up!" I was truly terrified, and I knew what he was capable of, but at that moment I just couldn't take anymore.

I have lot of faults: I talk too much, tan too often, and have too many pair of shoes, but cheating is not one of them.

I went to the ends of the earth to make the marriage work and to have a happy home. I gambled on the wrong response, and he backhanded me across the face. I let out a big "uh" but stood completely still. I didn't take my eyes off the ground. But it didn't matter, he was going to assault me anyway. He grabbed my face and came in close, nose to nose, pursing his lips together and glaring into my eyes.

He said, "You aren't f—ing worth it, Corine." I was shaking and bracing myself for what would come next.

Devin let go of my face and used his body to intimidate me. I turned toward the bathroom, and he pushed me in the back as hard as he could. I hit the wall headfirst, then bounced backward trying to catch my fall. I kept repeating, "I have to leave! Please stop!"

He started laughing and said, "I don't give a f—, and I want a divorce."

I could not believe what I heard.

I gathered myself, grabbed my bags, and walked out the front door. As I was getting into the car, he said, "We can split everything up when you get back." I started up the car and drove off.

When we landed in Iowa, it was one mishap after another. The temperature was below freezing, and snow and ice covered the ground. As we exited the bus toward the hotel, we looked more like ice skaters than cheerleaders. The first night in Ames, we went to dinner. Afterward, some of the squad members decided to go out and experience Iowa. That was pretty standard on away trips.

I usually deferred, but this time I didn't feel like being cooped up in my room, especially after what had happened. We checked around to see where Duck fans were at, jumped in some taxis, and ventured out. The tricky part was keeping the whole group together, given that some of the members were under twenty-one. Most of the time, we only brought the most senior cheerleaders on the road. But in this case, we had a mix.

We got to the club, and it was perfect. Persons twenty-one and over upstairs; spring chickens downstairs. We got wrist bracelets; the youngsters didn't. Like with every college town in America, the place had the party scene down to a science. There is never a doubt when a cheerleading squad is together. There is always someone dancing, singing, stunting, taking pictures of themselves, or all of the above. In some cases, simultaneously.

I walked into the big girl section with the three Amigos and other squad members. One of the male cheerleaders escorted the youngsters downstairs.

The bar was packed. The place was jumping, and people were dancing everywhere. Televisions were all around, and Iowa State memorabilia was on full display. I was approached right away to dance with a gorgeous guy. He was about my age and had an intoxicating smile. I didn't hesitate for a second and got right out on the dance floor. Before I knew it, Bob, Becca, and Frankie were right on my hip, dancing and laughing in their usual style.

We danced nonstop and had a great time. The funny thing was, we didn't see any Oregon fans at the club. None that we recognized, anyway.

It started getting late, and I decided to head back to the hotel. My dance partner for the night offered to join me. It had been a long time since I had enjoyed myself so much, and I missed the feeling of being wanted. How sad. It took a perfect stranger to provide what I was missing. Sometimes, I can still feel the rush of

Chapter Twenty-Six: On the Road Again

my heart beating like it was yesterday. How ironic! I was backhanded and berated by my husband for something I didn't do and threatened with the prospect of divorce.

That evening, I was prepared to accommodate him. I could turn all of Devin's conspiracies into prophesy.

It took everything I had to say no.

We said our good nights, and I headed for the hotel... alone!

I got back to my hotel room and was about to change for bed when I got a distress call from Becca. "Coach, we got a problem!" She gave me the cliff note version, "The girls are being arrested at the club."

I thought to myself, *how is that possible?*

Becca and Bob returned to the hotel in a cab to pick me up. We pulled up to the club and the first thing I saw was two police cars with flashing lights. As we got closer, I could see three of my under twenty-one girls were in handcuffs. I yelled out and tried to intervene, but Frankie grabbed me and began walking backward. I could see the look on my girls' faces as they were placed in the back of the squad cars. I learned later that they were far more afraid of me than they were of the police.

Right away, Becca made calls, trying to figure out how to get the girls released. I was pacing in the parking lot, considering whether to call the Athletic Director.

It was one a.m. This was not a good look. The University wasn't big on scandal.

Frankie and Bob were more worried for me than for the girls.

They hailed a cab, and we returned to the hotel. The entire squad went to their rooms, while I sat with the three Amigos to troubleshoot. Paying bail was not an option for me. I wasn't about to call Devin for anything. We canvassed our networks, came up with the money, went downtown, and posted bail, then jumped in a taxi and returned with the "packages." Not a word was spoken.

It was late, and we had an upcoming game. I wanted a great performance, so I decided to wait until we got back to Eugene before metering out justice.

The plan worked like a charm, right up until the story was printed in the sports section of Eugene's Register-Guard. As it turned out, a reporter from the newspaper had been at the bar that night. A copy of his article was on my AD's desk before sunup, along with a colorful photo of the girls in handcuffs. Apparently, once I left the club, the youngsters took umbrage and came upstairs. They walked into the bar without wristbands, then lied about their age once confronted. When their driver's licenses revealed the ugly truth, the police were called, and the girls were arrested.

Fortunately, I had a wonderful relationship with my Athletic Director and university supervisors. The band director was also fully supportive. Nevertheless, the situation was embarrassing for all of us, so there had to be consequences. The three girls were reprimanded but not kicked off the team. I had to set an example so there wouldn't be a repeat in the future.

We all grew as a squad. In fact, two of the girls eventually became team captains a few years later and turned out to be two of the most talented and respected leaders we ever had. It was a tough week for them, but something we can all laugh about today.

As for the cute guy at the bar, he came to the game the following day and greeted me like a longtime friend. We talked and laughed during halftime. Honestly, I was surprised but flattered that he took the time to come.

After the trip, I detected another internal shift. I was feeling more alive yet conflicted. A part of me had been dying a little every day. Living with abuse had become all consuming. It was growing harder and harder to hide the truth from the world. I was a fun, outgoing person but lived with a broken heart and a troubled soul.

Chapter Twenty-Six: On the Road Again

I dreaded the trip back home. I couldn't wait to see Haley, but the nausea of seeing Devin was inescapable.

Throughout the trip, I spent a lot of time with Becca. She was the oldest member of the squad. We were four years apart and had a real connection. Becca was so in tune with my feelings, she could almost read my thoughts. I found out later that she was studying early childhood development and working with abused women and children. Becca made me feel safe and allowed me to be vulnerable. She had noticed the bruises and began voicing her concerns. After the trip to Iowa, Becca officially became part of my inner circle. She also began babysitting Haley from time to time. Haley told her about the abuse in her own words. It was powerful testimony coming from a four-year-old.

The Bible says, "Out of the mouths of babes and sucklings hast thou ordained strength because of thine enemies," (Psalm 8:2).

Chapter Twenty-Seven
A Sordid Affair

In March 1998, Titanic won eleven Oscars at the academy awards, including for best picture. And in May, an equally compelling show got underway when the Department of Justice filed an anti-trust lawsuit against Microsoft. Now, that was a movie—Bill Gates versus Janet Reno. It was Goliath versus Goliath, two titans getting it on, like Ali-Frazier 4.

Sometime during this period, I got a surprise call from the athletic department; they needed me to attend an urgent meeting. It was rare for them to call my cell phone, so I left work early and headed over to the Casanova Center, which is the chief administrative building for the Oregon athletic department. I was directed into one of the boardrooms, and as I walked in, I saw the athletic director. Everyone absolutely loved him, including me. We had an excellent relationship, and I was happy to see him. He put his arm around my shoulder and said, "I'll be right by your side."

As I scoured the room, I recognized a few of the participants. There was someone from legal and another person from affirmative action. I didn't see my mom, who was my direct supervisor, so I was a little confused about the purpose of the meeting. To the best of my recollection, all the other attendees were men. But since we were in the "Casanova" Center, there was no reason to fret.

One by one, the participants introduced themselves. By the time they finished, I was still oblivious. Within minutes, my heart started racing. My stomach turned nauseous. Once again, I was thrust into an impossible situation, a pot of boiling hot water.

Devin was being accused of sexually assaulting a cheerleader on my squad.

The head of Devin's department began laying out the facts; it was an open and shut case. They questioned me about my knowledge of the accusations and about whether I could continue on as a coach, given Devin's involvement. Some of the questions were a bit insulting, especially given the fact that none of them knew that I was raped eight years earlier as an Oregon cheerleader. The victim and I had more in common than any of them could imagine.

They didn't know the massive impact this had on my mental and emotional health; it was like a form of PTSD. I assured them that I was a professional and that the victim would be treated no differently than before I walked in, no differently than any other girl on the squad. I told them that I loved her and that I was sickened and hurt by the situation. The participants could feel my pain and accepted my words as true. Career-wise, I lived to coach another day. Marriage-wise, bridges were starting to burn.

After the meeting, I was dying inside, especially knowing that some of the other squad members were aware of the situation. I went to eat with my mom and told her what happened. She was absolutely disgusted. I sat there in shock, numb, trying to figure out the next steps.

I heard someone once say, "Ten percent is the problem, ninety percent is your attitude." Crisis managers will tell you that what you do in the first twenty-four hours can be crucial. I called Devin and told him that we needed to talk. He seemed to expect it; he knew it was only a matter of time.

Chapter Twenty-Seven: A Sordid Affair

Soon after, I found the police knocking at my door. They asked what I knew about the accusations. They also wanted to speak to Devin, who was coaching on the football field at WHS. The police followed me to the school and allowed me to take the lead. I didn't want the kids to see Devin handcuffed and marched away. I walked over to my dad in the middle of practice and explained the situation. I told him that the EPD was there for Devin. He had to go down to the station to get blood tested and questioned.

Devin's version went something like this: While I was at the game in Iowa, the cheerleader invited him to her dorm room to hang out. They had some drinks together and one thing led to another. They had consenting sex, and she even gave him naked pictures of herself. Devin suggested that the next day, she probably got worried that I would find out and decided to report him to the campus police. Devin produced two naked pictures of her, which he had hidden in a duffle bag in the garage. It was enough to escape criminal charges but not enough to vindicate his infidelity and immoral behavior.

Later that week, I found out that while Devin was employed at the university, this was the third time he had been placed on administrative leave. All three times for accusations of sexual harassment or misconduct involving female students. I worked in the athletic department and never had a clue. While Devin was at the police station, my close friends Stephanie Vaughan, Steve Dade, and Hansen came to the house to keep me company. We had dinner and they played dominoes until Devin walked through the door. I didn't know what to expect, but I wasn't in the frame of mind to be alone. Later that night, we sat down to talk. Devin told me what happened at the police station. I acted like the empathetic wife, though I could hardly stomach the sight of him.

Not long after, Devin was terminated from the University. By this point, I was completely checked out of the marriage. I was living day to day, miserable, conflicted, zombie-like. Little did I know, I was not yet at rock bottom.

Shortly after the meeting in the Casanova Center, rumors about our relationship ran rampant throughout the athletic department. Coaches and administrators always treated me with respect, but Devin's behavior was like the pink elephant in the room. One particular acquaintance was not a fan of Devin's. He saw firsthand Devin's incessant womanizing and disparaging behavior. He interacted with him on a daily basis and knew that Devin was a serial sexual offender, that his indiscretions were almost an open book.

Toward the end of the marriage, I fell short as well. I stepped outside of my vows. After the latest revelation, I lost it. I crossed the line with someone outside our marriage. We had known one another for a while, and over a period of time became increasingly close. It wasn't planned, but it happened unexpectedly. One night, after hours of talking about what I had been through. He was there for me, and, honestly, I was feeling numb. We didn't have sex, but we walked right up to the line. When I got home, Devin knew that something was different. I tried to hide my body for several days. One day, he confronted me about why I wouldn't undress around him. I had hickeys and marks in several places, especially around the back of my neck.

As scared as I was, I told him the truth. There was a lot of yelling, screaming, threats, and intimidation. But that morning, he didn't lay a hand on me. He couldn't afford another run-in with the police. He was fresh off the rape allegations and still on

Chapter Twenty-Seven: A Sordid Affair

administrative leave. He also wasn't sure how much I had told my quasi-paramour concerning my physical abuse. Devin demanded to know who I was with. Initially, I didn't tell him, why get two people killed? After an hour of attacks and blistering interrogation, I broke down like a soldier who went AWOL. Devin put two and two together and figured it out.

As soon as I confirmed the identity, Devin went directly to his office and confronted him. My friend was the furthest from being intimidated and Devin knew it. My friend told the truth about everything. I was surprised at how forthcoming he was. They continued to work together until Devin was fired and, after that, they never spoke again.

The interlude was a one-time event, and we never went down that road again. Up to that point, I had been above reproach, like Caesar's wife.

After some time had passed, I reflected on my actions. There was no justification for what I did. Two wrongs don't make a right. I knew that despite the trauma I endured, I should have made a better decision. I also knew that people would judge me and attempt to find fault. Having lived in the public eye for a while, I knew that was just part of the game. Coaches, players, actors, politicians, and other public figures go through it all the time, but having your life on display for all the world to see is not easy. And having a husband accused of seducing and raping young girls doesn't promote fidelity either. By this time, I felt nothing for my marriage. I had nothing left to give. I had no remorse or regret. It was my cross to bear, and I was prepared to bear it.

Jesus once said, "He who is without sin among you, let him first cast a stone" (John 8:7).

In the end, there was a silver lining. I detected another shift. I had stood up for myself at the University; I told my mother the unvarnished truth; I confronted my husband directly; I let the legal process play out; I got a little dirty, but I didn't despoil myself; I told Devin the truth about my indiscretion in the face of fear and uncertainty; I endured the naysayers but didn't let them break me; and I reassembled my cheerleaders and continued to deliver excellent results. Something was changing inside, something more powerful than myself.

I was still in the tunnel, but there looked like a light at the end.

Chapter Twenty-Eight
Gotham's Reckoning

I was leaving for the gym on a Sunday morning as usual. I had to cover a women's volleyball game later that day, so I had to get in, get my workout done, and get back. Before leaving, Devin asked me to bring home some food from the Hawaiian Grill, which was located inside the gym. I agreed and went on my merry way. Before completing my workout, I walked over to the grill and discovered they were closed. My cell phone was in the car, so I called Devin from the front desk. He picked up and I explained the situation; that I was planning to stop by Subway. He moaned and groaned but accepted reality.

The call ended, and I went back to complete my last few sets of squats. Back then, home phones had caller ID and reverse dial features. So, sure enough, Devin pushed redial and started questioning the front desk clerk. He wanted to know who the two guys were who were talking in the background and whether I was working out with them? The clerk was put off but reluctantly answered. She even put one of the guys on the phone and Devin started questioning him.

Before I left, the two guys came over and gave me the "411" on their discussion with Devin. I was super embarrassed but thankful. Then, like clockwork, as I was leaving Subway, Devin called my cell phone and began screaming. I asked him to calm down so I could respond. He continued ranting and raving and slinging accusations about me and Shawn, the guy he spoke to at the gym. It was absurd, and a farce.

Devin had worked up a scenario in his mind and was completely out of control. He told me that he was going to kill me. He said he was going to let Haley watch him murder me. Nothing I could say was going to change that. He had a 9-millimeter handgun, and I knew he was capable of using it. I did the only thing I could do; I drove to the high school to get my dad and brother. Dad was the head coach at WHS, and my brother was the offensive coordinator. They were having a coaches meeting, but Devin was no longer on the staff. I pulled up to the parking lot and walked through the side entrance of the school.

The classroom door was wide open, and the coaches were watching game film. I stood in the doorway and asked for my dad and brother to come out. This was the first time I had ever gotten them directly involved. I reluctantly said, "Devin is out of control. I can't go home." They were both frozen. I told them that I needed their help. I had a plan. I remember vividly standing outside my car and explaining.

I said I wanted them to be very quiet and told them I would go through the garage and for them to enter through the front door. Before we left the parking lot, I said "I want you to see what's been happening."

We got to the house, and I entered through the garage and walked toward the bedroom. My dad and brother walked in through the living room. Devin was about to get in the shower. As soon as he saw me, he pulled me by my ponytail, threw me into the closet doors, and began punching me in the head repeatedly. My dad and brother came racing in and Devin was absolutely shocked. He thought we were alone. My dad started yelling and demanding answers. Devin tried to convince them not to believe their lying eyes. My brother went to check on Haley. My dad stood between me and Devin. He was so mad and so hurt. He felt betrayed. He had been good to Devin.

Chapter Twenty-Eight: Gotham's Reckoning

Dad ordered Devin to leave immediately before he called the police.

Devin was scheduled to work the graveyard shift that night at a juvenile detention center, so he got dressed and left. I gathered clothes and necessities for Haley so she could stay with my parents for a couple of days. With Devin working graveyard, I thought that I had plenty of time to get a restraining order before he returned.

Late that night, I received a call from one of the detention supervisors. He explained that Devin was so out of control that they had to place him in a holding cell. While at work, he told his co-workers he was going to kill me. He was in such a rage. Devin went into great detail about how he was going to shoot me with his gun. The supervisor was someone I had known for years. He was genuinely worried for my life and told me to get out of the house and go to a hotel. They couldn't keep Devin locked up. He hadn't committed a crime, so they had to send him home. Apparently, under the first amendment, threatening to shoot your wife in the face is not a crime.

I knew I had to get out and was trying to decide where to go. I was advised to avoid friends and family; those would be the first places he would check.

Suddenly, the nightmare began. Devin was already home. I was still lying in bed. My lights were out but the television was still on. He walked into the bedroom, grabbed my ponytail, and flipped me off the bed. He started punching me, and I was screaming for my life. He turned the lights on, then reached for the iron on the ironing board. I don't know where I got the strength, but as he was about to hit me with it, I started defending myself.

He got his gun out of the closet and brandished it in my face. He took my cell phone and the home phone from the bedroom. He went into the closet and threw every piece of clothing on the floor and bed. He told me I was going to iron every stitch until it was done. Ties, socks, shorts, T-shirts, hoodies, pants, dress shirts, sweaters, everything.

I put some water in the iron and got to work. It was the middle of the night. I remember watching the movie *My Cousin Vinny*. It's a great movie, but nothing was funny that night.

I began ironing, not knowing what came next. I was on a need-to-know basis until Devin was ready for me to die. Finally, he went into the office to play video games but periodically checked up on me to make ensure that the operation was being performed to his satisfaction. After a few hours passed, I finished ironing. I sat on the edge of the bed and periodically pushed the steam button, so he thought I was still working. The video games stopped, and I checked to see if he was asleep. I knew it might be my only chance.

I quietly got dressed and crept out the door like a Navy Seal, then I ran to my parents' house, and my dad drove me to the Lane County Courthouse to get a restraining order. I went before the judge and the order was granted immediately.

I called Women's Space, a domestic violence organization, and they gave me some powerful resources and information. I contacted a family law attorney, and she agreed to see me right away. I loved her from the start. She was the power and strength that I needed—my own personal Gloria Allred. She gave me the voice I had lost and helped me navigate the aftermath of the trauma.

I was contacted by the District Attorney's Office to answer questions, and I had the most amazing female Assistant DA on the case. I was simultaneously filing for a divorce, filing criminal charges, and getting a subpoena for his arraignment. The DA intended to hold him accountable to the fullest extent of the law.

Chapter Twenty-Eight: Gotham's Reckoning

I was worn out, traumatized by the years of abuse and violence. I had all the signs of PTSD, everything but the napalm. The chaos, the shame, the nightmares, I just wanted to hide.

A few days later, Shawn, the guy at the gym, called. He was disturbed by a conversation he had with Devin. Shawn was confused about some of the details but truly concerned for my safety. How ironic that the accusations and violence from Devin would drive me into the arms of Shawn. Right or wrong, I hadn't felt safe or loved for years. Shawn was the exact opposite of Devin: calm, gentle, reassuring. The first time he gave me a compliment, I wanted to jump into bed. The ink wasn't dry on my divorce filing and, already, I was head over heels for Shawn.

Before Devin was sent to jail, he was granted supervised visits with Haley. I agreed to the visits provided Hansen was there to supervise. Hansen had a daughter Haley's age, and she loved coming over. Hansen was put in a tough position. Devin was his friend, a former teammate and roommate, but he did everything by the book. He allowed Devin to stay with him after I got the restraining order and served as the go-between for a long time. Hansen helped make an impossible situation manageable.

A private investigator came to the house to serve Devin the divorce papers. Apparently, he went ballistic and started accusing the investigator of having an affair with me. He was always so jealous and controlling. In reflection, Devin exhibited what I've come to know as "projection," which occurs when an individual places their own views and behaviors on another under a similar circumstance. Because of Devin's numerous indiscretions, he couldn't conceive of anyone doing their job with no sexual connotations. The irony was that the private investigator lived right by Hansen, and I knew him from the gym. My attorney had hired him unbeknownst to me.

By the time the divorce was final and the criminal trial ended, I despised Devin on an almost indescribable level. The very sound of his voice was nails on a chalkboard. My four-year-old daughter had to be videotaped giving testimony about the abuse she had witnessed. Later, I had to put her in extensive counseling in order to rebuild her confidence. However, I never got the counseling I needed. Like always, I just soldiered on.

I decided to hold my head high, despite the ten years of extensive abuse, shame, and humiliation. I brushed aside all the whispers, gossip, and naysayers who never had to walk a mile in my shoes. Most knew nothing about what I had endured. They knew nothing about the rape, the cracked tail bone, the cracked ribs, the concussions, bruises, and mental torment. They didn't know what it felt like to plead for your life with a knife at your throat or gun in your face. They didn't know what it felt like to walk out into a stadium full of thousands of people and having to wave and smile, to shake hands with donors and sponsors, looking them in the eye with confidence when I was battered and broken. They didn't know that while I was giving hugs to the fans and taking pictures, I was praying to God to strengthen and protect me.

No one could have known the genuine love I had for every single cheerleader I coached. They knew nothing about why I was so protective of them; why I cared so deeply about their wellbeing. Why I went beyond the call of duty to keep them safe. They didn't know why I wanted my girls to be so good, beyond being the best, but angelic. Coaching became so much more than University tradition, branding, and game-day performances. All those were important, but much more important was the safety, confidence, and empowerment of our cheerleaders to enable them to pursue their dreams. We placed rules on our teams over the years that

Chapter Twenty-Eight: Gotham's Reckoning

probably seemed ridiculous at the time. If any of them read this book, I hope they now understand.

Postscript: through the many years of being with Devin, it was clear to me that he had an anger management problem. I intrinsically knew this. What remained a mystery was why I was always the source and outlet of his frustration. The problem became increasingly worse as time after time I failed to defend myself. In some ways, the fact that I didn't stand up for myself, may have emboldened his behavior. It certainly appeared to reinforce his ego and serve as fuel for further abuse.

Devin had a predator's instinct. Lions look for the weak, the sick, the old, and the isolated. In other words, they look for easy targets, where the potential risk of injury is low. Sometimes, predators are hard to detect. Sometimes they pretend disinterest, sometimes they hide in the tall grass in wait, and sometimes they come as wolves in sheep's clothing. In any case, it is important to stay alert, be diligent, and size up the situation correctly.

Deep inside, I always felt something was wrong, seriously wrong. Even before we got married, I could see some of the signs: the rage, the irrational behavior, the jealousy, and the lack of personal responsibility. He blamed everyone else for his problems. He blamed his mother for one problem and his brother for another. He blamed his football coach for not sufficiently going to bat for him with the NFL scouts; that's the reason he claims he wasn't drafted. His roommates undermined him, other teammates set him up. Someone was always conspiring against him; there was always a dark force lurking in the shadows. There was always a conspiracy against him for something; he was always being treated unfairly or unjustly accused.

Why did he brutalize me? The answer was as clear as the nose on my face. In many cases, abusers feel their own sense of victimization. This gives them a license to lash out and hurt others. Devin felt a constant sense of aggrievement. Hurting me was his way of recapturing his power.

I have to admit, I'm a slow learner. Some women get it right off the bat. But during the rape investigation, the light bulb finally came on. At this point, I knew that Devin had a problem beyond my capacity to help. It was a recognition far too late in the game, but I had deeply internalized all the rage, threats, disparagement, intimidation, lies, violence, extra-marital affairs, manipulation, abuse, and psychological warfare. I'm a hopeful, optimistic person by nature, but I realized that hope was not a strategy. Even faith requires work. It was as if all of my inherent qualities of loyalty, optimism, faith, and hope were being used against me.

I didn't write this book to absolve myself, I wrote it to enable others. I wrote it to reveal some of the patterns of abuse that may be manifesting itself in someone else's life. If so, don't ignore the signs. "Let the buyer beware." Again, ten percent is the problem, and ninety percent is the actions you take to solve it.

Finally, and let me be clear, I do <u>NOT</u> advocate violence or taking up arms against your husbands or abusers. I am not a trained professional, and I do not give specific advice. I am just an advocate for helping women to understand that they are worthy and for them to understand the implications of what I call, "The Unvirtuous Cycle" (more on that later). I am an advocate for women to do something constructive to protect themselves and to safeguard their children. I am an advocate for helping women avoid becoming disillusioned, battered, and spiritually broken. I am an advocate for calling your abuser's father, mentor, friends, boss, or whoever else can help. I am an advocate for utilizing your own family and friends, for involving mental health professionals, for reaching out to other women and women's organizations, for

Chapter Twenty-Eight: Gotham's Reckoning

going to women's shelters and joining domestic violence groups, and, when necessary, for calling the police.

I am an advocate for not living a life of pain and despair.

There are people out there to help you. I am an advocate for letting them!

Chapter Twenty-Nine
Showtime at the Apollo

Sometimes living can be a life sentence. That's how it can feel when you've been raped or are experiencing domestic violence. After the physical trauma, the mental trauma stays with you for a while. It doesn't matter how much time elapses, it's always in the back of your mind, embedded in your soul.

When I was raped in 1990, nothing ever felt the same again. No matter what I did, I didn't feel like the same person. I've had amazing opportunities since then, and, of course, I have soldiered on. But the trauma has never left. It's like a form of addiction, it always has to be managed. I would have many good days, then, out of nowhere, that sinister laugh would flash in my mind. The feeling I had when my attacker mocked and taunted me; it has haunted me for years.

I don't know how many times I stood in the mirror applying makeup, and the vision would appear, the eighteen-year-old Corine, the one with fraught makeup and tears rolling down her cheeks. Time and time again, for decades, I would see her in the mirror. WHY would she come? What did she want? I would scream inside my head. The vision was burned in my mind. When would enough be enough? When would it leave? At what point would I be entitled to peace?

I walked away from some important relationships over the years because I feared being vulnerable. I would rather suffer in silence than re-open Pandora's box. It was just easier to smile and portray myself as the girl who had it all together, even though it was a sham, even though I sometimes detested myself.

Battling the psychological repercussions of sexual assault can drain you, then being beaten by your spouse feels like getting runover by a Mack truck. The years of mental, emotional, and physical abuse I endured from the man I vowed to love, honor, and cherish flooded my head with toxic thoughts. It's a different kind of imprisonment. I spent a decade downplaying the abuse, maybe to justify staying in the relationship, maybe as a survival mechanism. Just because I eventually left doesn't mean I got away unscathed.

I was never the same after my marriage to Devin, it affected every successive relationship thereafter. There were times when I didn't know if or how I was going to survive. I didn't know if I would ever be able to trust again, love again, be happy again. I was in survival mode, which can be both empowering and disheartening.

When I peeled back the layers, I had transformed myself. A completely new me emerged. A stronger, more resilient but also less tolerant and less forgiving me. I had changed from who I was into who I thought I had to be. I could show you my heart but only if you acknowledged my value. If you lied about one thing, I assumed you were lying about everything. Everything was pushed to the outer edges: right or wrong, good or bad, friend or foe. There were no gray areas. Everything had to be concrete, ironclad, written in stone. If I had a dollar for every time someone told me that "you're such a strong woman," I could have bought a Russian yacht. Being strong wasn't a choice, it was a necessity. I believed that it was all I could be. This is what trauma does. This is how PTSD (post-traumatic stress disorder) feels. It's fight or flight. No justice, no peace.

It hadn't been more than three weeks after my divorce was final when Shawn and I had decided to be together. We were still getting to know each other, but our connection was undeniable. He was

Chapter Twenty-Nine: Showtime at the Apollo

an extremely charismatic guy, and I loved how he made me laugh and smile.

I came home after a long day of work, and Haley was singing and dancing to her favorite Disney movie in the living room.

Shawn was on his way over, so I started making dinner and setting the table. Haley absolutely loved when "Shawn" came over because she got all of his attention.

There were three loud knocks, and Haley bolted to the door.

"Boo Bear, ask who it is."

"Okay, Mommy. Who is it?"

A raspy voice emerged. "It's Shawn." Haley opened the door and Shawn swooped her up like a sack of potatoes.

We finished dinner and, as usual, I cleaned the kitchen to perfection. Shawn told me that he was going downtown to meet some friends at a club. He generally met up with two of his closest friends on Tuesday and Saturdays. I never thought anything of it, and both were good guys. We talked for a while, he took a shower, and started to leave. For some reason, I suggested that Shawn take my car. He intended to stay the night at my place and agreed. I was exhausted that night and could hardly keep my eyes open. I was relaxed and laid down to sleep.

A couple hours later, I was awakened by a knock on the door. I looked over at the clock on the nightstand and was surprised. It was only eleven p.m.

Shawn walked into the room and sat on the edge of the bed. I was surprised he was back so early, and he was steaming mad!!! I sat right up, and he had my full attention. He began telling the story, and I couldn't believe it. He said that when he pulled into the parking lot, a guy was looking at him kind of crazy. He didn't really think too much about it, but the guy was definitely trying to "act hard." Shawn walked into the club and met up with friends David and Tony. After some time, he noticed the same guy staring.

Shawn asked the guys if they noticed. Then, all of a sudden, the guy walks over and says, "Why you driving my frickin car?"

Shawn knew right away that it was Devin. They had never met in person, so he didn't know what Devin looked like. The conversation went back and forth, and on cue, Devin started making threats. He told Shawn how he was going to kick his a—. Shawn held his ground. He was unafraid and as cool as the other side of the pillow. Devin was completely infuriated. And like any good sociopath, he doubled down, threatening Shawn's life, "I'm going to kill you…then stick my…in your mouth." Devin was in full swing, using words that would make Sam Kinison blush.

At that moment, Shawn said the look on Devin's face was indescribable. Right then, he knew everything I had told him was true. Shawn had no reservations about me or our relationship and held his ground. And given Devin's legal trouble, and the number of witnesses, Devin wasn't going to do anything to anyone that night. Devin walked away and, after that, Shawn just called it a night.

It was the first time Shawn and Devin exchanged words but certainly not the last. And the confrontation had the reverse effect Devin intended. It actually solidified our commitment to each other. The following morning, Shawn and I dropped Haley off at my parents' house and went to the gym to work out. It was so nice to have someone in my life who enjoyed doing the normal things, fun things. I loved having someone who supported me and stood by me. And contrary to the whisper campaign around Eugene, my divorce was final.

But the criminal trial hadn't yet begun, and I had done such a good job of hiding my abuse and keeping my demons inside that I suddenly became the topic of barbershop talk. Various stories and theories ran throughout the Duck family of athletes. Some defended me at every turn and others spread conspiracies. To

Chapter Twenty-Nine: Showtime at the Apollo

some people, my marriage simply had run its course and I found a new athlete to date. To others, they knew the "philandering" Devin but couldn't see him hitting or abusing me. I was doing the only thing I knew how to do, "**SMILE**, *Chin Up*! Move forward!"

I continued to go to work and practice like I had done for years. I made sure to put Haley in counseling and keep my eyes open for any signs of trauma. But I continued to repress my own feelings and deny myself the help that I needed. At least, I thought I would prevent any lingering pathology in Haley, even though I was a pro at disguising mine.

The one thing that continued to cause a stir was the fact that Shawn was also a former football player at the University of Oregon. He was two years younger than me and six years younger than Devin. But the fact that they both graduated from Oregon; both played defensive back; and both were from the Los Angeles-Long Beach area was too much for some people to resist. It was like manna from heaven.

Gossip is funny; give it a hint of truth, and you can take it around the world in eight days. People hate because it's easier than showing empathy, or because they don't realize the self-inflicted harm. I'm a people person. I think of myself as a helper and an encourager. Although imperfect, I took comfort in the fact that I wouldn't wish the abuse I endured on anyone, not even my worst enemy.

Chapter Thirty
Let the Church Say Amen

Some of the best years of my life were spent at Jubilee World Outreach (JWO). Shawn and I had been married for about a year when we were first invited to attend. I remember walking into this little storefront church and hearing the most unbelievable music. As a little girl, I had grown up in the Lutheran Faith and always loved Bethesda Lutheran where I was baptized. My mom was in the church choir, and I could pick out her voice from the rafters. Mom had a beautiful almost operatic voice. My dad loved sitting up in the balcony so he could savor her solos.

On most Sundays, by the halfway mark, Rick would put the hymnal on his lap, grab a pencil, and an offering envelope, and start playing tic-tac-toe or a couple rounds of hangman. My dad always had a pack of mints or Tic Tacs in his pocket, and by the end of the service, I would have eaten them all. I appreciated the message, but until I got older, it was mostly ritual.

I loved singing from the hymnal, reciting prayers with the congregation, and had a genuinely strong connection to God. We lived our lives as Christians in every sense of the word, but, in 2001, I felt a deeper relationship with Jesus.

Shawn, Haley, and I walked into the service at JWO, and it was like a new experience. I recognized so many people, including many young and interracial couples like us. I was overwhelmed by the music. I had never been to a church that had a live band and so many praise and worship singers. I had never experienced a music ministry, let alone a ministry by music. I was accustomed to the choir, organs, and piano, but JWO was a whole new awakening.

Haley was hanging onto my arm, and her eyes were open wide. She was created to sing and dance; God gave her a gift of writing songs and poetry, and her senses were clearly stimulated.

I remember thinking *how have I only just now heard about this church!* The answer came swiftly. The Pastor of the church was Keith Jenkins "PK," a young man who had recently moved his family to Eugene. PK's beautiful wife was named CoCo, and they had three gorgeous children, all around Haley's age. Once the three of us were settled in our chairs, I couldn't help but stand up and join in the clapping and singing. It felt like home. I knew this was exactly where I was supposed to be. After about twenty minutes, something moved inside me. The music slowed down, the atmosphere was calm, and I heard the voice of an angel.

"In awe of you, we worship and stand amazed at your great love." I don't know what drew me in more—the lyrics or the voice. There were rows of people standing in front of us, so I couldn't see the woman singing. I closed my eyes and listened as the song captured my heart. A few minutes later, I heard the words, "Blessing and honor and glory and power forever and forever."

The words were sung prophetically, over and over for minutes. I raised my hands as tears poured down my cheeks. I was unable to stop crying. My body felt numb, almost weightless. I had never had a spiritual experience like that before other than the time I saw Lisa Flormoe at the foot of my bed.

Every ounce of pain I felt from the physical and mental abuse came rushing through my body. My heart felt like a thousand knives stabbing me all at once, and the tears flowing down my cheeks, leaving the feeling of euphoria.

By the time the songs ended, I knew I had felt the presence of God.

Pastor Keith has a booming voice. He began to pray, and I received his prayer deep within my soul. I fell in love with Jesus

Chapter Thirty: Let the Church Say Amen

that morning in a way I hadn't known. It wasn't about believing anymore; it was about knowing. "The Lord is my shepherd; I shall not want" (Psalm 23:1).

The service just got better and better. The voice I heard singing wasn't that of an angel but Karrissa Stavros. She was one of the cheerleaders at Willamette High School, where Mom and I had previously coached. She was a preacher's daughter and one very talented and smart girl. I later learned that she, as a teenager, had picked up on the issues I was having with Devin and prayed for me. She never said anything directly, but it bothered her deeply that I didn't seem safe. I had never heard her sing before, but her prayers were answered that day.

God really does have a sense of humor, and part of it is in His timing. After church service, Shawn reunited with several of the guys that he played football with at Oregon. We invited about ten people over to eat and hang out, including Derrick and Eileen Deadwiler, both Oregon alumni. They were the couple who invited us to Jubilee and two of my most favorite people in the world. They were also youth pastors at the church and had three daughters around Haley's age. They came over to the house and brought along Pastor Jenkins' kids. Haley hit it off with them instantly and, before long, we were inseparable.

We had been attending Jubilee World Outreach every Wednesday and Sunday for about six months before we had been called to serve. We had been closely involved with the first family and the other pastors in the kids, youth, and music ministries, and I was asked by the music ministers if I wanted to be on the praise and worship team! I couldn't believe they were offering me such an important role in the church, especially so soon. I was so honored to be called in a capacity that brought me the most joy. I took my role extremely seriously and made it a top priority.

I was a wife, mother, marketing manager, and cheerleading coach; my plate was full. I remember feeling like I could do anything. I also drew strength from worship on days I was struggling with past trauma.

Shawn took on the role of being the pastor's armor bearer, part of the security team. He was so honored. He had great respect for Pastor Keith and took the job seriously. Shawn grew so much in his faith and learned so much about being a father and husband. He and I built our first house together, and it was absolutely beautiful. I designed it in part so that we could entertain. I remember calling Pastor CoCo and Pastor Keith to come to bless our lot. The builder was about to pour the foundation, and we placed a Bible on all four corners of the slab. The two pastors prayed and blessed the house, and we knew it was built on the Word of God, literally.

Once the framing was complete, Shawn and I went around and wrote scriptures and Bible verses on the framing. I remember looking up at him standing in the loft. He was so proud, and we were so happy.

Haley was ten years old and in fifth grade. She was doing really well considering what she had endured. She had wanted a sibling for some time, and we decided to oblige her. Our house was about two blocks from "PK's" house, so it was a perfect location. All of our children became really close, and it felt strange when there wasn't two or three in tow.

Just before we moved in, we added a new addition. I had a beautiful baby named Jaden. The delivery was perfect and, unlike the ordeal with Haley's pregnancy, everything fell right in line.

Jubilee started to grow like wildflowers, and we had to move out of the storefront location to the Powers Auditorium at Willamette High School, my alma mater. The school had an absolutely gorgeous auditorium, and once we moved in, we were

CHAPTER THIRTY: LET THE CHURCH SAY AMEN

able to invite multiple times our existing congregation. We had a full choir, band, and praise team. The sound system was topnotch, and when PK preached, it sounded like we were in Carnegie Hall. The location opened up our ministry to perform outreach in the community, and we took full advantage.

One thing I loved about working in the ministry was the opportunities for leadership. I had spent my entire life dedicated to dance and cheerleading. I was a natural born leader, but my spirit showed me more, and my church family supported and encouraged me on a level that's hard to convey.

The Deadwilers, Strouds, Stavros, Coles, and the rest of my praise team family gave me the courage to expand my ministry beyond the walls of the church. They knew and accepted that I was wounded. They knew I had struggled with night terrors and self-shame from PTSD.

They loved me through every ounce of trauma and accepted my faults, but they also expected me to do the work and learn to love myself again. I loved them for that. There was a genuine bond between us. There was also clean, good-natured trash talking.

Pastor Keith had a great sense of humor, and it was reflected in the rest of the church.

PK and CoCo became Jaden's God Parents. It was the best of times, and the memories still resonate deep within.

Chapter Thirty-One
Wakeup Call

I work out five to six days a week and have for nearly twenty-five years. I am an early riser, so I usually set the alarm for three-thirty a.m. in order to be at the gym by four. I enjoy working out, it's my respite from the storms. Also, staying healthy and being in good shape has always been important to me.

Julie Kaanapu is my workout partner. She is just as dedicated and, some say, just as crazy! Since we were best friends and next-door neighbors, we have it down to a science. We alternate driving every other day and change our workout routine about every six weeks in order to avoid boredom and maximize our muscle response system. We are extremely disciplined and are always challenging ourselves and one another.

Before Juile was Julie Kaanapu, she was Julie Hollingsworth. We met in my senior year in high school, and she was just a little Barbie Doll eighth grader. Our mothers worked together in the resource room at Willamette High School. I had gotten to know Julie's mom, Connie, extremely well because she and my mom were such close friends. Julie's brother Don was in my graduating class of '89, and he was always a fun-loving person. Julie's dad, Will, also worked for the city of Eugene, along with two of my uncles, both named John. Our family had a close connection, so Julie and I becoming the best of friends was more of an inevitability than a surprise.

Beyond family connections and logistics, Julie and I shared a common interest in our unwavering love for cheerleading and dance. When I made the cheerleading squad at Oregon at the end of my senior year, Julie was gearing up for cheerleading tryouts at Willamette High School. Mom was the coach, and my first real interaction occurred after I watched her at tryouts. I saw so much of myself in Julie and recognized her sheer talent. Julie was the shining star. We had never allowed a freshman to make the Junior Varsity squad before, not even me. We always thought it best for freshman to stay with their peer group. But Julie's talent was so far above anyone else in her age group we made the lone exception.

In fact, we wanted to put her on the Varsity squad but decided the age difference might pose too great an issue. The next three years, Julie made the Varsity squad and became captain. She was awarded the most valuable cheerleader by her peers and received the coaches award all four years. Julie was a huge factor in leading her squad to multiple first place titles at various cheerleading competitions, including at the OSAA state cheerleading championship. Like me, Julie was also named to the OSAA All-American team her senior year.

In Julie's junior year in high school, I came down with the Trailblazer dancers and performed at a WHS student body pep rally. It was so much fun to return to my alma mater and put on an electric show. The student body and staff had never seen anything like us at the high school. I remember Julie telling me how much it motivated her to try out at the University of Oregon. The following year, she did indeed tryout for the Ducks and made it as an entering freshman!

The summer before college, the WHS cheerleaders were invited to the Universal Cheerleaders Association cheerleading camp, where I was the head instructor. Julie was selected by camp staff to the UCA All-Star team, and I enticed her to be an upcoming UCA instructor!

Our bond grew even closer when Mom and I became the coaches at Oregon during Julie's sophomore year. Julie and I were

Chapter Thirty-One: Wakeup Call

afforded the opportunity to be around each other several days a week at practices, games, appearances, and general girl time. By the time Julie made the squad at Oregon, I was already married to Devin.

One year, at the Rose Bowl in Pasadena, I mentioned to Devin that Julie was dating Todd Kaanapu, also known as "TK." Devin was shocked because TK went to college with us and played at the Independence Bowl in Shreveport. Devin gave TK props, saying he was one heck of a lineman and teammate. On this occasion, TK was at the Rose Bowl as a grad assistant to Coach Jimmy Radcliff, another legend at University of Oregon. Jimmy was the strength and conditioning coach and revered by every Oregon player alive. Coach "Rad" was part of the Oregon coaching staff when I was a cheerleader and throughout my fifteen-year coaching tenure at Oregon. He was a fixture in the athletic department for decades and undoubtedly one of the most beloved coaches of all time.

Devin and I were super happy for Julie and TK, and even more so when they got engaged! I was a bridesmaid in the wedding, and Haley was the flower girl. We had such a close bond; more than friends—we became extended family.

As the years rolled by, Julie and I became partners in choreography and coaching. We went to Orlando Florida together to coach WHS in the national UCA cheerleading competition at Disney World Magic Kingdom. Later, Mom and I brought Julie on as an assistant coach, and we had an absolute blast for years!

Julie and I continued working out at the crack of dawn for decades. We always had common physical fitness goals, and even to this day, she pushes me to the limit. Julie is my pillar of strength, sometimes my conscience, and always my confidant. We absolutely love and adore each other's children as though they were our own.

Our kids grew up together and think of each other more as cousins.

Julie and TK went through the best and worst of times with me. They were by my side through thick and thin, year after year, no matter what. The love and support I received from them through three decades were a lifeline at times, and they have proven to be my most cherished friendships. We even built houses together, side by side, just to be more present in each other's lives. Julie has been my closest and best friend my entire adult life. We share a love and bond so much stronger than most could imagine. We don't share the same DNA, but if you said that we were closer than most sisters, that wouldn't be an understatement.

During football season, TK would go to the gym in the early morning, which meant that on Wednesdays, Julie stayed home with her two kids. She and I were constantly being pressed at the gym to use a personal trainer, but we would just laugh. With Julie's degree in Exercise Movement Science (EMS), both of our husbands being former division one football players, and our own expertise in fitness, we were less than enthusiastic. Nevertheless, during football season, I had to go it alone on Wednesdays. On one occasion, I was lifting heavier than usual, and a personal trainer ran over and gave me a spot. He was super encouraging, and I appreciated his help. He asked about training me and, like a thousand times before, I demurred. But he was super friendly, and I knew some of his family. He seemed knowledgeable and hardworking, so I told him that I would think about it.

Later, I mentioned it to Shawn, and he had no objection. So, the following morning, I showed up at the gym and paid for ten training sessions. Every Wednesday for ten weeks I was scheduled to work out with my trainer, Lennie, at four a.m. The morning manager was very professional and conscientious. He always

Chapter Thirty-One: Wakeup Call

greeted us with a hearty, "Good morning, Ladies" and went out of his way to help all the members.

For our initial session, I walked into the gym about ten minutes early and started talking to the front desk manager. Lennie arrived a few minutes later with his usual upbeat personality and said, "Let's Go!" We walked into a side room just off the weight room. It included a couple of file cabinets, a desk, a scale, some resistance bands, and other workout paraphernalia.

Lennie pulled a tape measure out of the desk drawer and began discussing my fitness goals. He took my weight and measurements so that he could begin tracking my progress. The door was propped open, giving us a partial view of the weight room and a direct view of the front desk. Julie and I had watched dozens of members go in and out of the room during our morning workouts, and it wasn't uncommon to see them being weighed or measured. Once Lennie finished with the measurements, we went out into the cardio area, and I began to walk on the treadmill. He advised me to warm up on the treadmill or elliptical machine for ten minutes prior to the commencement of our sessions.

Several weeks had passed, and I was making great progress. Although Julie and I consistently put in maximum effort at the gym, it was nice having accountability to Lennie. Knowing he was tracking my progress made it more of a challenge and, frankly, more fun.

Around week six, we had decided to take my measurements and weight before the session. I arrived around a quarter to four in the morning and talked with the front desk associate until Lennie arrived with his usual, "Let's get to work." He said that we would do the measurements after. I didn't care about the order, so we got right to work. Lennie put me through a grueling workout; I was so proud of myself. I knew without a doubt I was stronger and leaner than I had been in years. I remember exactly what I was wearing. I had on black yoga pants, an Oregon cheerleading sports bra, and a white NIKE tank top. I was absolutely dripping with sweat. My clothes were soaking wet from perspiration. As he led me into the side office, I even said jokingly "Are you sure you want to measure me right now!" He flashed a big smile and giggled under his breath. Lennie took my weight, then reached into the desk drawer and grabbed the measuring tape and calipers (used to measure body fat). Like every other occasion, the door was propped open. It never crossed my mind to be wary, and there was never a concern about being alone with Lennie or anyone else. It was common practice, routine.

I was really excited about getting the results. First, Lennie measured my biceps and triceps. Then, he asked me to raise my tank top so he could get an accurate measure of my waist. I stood in the center of the room, grabbed the bottom of my tank top, and pulled it over my chest. Lennie squatted down and measured my lower body. Then, he asked me to scoot back, where I was standing with my butt pressed against the desk. There was no one in the weight room at this point. The only people present were standing near the front desk. Lennie instructed me to pull my tank top higher so he could accurately measure the diameter of my chest and back.

Like an army recruit, I did as commanded. I pulled my tank top above my clavicle, just below my neck. Sweat was still streaming down my back, and I was starting to feel sticky. Lennie told me to place my arms above my head and behind my back. Once again, I did exactly as instructed. Now, I was pinned against the desk, with my arms overhead, clasping my left wrist with my right hand. Lennie sat down on the lower file cabinet with his at eye level with my chest. Then, without warning, he grabbed the bottom of my sports bra and ripped it up around my neck, completely exposing my breast!

Chapter Thirty-One: Wakeup Call

Lennie's face was about three inches from my naked breasts. It took me a few seconds to process what was happening. Then I realized what he was doing and I quickly grabbed the sports bra from around my neck and tried to yank it back into place. But the bra was so wet that I struggled to get it down. I couldn't turn around or away because I was pinned against the desk. I yelled out loudly, "Oh my God!" Finally, I got my bra and tank top pulled down and I ran out of the room and straight to the front desk. Thank God! The front desk associate had witnessed the entire affair and had already picked up the phone to call his manager.

I was shaking, and I couldn't stand still. For some reason, I was pacing back and forth in circles. I was so confused and absolutely panicked. I watched Lennie walk right past me with his head down. He was speed walking toward the men's locker room. I fumbled my cell phone, trying to dial. I finally got a hold of Shawn and could hardly talk. Eventually, I was able to catch my breath and explained what happened. Shawn was out of his mind with rage. He told me to get home to be with the kids and that he was on his way. Shawn was so upset that he called Pastor Keith and Joshua Stroud at around five-thirty in the morning and asked them to meet him at the gym.

He grabbed one of his golf clubs and told Joshua that he wasn't going there to have ice cream. PK and Josh knew that Shawn was a levelheaded guy, so if he was going ballistic; they knew they had to take it seriously. By the time I left the gym, Shawn had arrived, but Lennie was gone. The guy at the front desk sat down with Shawn and explained what happened. The manager suggested that I file a formal complaint with the company, and Joshua recommended that we also file a complaint with the police. So many times, in situations like this, it ends up being the victim's word against the perpetrator. Thankfully, in this case, I had an eyewitness.

About an hour had passed and no one could reach Lennie. Shawn suggested that I call him on his cell phone. It rang twice, and he picked up. Lennie said, "Hello," and Shawn took it from there. Lennie began apologizing profusely, telling Shawn how sorry he was. He said he didn't know what came over him. Lennie said that he had never done anything like that before and just lost it for a moment. Shawn called BS on the story and told Lennie to be thankful. He demanded that Lennie apologize to me and return my money immediately. Lennie agreed, but I was in no mood for an apology.

That afternoon, I filed a formal complaint with the gym and the police. I received a full refund from the gym for my fees, and Lennie was fired and banned from the gym and all of its locations. I was told that sexual harassment wasn't a crime, so they couldn't arrest him. Sexual harassment? Are you kidding? He pulled off my bra, and who knows what he was planning. It was sexual assault, pure and simple. At a minimum, he had me pushed against a cabinet, in violation of my civil rights! That's how I saw it, anyway.

Some people thought having him fired was enough, and I was asked on multiple occasions by multiple mutual acquaintances why I demanded that Lennie be fired. To be honest, I thought the question was offensive. I had spent many years fighting the ravages of self-shame and PTSD from the brutal rape and domestic abuse and, in my view, empathizing with Lennie placed you on the wrong side of history and on the wrong side of the moral equation. In fact, in my view, that kind of thinking was part of the problem, part of the reason that sexual harassment and violence against women is still so prevalent. It's an argument against accountability, and without accountability, there can be no justice. And without justice, there can be no redemption. To be honest, I was ticked off!! When in the h— was this going to stop! Why did I always feel pressured to just get over it! I'd had it!

Chapter Thirty-One: Wakeup Call

I didn't hold my rapist accountable, or my violent ex-husband. I was quiet and ashamed. I internalized the experiences, made excuses, and didn't report it to the authorities. When I did, it was much too late. In some ways, I enabled them to perpetrate the same offences on someone else. This weighed heavily on my heart. Accountability is a two-way street. It means holding others accountable but being accountable yourself. As I internalized this, I began to recapture my power. I became an advocate for women's empowerment, which meant I became an advocate for taking action. Empowering yourself means positioning yourself to take action. You can't always control what happens to you, but you can always control your response.

So, in the end, the answer to the question was easy: accountability. I wanted Lennie to be held accountable and, as it turned out, this clown had also tried to assault a friend of mine.

Chapter Thirty-Two
Pandora's Box

It was the year 2000; the country survived Y2K, but in a major legal standoff, Janet Reno sent five-year old Cuban refugee, Elián González, back home. The case garnered national attention, maybe even international. It had everything: a harrowing trip across shark invested waters to Florida, huge protests on both sides of the political aisle, high-stakes legal wrangling, and a showdown with Castro. All that was missing was a velociraptor and a steamy scene with Sharon Stone.

Closer to home, a very important young man at the University of Oregon named Tyson came into our life.

Tyson was from Southern California and played quarterback at Beverly Hills High School. He was recruited to Oregon, where he played running back. Tyson was off to a great start until he received some devastating news. He was told that the bone in his ankle was dying. There wasn't enough blood supply getting to his foot, and he would no longer be able to play football. It was heart wrenching to watch him go through this. Not a dream deferred but a dream snatched away in darkness. But Tyson loved Jesus and stayed strong. He quickly became a part of our family and would come and go as he pleased. "Mi casa es su casa."

Tyson also attended JWO. He was a magnet; people were drawn to him. He prayed with people and hugged those in need. He was a light that lit up the room.

As the months turned into a year, Tyson decided to attend our cheerleading practice and learn how to do partner stunts. He was built like a Mack truck and had unbelievable strength. He had so much natural talent and was phenomenal. The cheerleaders, male and female, loved having him on the squad.

By nature, Tyson was extremely protective of me. He didn't like hearing "locker room talk" about me, regardless of who it came from. He wasn't cool with guys catcalling or any of the usual funny business. If people didn't know, they could easily assume that Tyson was my husband, in terms of the way he always opened doors for me; the way he stood by me when other men approached, especially if Shawn wasn't around; and the way he waited on me hand and foot no matter where we were. He would introduce me as family, and Shawn absolutely loved him.

After Tyson graduated from Oregon, he decided to become a parole and probation officer and was hired by the City of Eugene. Tyson's boss was one of the most influential women in the county. She was a strong and respected black woman. Everyone who came into contact with her loved or feared her or both. She was instrumental in my case against Devin and was his probation officer after he was released from jail. She genuinely cared about me, and I was lucky enough to call her friend. She knew the unvarnished truth about Devin and our situation. She helped countless young men in the city, but had no tolerance for violent or criminal behavior.

One of her roles as a supervisor was to train the new hires to read case files. Because Tyson was working directly with her, he was privy to her caseload.

One day at work, Tyson ran across Devin's file. He mentioned to his supervisor that he was a close friend of mine. She told him that it was in his best interest to stay out of the file. She felt it may be way too personal. Tyson was a big, tough guy and didn't see it as a problem, especially considering he knew a lot about Devin from stories I shared.

Chapter Thirty-Two: Pandora's Box

Tyson didn't think too much about it, but when he came over that night, he told Shawn and I about some things that he had heard about Devin. I made dinner for the family, and we stopped talking about it while Haley was in the room. She was about seven at this time. I remember cleaning up the dining room table and putting the dishes in the dishwasher. Haley gave them her goodnight kisses and hugs, then we hustled her upstairs. I could hear the guys talking in the living room about my past. Shawn was matter of fact about the pain I had been through.

As sometimes happens, when men speak, their inside voices tend to carry loudly. They were sitting in the living room playing Madden 2000. The sound of laughter and trash talk meant a normal night in our house. There were many nights when Shawn, Memphis, Tyson, and others would be downstairs playing video games for hours. It was important for Shawn to have his guy time, but when I looked on, the competition always intensified.

This particular night, I overheard Shawn telling Tyson about my nightmares. On multiple occasions, he had to wake me from some dubious situations. For some reason, listening to Shawn describe the nightmares to Tyson kind of shocked and scared me. I knew the nightmares were bad, but I didn't know the extent. I also didn't know how deeply they affected Shawn. I heard him say: "Bro, she will be laying there in a dead sleep and can't breathe. It looks like someone is on top of her, strangling her. Sometimes, I can just nudge her and she wakes right up. Other times, it feels like I'm fighting to get someone off of her. She's throwing punches, trying to run. It's crazy."

Shawn's voice started cracking, and he began to tear up. There was complete silence for about a minute, then Shawn said, "I know it's him, and I'm afraid one day she won't wake up from the terror she's experiencing." I didn't really hear Tyson respond. I walked into the living room and they both stopped talking. I told them I was going to sleep since I had to get up early in the morning. I gave Shawn a kiss and said good night. I got a huge bear hug from Tyson and told him, "That's all in the past, and I'm going to be okay." I looked him in the eye with a big smile and asked him not to look at my case file. He agreed, and I went to my room.

The following night, we were sound asleep. It was about ten-thirty p.m., and there was a loud banging on the door. We woke up simultaneously, I threw on one of Shawn's T-shirts, which hung down to my knees, and looked out the peephole in the front door. The porch light was on so I could see that it was Tyson. As I opened the door, Shawn came around the corner.

Tyson was distraught. I didn't know what was wrong. He threw his arms around me and squeezed me tight. He started sobbing so hard he could barely stand up. The weight of his body was too much to withstand, so we fell to the floor. I had never seen Tyson cry. His distress was breaking my heart. He had his head pressed against my stomach and his arms were wrapped around my legs. I kept asking over and over what happened. I was getting scared.

Tyson was devastated. I thought maybe something had happened to his daughter. He started catching his breath, and we made our way to the couch. Tyson sat back with his head in his hands, I sat on the edge of the couch and Shawn sat right next to him as we tried to make sense of his pain.

Suddenly, Tyson blurted out, "I read it! I read your file! I'm so sorry about what happened to you. I'm so sorry he put you through that."

He wanted to know why I hadn't told him. His tears became anger and his questions, although forceful, were coming from a place of love and concern. "I knew you had been beaten, but I didn't know the extent of what he did to you."

Chapter Thirty-Two: Pandora's Box

I grabbed his hands and said, "This is why I didn't want you to read my file. This is why your supervisor told you not to as well."

Tyson looked at Shawn and asked, "You knew about all of this?" Shawn looked at me and said, "Corine's never told me everything." I stopped the conversation mid-sentence. I knew that once you open Pandora's Box, it's hard to put back the contents. I didn't want Shawn to think about me that way. I had a need for normalcy and couldn't continue to revisit the past. We talked for another hour and Tyson went home. It was a long night for Shawn, but I reassured him that I would be okay.

I never talked to Tyson about that night, again. We just moved forward and, if anything, we became even closer. You never know how your life can affect someone else, either positively or negatively. When a survivor is asked questions by someone they love about abuse, it generally goes one of two ways. They want to know why you stayed so long or how you got in that situation in the first place. In this case, I also had to explain why I didn't lean on them for support and why I repressed the trauma. The answer was simple: at that point in my life, I had to focus on thriving, not just surviving. Focusing on the trauma would have kept me tethered to the past and eaten me alive.

Sometime later, Shawn and I would split. It's been said that some people come into your life for a reason and some people only for a season. Shawn and I spent eight years together, most of them wonderful. We had a child together; we bought several homes together; and we both grew spiritually and otherwise.

Sometimes events overtake your life. One of those events was social media, specifically "My Space." It opened a gulf between us that couldn't be closed and ultimately led to the termination our marriage.

Shawn and I signed a peace accord and parted ways.

Of course, we continue to co-parent together as best we can. Our relationship was incredibly challenging for quite some time. This was another hard moment, but I put on a smile and soldiered on.

Chapter Thirty-Three
Cheerleaders are Heroes Too!

On August 28th, 2005, the gulf coast was hit with a category-five hurricane known as Katrina. The following day, Katrina was downgraded to a strong category-three hurricane and made landfall in New Orleans. Katrina caused enormous destruction and significant loss of life. At the time, it was the costliest hurricane to ever hit the United States. In all, Katrina was responsible for more than 1,800 fatalities and more than $100 billion in damage.

By August 31st, 2005, an estimated eighty percent of New Orleans was still underwater.

That morning, the University of Oregon cheerleaders, band, football team, and members of the athletic department boarded a charter flight for Houston. It was early, but our energy was high. The Oregon Ducks were playing the University of Houston in a pre-season game at NRG Stadium, the home of Houston Texans. I was super excited because I had never been to Houston, and the thought of performing in an NFL stadium was like a dream.

Finally, we landed in Houston and went through the ritual of gathering our belongings and loading them into the caravan of charter buses. Once we were on the bus, I handed out the per diem money to all the cheerleaders and mascot. I had a list with everyone's name, and each individual had to sign before receiving their envelope. The athletic department wanted to make sure that everyone had enough money to eat while we were on the road. But the way in which they managed their money was completely up to them.

We cruised from the airport to the hotel, noticing some of the devastation. Before arriving at the hotel, unlike usual, we pulled into an adjacent parking lot across the street. I remember seeing a Kroger's grocery store and some other small businesses. Not reading too much into the situation, we patiently waited. As time passed, our bus became increasingly quiet. We began looking out the windows, trying to make sense of what was happening outside. I was in disbelief. If you've ever seen the motion picture *The Impossible*, that's what comes to mind.

There were hundreds and hundreds of people standing and sitting in the parking lot. Commercial buses continued pulling in; they were filled with more and more desperate people. Women holding babies and walking alongside their children. The more I concentrated, the more I began to understand. These people had been displaced from their homes. They had nothing, no belongings whatsoever! They were in dire straits! Our driver got on the intercom and confirmed that the bulk of the people were indeed refugees. They had been bussed in from New Orleans and Mississippi. All of these beautiful people, desperate and seeking refuge from Katrina.

It became increasingly painful to watch. I was absolutely sickened by the looks on their faces. They were completely devastated. No more than ten minutes passed and one of our male cheerleaders said with great conviction, "I'm not going to just sit here and watch!" He stormed off the bus and approached a group of people outside. He was hugging small children and asking the adults how he could help. Within seconds, the rest of the guys followed suit. Before long, all of us were outside trying to help. I've never felt so overwhelmed in my life! I didn't even know where to begin.

After talking to several of the refugees, it was abundantly clear that most of the people had no money. Babies with soiled diapers,

CHAPTER THIRTY-THREE: CHEERLEADERS ARE HEROES TOO!

children with nothing to eat or drink. We were in the middle of a living nightmare! I remember looking up and seeing one of my guys handing out his per diem money. One cheerleader turned into two, and two turned into four. Before long, most of the cheerleaders were parting with the money I had given them. Some of the squad members went into the grocery store and began to buy cases of bottled water and other products. I was watching these selfless college students act without regard for themselves. It was the best of my cheerleading squad and the best of America. I had never in my entire life been more moved or proud of these amazing human beings.

After what seemed like an hour, I got on my cell phone and called Curtis Irving and David Driskill, the owner and President of my company, American Title Group. I explained the situation and asked if I could use my company credit card to help. Without hesitation, they both agreed. I spent a couple thousand dollars on diapers, baby formula, food, snacks for the children, water, and other necessities. I was so thankful to both Curtis and Dave for stepping up in such a big way. This gave real meaning to the passage "love thy neighbor as thy self."

I was glad that I was able to help in some small way, and it proved to be one of the most meaningful days of my life.

The following day, Oregon was gearing up to play the University of Houston in NRG Stadium. Everyone was hyped for the game, but there was a real sense of compassion about what was happening around us. We walked into the stadium and began warmups, just as we had done a thousand times before. We didn't expect a huge crowd because there was no rivalry between the two teams, and there was nothing at stake.

The stadium was huge. But to our surprise, it started filling up like a Bruce Springsteen concert. One of the sideline officials pointed out that most of the people were refugees and had on yellow wrist bracelets.

There was some sort of collaboration between the two Universities and the Houston Texans that made it possible for the refugees to attend the game and receive food and beverages. This was such an amazing gesture, and the smiles on their faces far outshone our 38-24 victory.

Chapter Thirty-Four
The Making of an Oregon Cheerleader

At the 80th Academy Award show in February 2008, the movie *No Country for Old Men* won the Oscar for Best Picture. If you haven't seen it, you should. The Javier Bardem character is an absolute nightmare, a combination of Scarface (without the drugs) and Nino Brown. The dude was relentless; he reminded me a bit of my ex-husband Devin.

A couple months later, I walked into Macarthur Court to begin day one of tryouts for the new University of Oregon cheerleaders.

It was an exciting time, a madhouse as usual, but this year was going to be a little different. We were filming an eleven-week reality television series with Comcast Sports called, *The Making of an Oregon Cheerleader*. The film crew followed me around from sunup to sundown. They also filmed various aspiring cheerleaders from all over the state. The cameras got up close and personal, giving viewers an inside look at what it took to become an Oregon cheerleader: the physicality required, the grueling workouts, and the level of pressure. Even members from the Oregon athletic department had renewed respect for our program.

Throughout the series, I began to attract thousands of followers on my Facebook page, including from different Universities, production companies, and media outlets. It started opening doors and new opportunities. By the time the series aired, the Oregon cheerleaders had appeared in *Sports Illustrated* and were voted as the one of top ten reasons to watch college football on ESPN. As the series rolled on, I gained greater public exposure. I can remember thinking, *What a blessing.* I was in my element: cheerleading, dancing, encouraging young girls.

There were also times when I thought about who might be watching.

The cameras began rolling, and I looked up to my sound guy and gave him the thumbs up. My microphone was attached to my sports bra and the battery pack was clipped to the back of my leggings. I was set in my beginning pose with my head looking down, visions flashing in my mind as I took a deep breath. Music from the group Day 26 started, and my voice boomed, "Five, six, seven, eight!" No one could understand, while I was dancing and coaching, the kinds of thoughts running through my mind. I wondered if my rapist would recognize me. I wondered if he even knew my name. I wondered if he ever thought about his actions. Because I couldn't stop thinking about him. I walked into this very same arena as a seventeen-year-old high school senior, not knowing what my life would become. Now I was in my fifteenth year of coaching girls hoping to fill my shoes. I wondered if I hadn't been raped where I would be. Would I still be coaching or somewhere in an ivory tower?

I could count the number of times I wanted to speak out about my rape. How badly I wanted to tell the cheerleaders why I was so hard on them; why certain safety rules were in place. I wondered if they would listen if I made myself vulnerable. I became incredibly close to my squad members year after year. They confided in me about so much of their personal lives. I dealt with everything from heartbreak to eating disorders. Besides the horrifying issue with my ex-husband, not once did any squad members ever mention sexual assault or domestic violence.

Sexual harassment was addressed every year because of the nature of the job and the prevalence of alcohol. And though that memory flooded my mind, I took great pride in the fact that my

Chapter Thirty-Four: The Making of an Oregon Cheerleader

attacker hadn't broken me. I was still doing what I loved most and what God gifted me to do. My rapist was now incarcerated in an asylum, and his mind was imprisoned with schizophrenia. I didn't take delight in this, but it prompted me to review the definition of poetic justice: "An outcome in which vice is punished and virtue rewarded usually in a manner peculiarly or ironically appropriate."

We shot eleven wonderful episodes. The cameras followed me both on and off campus, at work and at home. The Comcast crew were so professional, and the cheerleaders were absolutely amazing.

During the shoot, something unusual happened. On the first day of tryouts, we had the most outstanding candidate perform. This girl was totally amazing, athletic, and a fabulous dancer. Unexpectedly, she got sick and wasn't able to complete some of the subsequent requirements, even skipping the personal interview.

Normally, not running through all the hoops was an automatic disqualifier. But in this particular case, we allowed her to come back and compete in the finals. She was absolutely phenomenal and made the team. This was a first for me. I broke all of my own rules, and, in doing so, I learned something. Sometimes the rules are made to be broken, especially if it helps propel someone forward in a positive way. I had a reputation for being really hardcore, Marine Corps tough, no-nonsense. But in this situation, I grew.

As we counted down to the final selection, the tension and excitement grew. The series was shown throughout the pacific northwest and was a huge success. So much so, for the next season, the Blazer dancers shot a similar series, it was fabulous as well. But, by that time, I was long gone.

Here is a summary of some of my cheerleading highlights:

- Member of Willamette High School cheerleading team: 1985-1989.
- Selected as 1988 Hula Bowl All-Star Cheerleader.
- 1999 Oregon State Athletic Association Co-Ed Cheerleading Champion.
- Selected in 1999 as Oregon State Athletic Association All-American Cheerleader.
- Member of University of Oregon cheerleader team.
- Cheerleading instructor for Universal Cheerleaders Association.
- Cheerleading instructor for Power Cheerleading.
- Member of Portland Trailblazer Dancers: 1991-1994.
- University of Oregon cheerleading coach and choreographer: 1994-2009.
- Coach and choreographer for University of Oregon - USA National Cheerleading Stunt Champions: 2005.
- Coach and choreographer for University of Oregon - USA National Champions in the hip hop dance division: 2009.
- Principal cast member of *Making of an Oregon Cheerleader* series.
- Judge for numerous state and national cheerleading competitions.
- Founder and CEO of P3 Company, providing cheerleading and dance choreographer internationally.

***

Chapter Thirty-Four: The Making of an Oregon Cheerleader

I was at home working up a dance routine in the living room when Haley came downstairs. She told me she was on the phone with her dad, and he wanted her to fly to Atlanta to see his new house and meet his new girlfriend Erika. Haley was so excited. I knew it was important to allow her to bond with her father, and I agreed to let her go, provided I flew with her. My boyfriend of four years lived in Tampa, Florida, so we made a plan. I would fly to Atlanta with Haley, then continue on to Tampa.

On the morning of departure, Haley and I grabbed our suitcases and headed to the Eugene airport. It had been about twelve years since my divorce from Devin. He was happily engaged and starting a new family. After Devin was released from jail, we communicated a lot over the years because of Haley. We weren't friends, but we did our best to work together in her interest.

Erika was okay with me coming out and staying overnight. Devin also suggested that it would be a good way for Erika and I to get to know each other. I was hesitant at first, but Haley wanted me to stay, too.

We landed in Atlanta and navigated our way through the airport. Devin arrived to pick us up, alone. I was surprised. I never imagined I would be alone with him again. I was reluctant to get in, but my ticket to Tampa was scheduled for the following morning. Haley was fourteen and had a cell phone, and I was favored with good friends in Atlanta. So, if anything went wrong, we could abandon the mission and stay with them. So, reluctantly, we put our luggage in the trunk, got in the car, and began the forty-five-minute drive to Devin's house.

I can't tell you how strange it felt to be riding through the city, just the three of us. It was the first time in over a decade that we had been together. The anxiety was almost overwhelming, and I think Devin was also uncertain. He was driving a beautiful Mercedes Benz and had the music on low so he and Haley could talk. We passed by Georgia Tech, and he began giving her a rundown of the city. His demeanor became more relaxed, and he was extremely soft spoken. By the time we pulled into his subdivision, the vibe was good.

As we were nearing the house, Devin said, "Hey, Corine, this is where Bill Musgrave lives." Bill was the quarterback at Oregon when Devin played. He was an amazing player and led our team to the Independence Bowl in 1989. Billy was the quarterbacks' coach for the Atlanta Falcons. Devin moved into the neighborhood, in part, because they were friends.

Finally, we pulled up to the house, and I took a deep breath. Devin grabs our bags, and Erika greeted us at the front door. Haley was smiling and instantly obsessed over the beauty of the house. They gave us a tour and showed us our bedrooms. I got myself situated in the guest room and gave Haley some time to visit with them alone. It was awkward, not because of anything specific, but my intuition was percolating. I had been through a living nightmare with Devin, and now I was sitting as a guest in his house. Sometimes the truth is stranger than fiction.

None of my family could believe I was there. "Are you crazy?" was written all over their faces. But I would never have allowed Haley to travel there alone, not for the first trip.

I called my boyfriend and walked him through my itinerary so he could pick me up the next morning. He picked up on my uneasiness and tried to remind me that I was doing the right thing. I hadn't seen him in over a month, and all I could think about was getting to Florida. While I was on the phone, I received a text message from Devin. He asked me to come downstairs and join them. I got off the phone and decided to make the best of a potentially uncomfortable situation. I walked into the kitchen, and Erika reluctantly struck up a conversation; it was like pulling teeth.

Chapter Thirty-Four: The Making of an Oregon Cheerleader

I remember wondering as she spoke if she had a clue what he put me through. Did she have any knowledge of the level of abuse that I endured? Haley had been only five months old when he beat me the first time. Did he treat Erika well or did he abuse her, too? I couldn't really read the situation between them. But the more she spoke, the more I liked her. There was an inner beauty. She was an incredible woman, but I couldn't get past the past. I didn't believe that anyone with his degree of narcissism could undergo such a dramatic change.

But hope springs eternal. And I hoped that Erika, unlike his ex-girlfriend Beatrice, would be treated right.

It was getting late, and I had to get up at five a.m. to fly out to Tampa. I wished them goodnight and made my way to the bedroom. Haley went to her room, which was adjacent to mine. Before I could change my clothes, I got a text from Devin, asking if he could come to my room. I immediately went into Haley's room. She gave me an awkward look and I whispered, "I have to stay in here with you!" She got it, and we both laughed. I showed her the text and, as she was reading, another one came through. Devin was telling me how beautiful I looked and how he wanted to spend more time together. Haley said, "Oh, heck no!" I grabbed the phone and texted him back, "I am already in bed with Haley; we can talk on the way to the airport."

This was unbelievable. Devin had this amazing new woman and a fresh start on life. He finally appeared to have it all together. I thought that maybe he was wanting closure, or maybe he just wanted to apologize for the trauma that he put me through. But I dismissed this immediately. Although his motives were uncertain, my mind was clear. I had to err on the side of caution. He wasn't texting to reminisce.

Suddenly, a dark thought came to mind. Maybe he hadn't changed at all. I lay there for an hour, snuggled up to Haley, concluding that mischief never sleeps. But it wasn't my problem anymore; this was a chance to smooth the waters for Haley, and we were off to a good start.

The alarm on my phone went off loudly in my ear. I had fallen asleep with the phone on the pillow. I quickly got up, showered, and underwent my usual ritual to glam up. I was feeling secure about leaving Haley. Devin had never hurt her, and I couldn't imagine he would start now. As for me, I couldn't get to Tampa fast enough.

We got into the car and zipped through traffic to the airport. I thanked Devin for the ride and kissed Haley goodbye. "I'll be back in a few days, baby girl."

For the return trip, the plan was to meet outside of airport security, then fly back to Eugene. It was a long trip, but I was glad we did it. Haley looked happy, and it was a giant step in helping to repair their relationship. I had to take myself out of the picture and do the right thing.

I learned a huge lesson and discovered how resilient I had become. I was smarter, wiser, and more confident than before. I was on the path to becoming a strong, independent woman, an example I wanted to set for my kids.

I picked Haley up at the airport and we flew back to Oregon a few days later. Aside from the late-night hiccup, everything went according to plan, and there was no baby-mama drama. Thank God!

Chapter Thirty-Five
The Night Stalker

Leesa Wilder is my "ride or die" and a business partner. She is the epitome of strength and class. We first met at a business meeting. She had a preconceived opinion of me before the meeting, and not in a good way. Afterward, we had a chance to talk and hit it off instantly. From then on, there was never a moment of silence between us. We are peas in a pod. So much so that we sometimes refer to ourselves as Chloe and Jasmine, our alter egos! And, believe it or not, we sometimes use these aliases when we travel or want to stay under the radar. It's really kind of silly, but it's our thing. A modern-day Thelma and Louise, minus the criminal element.

Anyway, it was March 2009, and Leesa and I were preparing to film a trailer in Las Vegas for a concept that I created called, *Outside the League*. *Outside the League* was a series of interviews that I was conducting with professional sports figures to highlight their philanthropic, business, and other endeavors outside the arena. We were preparing to interview our friend Deral Boykin, as he orchestrated a birthday bash for Heins Ward and best friend Jerome Bettis. Deral was a veteran player in the NFL but also a legend for his promotional events. Leesa and I were scrambling, working non-stop to get ready. The production was scheduled for a five-day shoot.

Leesa and I were working from home, and I was on a conference call, while she was fine tuning the budget. She received a call from her lawyer about a family matter that required quick action. Leesa took the call and walked outside because I was working on the schedule with our producer, Vanessa, trying to decide if we needed to obtain permits to film inside the casinos. Deral had booked two of the biggest clubs on the Las Vegas strip for birthday bashes and always wanted everything done to perfection. So, I knew we had to dot every "I" and cross every "T."

Shortly, Leesa returned with a look of defeat. Uncharacteristically, she sat on the couch, put her head in her hands, and said, "I don't know what we're going to do." It was a rare day when Leesa wasn't climbing mountains, pushing through walls, or blazing new trails. It was always full speed ahead with her hair on fire.

I got off the phone and asked, "What do we need to do?"

She looked me in the eye and said, "Find a lawyer!"

It was a Wednesday, and on Wednesdays we religiously ate lunch at a place called "The Prairie Schooner, or Schooner's." The prime rib at Schooner's was to die for, and on Wednesdays, it was the place where University of Oregon donors near and far descended like pigeons at the park. Most of the donors knew me as the cheerleading coach, and they knew Leesa from business. She and I arrived around noon, and a table of regulars had already arrived. During this time, most of the big supporters were men. But over the years, that too has changed, and rightfully so. Leesa and I would always stop and chat with the donor crowd about various projects, university business, and "must know gossip." Oh, yes, men gossip, too!

Leesa was summoned to one side of the table, while I occupied the other. I generally chatted with a prominent attorney in town and his buddy, a well-known accountant. They loved to give us a hard time, and we got a kick out of their macho one-upmanship. It was all in good humor and harmless... so we thought. We walked in intending to troubleshoot Leesa's legal

Chapter Thirty-Five: The Night Stalker

trouble and saw Paul sitting front and center, a high-powered attorney. Leesa and I had a mind meld—problem solved. We exchanged our usual hugs and pleasantries, then Leesa gave a general explanation of her need. I knew Paul's friends would be arriving soon, so I asked him directly. He didn't hesitate and told us to call his secretary and schedule an appointment. We were both relieved that he was willing to help, and we thanked him and walked over to our table.

We sat down, and Leesa called and made an appointment for the following afternoon. We had a packed schedule that week, but this was a priority.

The next day, Leesa pulled up in her maroon Ford SUV, and I grabbed my purse and headed for the door. We were discussing the production schedule for Las Vegas as we pulled up to the law offices and parked near the front door. Paul heard our voices in the reception area and came out to greet us. We walked back to his beautifully appointed office and sat down.

Like many successful people, Paul definitely had an ego. But one thing I appreciated about him was he treated us with respect. I never got the sense that he talked down to people, even with his abundant display of self-confidence.

Leesa got right to it. She and Paul talked for about thirty minutes as I sat back, spectating. Occasionally I injected a word or two, but I had my own legal issues. I was texting a friend, trying to make some decisions about whether to stay in my current home or move to a new one. My house was everything I wanted, I loved it. But it was a lot of house for just me and the kids, and the mortgage payment was steep. I was really torn on whether to downsize and lower my payment or tough it out and stay put. This was my second home in five years. It was two houses down from the one I had built with Shawn. So, a third move in seven years, in the same subdivision, seemed a bit pointless.

I heard Leesa's keys rattle as she completed her business with Paul. They briefly discussed next steps and gave hugs goodbye. I was up next. Paul asked me why I had been so quiet, and I explained my predicament. He looked surprised to learn that I was separated from my husband. I hadn't told many people at this point because I hadn't really decided what I wanted to do. Paul invited me to lunch at "Kowloon's" for some Chinese food, but Leesa and I had a prior appointment, so I had to take a raincheck. One way or the other, I needed sound legal advice, so we agreed to meet the following day.

Over the next several weeks, I met with Paul three times regarding my separation. I knew that either I had to make a decision. I needed to try to reconcile with Shawn or file for divorce. It was extremely difficult for me. I had already been through this once before, although under very different circumstances. In the end, staying separated no longer seemed tenable, so I decided to file.

One afternoon, I got a call from Paul, and he left a voicemail message. I was surprised when I heard it because he sounded intoxicated. I listened to the message twice just to be sure. His words were slurred, he called me baby, and asked me to sit on his lap. I pulled the phone away and stared at my blackberry in disbelief. I stood on my front porch debating whether to go next door to Julie's and play the message for her. It really rubbed me the wrong way, but I thought maybe Paul dialed the wrong number by mistake?

The following morning, I played the message for Julie on our way to the gym. The look on her face was priceless. She had this, "What the frick!" expression. We shared an uncomfortable laugh and sort of shrugged it off as a drunk dial.

Later that day, I received a call from Paul's secretary asking me to come pick up a document at the office. I was feeling a bit

Chapter Thirty-Five: The Night Stalker

awkward about the situation, and Leesa rode with me in case there was some drama. Fortunately, I picked up the document and Paul was nowhere in sight.

Several days later, Leesa and I went to the Oregon Club to have lunch and to network, as we did most Monday afternoons. We sat at a table close to the back because we had to leave early that day. I walked through the buffet line and filled my plate. I loved the food there and I was particularly hungry that day. There were easily a hundred club members already seated, eating and telling tall tales.

The place was packed, so we left our purses and blackberries on the table to hold a spot. By the time we made it through the line, I looked up and spotted Paul and a couple other members sitting at our table. Leesa noticed them, too. I glanced over, and the way she was squinting said everything.

It wouldn't have been a big deal, but Paul had placed himself in between us. He had moved her things over in order to sit next to me. Immediately, a red flag went up. As lunch proceeded, Paul began leaning in close to talk to me. He kept whispering things in my ear, as if we had a special connection. It started to bother me immensely, and he was getting a little too comfortable. Paul was friendly to everyone; but this was too much.

After the requisite speeches by the various coaches and athletic department staff, I said loudly to Leesa, "Let's go!"

Before I could remove the napkin off my lap, Paul placed his left hand on my upper thigh and said, "You don't have to go yet, do you?"

I grabbed the napkin and said firmly, "We're leaving."

All of Paul's whispering gave me hives. I had to bite my lip to keep from cursing. I was fuming and marched straight to the ladies room. Leesa was confused. I started pacing and told her what happened. She was as upset as I was and ready to go back in there and cuss him out. But we both gathered ourselves and decided to get the heck out of there.

About two weeks later, at six a.m. on Christmas morning, the doorbell rang. I put my sweatsuit on and went to the door.

Jaden was about three and Haley was thirteen. The doorbell woke both my kids, and Haley was already downstairs. She said, "Mommy, some strange man is at the door." I had a front door with a glass window and wrought iron design. It was somewhat difficult to recognize the person, so I opened the door, with the kids standing behind me.

Low and behold, there was Paul.

Like Santa Claus, he came bearing gifts. I couldn't believe it. He said, "Merry Christmas," and I'm not sure what I said, but I know what I thought.

It was completely disturbing on so many different levels, particularly given that Paul was Jewish and didn't celebrate Christmas.

He brought Dutch Brother's mocha coffee for me and hot chocolate for the kids. It would have been a wonderful gesture if he hadn't put his hand on my thigh two weeks earlier or left an inappropriate drunken message prior to that.

It was an awkward moment.

Luckily, Julie was awake and saw him standing at my door. She was completely weirded out and called immediately. Of course I told her to come right over. Jaden was too young, but Haley could tell I was uncomfortable. Julie came over like one of Santa's helpers. Paul didn't see that coming, but I wasn't about to let him in, and Julie had no intention of leaving. Paul grew visibly nervous and bid us farewell.

I was becoming increasingly disturbed by his behavior.

Chapter Thirty-Five: The Night Stalker

Notwithstanding the fact that he was my lawyer, Paul was calling incessantly. There was absolutely no reason for him to be contacting me at all hours of the day and night.

Leesa and I stopped going to Schooner's on Wednesdays, and I didn't go to the Oregon Club for weeks. I could tell that Paul was drinking heavily. His drunk voicemails were completely inappropriate. It got to the point where I simply had enough. I told Leesa and Julie that I had to terminate my professional and personal relationship with Paul.

A week or so later, I walked outside to put Jaden in the car seat, and Paul was parked down the street, sitting in his green SUV. It was just before eight a.m., and he was watching my house. I acted like I didn't see him, got into my car, and immediately called Leesa. I was shaking with fear and frustration.

I kept repeating over and over, "This is crazy."

Leesa said, "This isn't a coincidence, Corine. He's stalking you."

I didn't disagree.

We decided to call a friend of ours who was a private detective. We wanted to get his opinion. He advised me to write down everything including times, dates, witnesses, etc. He also instructed me not to delete any voicemails or personal correspondence. I couldn't believe it had come to this! I had done nothing to give Paul the wrong impression. Our relationship had gone from friendly banter into a full-blown obsession. It was getting out of control.

Several days later, I made the decision to move out of my house. The builder of our subdivision, who I loved dearly, built several new homes in the cul-de-sac behind us. We worked out a deal, and two weeks later I planned to move into a new house.

The week before we moved, Haley was in my bedroom watching television in bed. It was around seven p.m. I was folding laundry and the blinds on the sliding glass door were open. I could see my reflection walking back and forth to the closet. The seventy-two-inch flat-screen television illuminated the room brightly. Suddenly, my dogs started barking. I was putting clothes on the hangers and looked outside and saw a man.

Initially, I thought it was my dad, wondering, *Why is he here?*

I went over to unlock the sliding door and realized that it wasn't my dad. I grabbed the chain to close the blinds and told Haley to get into the bathroom and lock the door. I ran down the hallway and checked the front door to be sure it was locked. I always kept my doors and windows locked regardless. It was dark, but I heard a car start. I looked outside and saw an SUV pulling off.

I called Julie and told her, "Paul was outside my bedroom!"

Julie was in disbelief. I had both my kids sleep with me that night, although I didn't sleep a wink.

I saw Paul parked outside my house on two more occasions. Now, he was stalking me at my new house.

Julie and Leesa told me I had to take action.

Leesa saw him parked outside the house one morning when she came to drop something off at my house. Julie saw him parked outside the house when she came home from the gym on another day. I knew they were both right. I didn't want to go head-to-head with a prominent attorney, but he gave me no option. I had multiple voice messages from him saved on my phone. All of them of a sexual and disturbing nature.

I contacted my family law attorney, Mindy, who knew me well, and I trusted her judgement. Mindy was in high demand, but I had to contact her anyway because Shawn and I decided to part ways.

Mindy knew Paul well from decades of practicing in Lane County. I made an appointment, and Leesa and I went to see her.

Chapter Thirty-Five: The Night Stalker

I told Mindy the story and played the voicemail messages. She was furious and referred me to an attorney who specialized in this type of situation. I told him the story and provided him with the voicemails. We then made the decision to contact the Oregon State Bar. I wasn't trying to ruin Paul's practice. I just wanted him to STOP! I found out a few days later, that I wasn't the only woman Paul had stalked. Another formal complaint had been filed a year or so before mine.

I didn't hear from Paul again after I filed the complaint. I knew that stalking was serious business and wasn't taken lightly. As a result of the fear and anxiety it caused, I began researching national statistics. I wanted to understand and be able to identify the characteristics and implications of this type of behavior. I learned that an estimated fourteen in one thousand persons age eighteen or older were victims of stalking. About half of stalking victims experienced at least one unwanted contact per week from their stalker. The risk of stalking victimization was highest for individuals who were divorced or separated, and nearly three in four stalking victims knew their offender in some capacity. Overall, an estimated six to seven million people are stalked annually in America and nearly one in six women and one in seventeen men experience stalking victimization at some point in their lifetime.

Later, I learned that Paul was a severe alcoholic and in failing health. A few weeks later, he was hospitalized and died. Regardless of what I experienced, I never wished him any harm. Paul was once an accomplished attorney who did a lot of good for a lot of people. In the end, I think he was probably harmless and just lonely. Unfortunately, this is not always the case.

As I reflected on my own situation, I also reflected on the death of actress Rebecca Schaeffer, who was shot and killed in 1989 at her home in West Hollywood. Schaeffer was murdered by a nineteen-year-old fan who had been stalking her for three years.

The man had written Rebecca numerous letters and traveled to Los Angeles hoping to meet her. Apparently, after watching her in a black comedy, he became enraged and concluded that she had become just another Hollywood wh—. This story hit home with me because Rebecca was from Eugene, Oregon and was just a few years older than me when she died.

In doing research for the book, I also came across the story of Mieke Oort, a twenty-one-year-old woman from Winchester, Massachusetts, who was studying in the Netherlands. Mieke was fatally stabbed in March 2022 in the city of Leeuwarden. Her sister told the media that, "She had the most beautiful soul." A twenty-seven-year-old suspect was in custody. He had stalked Mieke for some period of time by putting a tracking device on her bike. It was another horrible tragedy. Unfortunately, one that happens all too often.

The more I learned about stalking, the more adamant I became about bringing awareness to this behavior. I'm not a criminologist, but what struck me was the fact that stalking appears to be a gateway activity. It's not that all stalkers are violent, but stalking can definitely signal danger and dysfunctional behavior; it's part of a continuum of fear, harassment, violence, and abuse experienced by too many women.

Part Four
The Awakening

Chapter Thirty-Six
Déjà vu

It was early 2010, a milestone had just been reached. *The Hurt Locker* won six Oscars at the academy awards, including for Best Picture and Best Director. The film was directed by Kathryn Bigelow, and it was the first time a female had won in the Best Director category.

I had transitioned from coaching at the University of Oregon into radio and television production. On this particular day, I was at home working on an upcoming golf event to be held in Chandler, Arizona. The event was to be held at the Wild Horse Pass Hotel and Casino and involved a number of former NFL players. I was on speakerphone with my Co-Host and close friend Mark McMillian. Everybody called Mark "Mighty Mouse" because he was only five foot seven but had an incredible vertical leap. He played cornerback in the NFL for eight years, including a stint with my favorite San Francisco Forty Niners. We were talking about how I could be most effective during the celebrity golf tournament. Mark and Byron Evans had an amazing foundation that raised funds for various children's charities.

Hard Hittin' Radio was their sports show, produced in Phoenix. My primary role as co-host was to interview professional athletes on a designated segment. In addition to appearing with them on air, I traveled to various NFL stadiums doing live remote broadcasts, tailgate events, and public appearances around the city. I spent most of my time looking at the phone, talking, texting, and posting to social media.

Part of God's gift basket was my ability to communicate. I always had a way with people. I genuinely love all people. I never met a stranger, at least not for long.

On any given day, I would be on conference calls with three or four people at a time. Professional athletes, entertainers, agents, producers, and wall street executives. It was exhilarating, and I learned so much about business and finance from some of the most talented and brilliant minds in the world. I didn't have my college degree. I walked away from college after the rape and never returned as a student. But I was a sponge; I soaked up every conversation. I had more on the job training than most people could imagine.

It always amused my business manager, Marcus Nettles. He marveled at some of my conversations. I was adamant—I didn't let anyone or any title intimidate me. I embraced the challenge but remained true to myself. Some of those same people have no idea how empowering those conversations were for me. I started recapturing my power as a result of the company I was keeping. I had valuable things to say and the platform and support structure to say it. I felt heard and respected, especially from Ryan Jeffries.

Ryan was one of the most influential people in my life. He was effusive with praise and encouragement and inspired me to be the best that I could be but also quick to put me in my place. He was truly the catalyst in helping me find my strength, face my fears, and apply my talents. Everybody needs a Ryan Jeffries in their life.

While Mark and I were brainstorming ideas, I had an incoming call. I did a double take because my former sister-in-law, Glenda, was calling. She and I hadn't spoken for quite some time, but we still loved each other very much. I told Mark I had to take the call and I would get right back to him.

I accepted Glenda's call and excitedly said, "Hey, Sis! What's going on?"

Chapter Thirty-Six: Déjà Vu

The usual upbeat tone in her voice was gone. Generally, Glenda was smiling ear to ear and very welcoming. On this day, however, she sounded stoic. "Hey, Sis, you have time to talk? I'm on a two-way call with Mom." I was completely caught off guard. I was always happy to talk to Mama, but I had an uneasy feeling.

"Hi, Mama" I said with a shaky voice.

She said, "Hello, daughter."

My heart started beating fast. I could tell something was wrong.

What Glenda said next had the hairs standing up all over my body. "It's my brother, he did it again. He attacked Ericka!" She was so hurt by what Devin had done, and I could hear the anger in her voice. Glenda was an extremely loyal person, especially to family. She loved her brother, but she wasn't one to sugarcoat things. I asked about Erika and their baby daughter Kaitlyn. They told me that Erika had Devin arrested and she was on her way to Seattle.

I could hear the disgust in Mama's voice as she began to describe the details. She was sick and tired of Devin's abusive behavior. He had not one but two chances to do right by his daughters. Not everyone believed me when I pressed charges. But as the years went by, they began to see the patterns of violence and womanizing firsthand. It was much easier for him to lie and manipulate his family when he lived in Oregon or Atlanta. But when he moved back to Los Angeles, the covers were pulled back for all to see.

Some time passed before I received another call from the family. They wanted me to know that Devin was in Eugene to attend an Oregon football camp. They knew he was mad because I had given information to the authorities in California about his history of abuse. They were building a case against him for his violence against Ericka. At this point, I hadn't seen Devin in a couple years. The two prior times, I had been around other people, and I didn't feel threatened in any way. Sometimes I would get triggered when my mind wandered to the past. I still harbored trauma and had nightmares from time to time. With him living in Los Angeles, I could mask my fear. But they knew he wanted to confront me, and the family was genuinely concerned.

I remember getting off the phone and feeling panicked. I thought I had a grip on my fear, but everything came rushing back. I picked up the phone and called my friend Ed, hoping he could swing by the house so I wouldn't be alone. Ed was tied up but said he would come as soon as possible. He was familiar with my history with Devin and knew that I was nervous from the tone in my voice.

Not long after, Devin was standing outside the house, in the flesh. I remember looking at my cell phone to get the time. I wanted to make a mental note of when he arrived. I could see him through the glass in the door, and he saw me, too. I didn't want him coming into the house, especially while I was alone.

I picked my car keys up off the coffee table and headed to the door and walked out as if I needed something from my car. I shut the door behind me, said hello, and asked what he was doing. He told me he was in town for the game and needed to talk to me. It was clear that he was trying to feel me out to see what I knew.

Immediately, he started questioning me about his relationship with Erika. He wanted to know what I said to his family and if the authorities from Los Angeles had contacted me. I told him I was aware of the situation, and I didn't want to discuss it or get involved. He was extremely agitated, pacing back and forth in front of the garage. I had gotten inside the driver's side of my car. The door was ajar, and my leg was hanging out. I was purposely trying

Chapter Thirty-Six: Déjà Vu

to appear distracted, feverishly looking for a mythical something. I knew Ed would be driving up soon, so I stalled as long as I could.

We continued our cat and mouse game, and I kept up the pretense of searching for something in the back seat of the car. Finally, I walked toward the porch, and Devin cut me off and obstructed my path. I was extremely uncomfortable. We were inches apart. I began to back up, and he grabbed my arm.

I said, "Hey, hey," and he quickly let go.

He was pressing me about the case, and the more I dodged, the more he tried to convince me that Erika was lying; that he was being set up and falsely accused. I couldn't believe that Devin was seeking my help. Somehow, he had convinced himself that I could be manipulated or intimidated. As narcissists tend to do, Devin weaved a tale so fantastical and far-fetched that it had to be rehearsed or he was borderline delusional.

As fate had it, Erika and I had just had a conversation a few days earlier. It was the first time we had been able to speak candidly and the first time that she realized that everything she heard about me was a lie. Devin's family had told her the truth about our marriage and the horrendous torment that he put me through. Nevertheless, it wasn't until she had stepped into the same nightmare that we were really able to talk.

Devin was completely desperate at this point. He had no clue that Erika and I had been in contact. I was a squirrel with a limp. He never considered the possibility that I was already helping her and Kaitlyn.

About twenty-five or thirty minutes had passed, and Devin was getting increasingly comfortable with his Nino Brown routine. His agitation bordered on arrogance. His aggressive tactics weren't working, so he completely changed course. He went from pacing and ranting to "Mr. Suave and Debonair." He pulled out all the stops. The smooth talk flowed like a gentle stream. It was truly bizarre. Devin really thought he was going to pull off the Jedi mind meld and lure me into his web.

I was becoming incredibly nervous. His behavior was bizarre, and I didn't trust his motives.

Thankfully, and not a moment too soon, Ed pulled up to the side of the house. Ed was well-known in the community, and his family had clout. When Ed walked in a room, people paid attention.

He got out of his car and asked if everything was okay. I told him everything was fine, and he walked inside the house.

In a loud, booming voice, he said, "We have work to do, let's go!"

I simply replied, "Okay." I told Devin that I had to go, and I would be in contact with his sister. He got in his car and drove off.

When I walked into the house, I was absolutely shaking. I was so happy Ed took time out of his day to help. He knew I was in a really tough situation and told me, "That's what family does."

He got in his car and headed out, leaving me with a little more pep in my step.

I had surprised myself. I was scared but strong. I dealt with the pressure of being alone with Devin; I was nervous but not neurotic, shaken but not stirred. I saw right through him, all the misdirection, the smoke and mirrors, the lies, the threats, the manipulation. He tried his whole bag of tricks, from charisma to coercion, but I had the kryptonite. It had been more than a decade since that last fateful beatdown from Devin. I was in a completely different place.

Unfortunately, Devin was still in the same place, swimming in legal troubles with a new wife and daughter. He had escaped a great deal of accountability for his crimes against me. He got off with only a ten-year restraining order. He had a brand-new start at life,

Chapter Thirty-Six: Déjà vu

with a beautiful family, but he couldn't shake the demons; they had infected his body like a COVID 4000.

Sometimes you don't know how much you've grown until a situation presents itself. In this case, I was able to react quickly: I reached out to a friend, I took evasive action in the garage, I refused to be manipulated or co-opted into Devin's scheme, I assisted another victim, I protected my daughter, and I survived.

Below is an excerpt from a letter that I received from Erika when I told her about the book. For those of you undergoing abuse, the extended version is included in the Epilogue. I recommend you read it.

> *"... For months now, I had been trying to convince Devin for us to go our separate ways. I would point out how he could be free to enjoy the LA life as a single man. I promised I would never deny him access to our daughter. I tried to paint a picture of great co-parenting possibilities. All my pleas fell on deaf ears and always ended in death threats to me and my family. He repeatedly told me I wasn't going anywhere with our daughter, especially because it was me who had "wasted his time" with my fake love.*
>
> *There was no reasoning with him. He was not a rational actor. Every time we had that conversation, I was appalled by his ability to blatantly lie to himself and to me. As if I had not just witnessed for myself what a piece of sh— human being he was. He had the gall to paint himself as the victim, as the one who had been duped into the relationship. That night, I was fed*

up and I had resigned myself to not backing down, even if it meant taking a beating.

My time in Los Angeles led me to the conclusion that the only way that I was going to get out of this relationship was after a major physical assault, one that I may not survive. Sure enough, we argued, and I didn't back down. He became enraged. He lunged at me, and I managed to barely escape his grasp but found myself back up to our daughter's crib. He lunged at me again and tried to grab my hair. Instead, his fingernails scraped down the side of my face. I felt a sharp sting followed by a wetness rolling down my face. By now, his sister had heard the commotion and walked into the room just as he had lunged at me and scratched my face.

She grabbed Devin and tried to hold him back. He was cursing and calling me names the entire time. I ran to the bathroom, and I saw my face. There were red marks and blood streaking from my forehead, over my eyelids, and down to my lip. As I looked closer, I could see that he had scratched the skin off my face. I became enraged and came out of the bathroom ready to attack, I yelled something like "You scarred my face, you f—ing fat b—!" During the time I was in the bathroom, his sister had pushed him out of the room and locked the door. Devin was out in the hallway, cussing and yelling profanities. I yelled back, "I'm calling the police." I asked for my phone and couldn't find it, then I asked his sister to call the police. I yelled back in response to his

Chapter Thirty-Six: Déjà vu

insults, "F— you, I'm done, I'm calling the police, and I'm pressing charges!"

This whole time, his sister was making every effort to calm both of us down. She kept telling her brother to calm down, shut up, and leave the house. His sister is a nurse, and it was her instinct to want to take care of my wounds. She asked me to calm down; she said that she needed to treat me and we could talk about it afterward, and if I still wanted her to call the police, she would. It was clear to me that she was in "protect my brother" mode. It also began to dawn on me again that I was all alone in this mess. If I called the police, I would have his entire Los Angeles family to face. And his most loyal and ardent supporter was his sister, and she was under the same roof.

I did not call the police that night and finally achieved my escape, but a few months later, there was no one to stop me, and I had his sister and brother's support. It turns out that Devin is not just a despicable partner, he is also the worst kind of son and brother as well. He accused his sister of being a freeloader... actively encouraged his brother-in-law to... He slept with his brother's... He hid money from me... and was accused of sleeping with various High School girls. By the time I left, the house was on the brink of foreclosure, even though Devin withdrew money from our account every month to pay the mortgage. Money that came primarily from my income...

... To make a long story short, I successfully left the state of California with my daughter, filed a criminal complaint, and pressed charges. Devin was arrested on his return flight from Oregon after a week of football camp. He had no idea I had left, and when he found himself in jail, he called his family and told one of his female cousins to "go see her" and get her to "drop the charges." If I refused, he alluded to being okay with them putting their hands on me. He called former Oregon co-workers and football players and coaches, begging them to bail him out. He was unsuccessful.

And when I was summoned at court, I heard him plead guilty to assault resulting in bodily injury and making terrorist threats. The judge also granted a ten-year criminal no contact order because of his prior history of physical abuse toward his first wife Corine Lewis. Like most sociopaths, Devin had what I can only describe as a 'memento" envelope. In it was a pristine copy of the court documents from his Oregon criminal case, including the details of the charges and a summary report of the injuries suffered by Corine at his hands.

August 18, 2009, was the day he was found guilty and sentenced to one year in prison with five years of probation afterward. That was the last time I ever saw Devin, and sadly it was also our daughter's birthday.

Since then, I have moved on and bettered my life and that of my daughter. I have also tried to

Chapter Thirty-Six: Déjà vu

keep my daughter in touch with Corine's daughter Haley. During my time with Devin, Haley visited us twice, once when we were in Georgia, before I knew I was pregnant with Kaitlyn, and once when we were in California and Kaitlyn was a little over a year old. Since we have been in Washington, we have traveled to see her in Oregon, once just the two of us, once with their grandmother Pearl, and the last time with my husband.

Each time, Kaitlyn has bonded with sister Haley in a new way, and each time I have been impressed and touched by Haley's desire to connect with her "Sissy." It is a joy to see the ease with which they pick up and just be with one another. And I am forever impressed with the young lady that Haley has been striving to be every time I see her, especially because I have an idea of what she has been through when it comes to her father.

Over the years, Kaitlyn struggled to reconcile in her heart and mind who her father is and what he represents to her. Fortunately, my husband has shown her what a real father is and how a real father loves. In the process, he has earned her love and respect. She has accepted him as her father and released Devin and herself from the pain that he represented in her life. Today, I am grateful for my daughter and focus on the blessings that got us here and not on what we went through.

I am grateful that I got a second chance to get it right in love and family."

Respectfully,
Erika Ramos

Erika and I were abused by the same man, and our daughters share the same DNA, but we became family by choice. It was because of our inner strength and determination that we came together to be examples for our daughters and millions of other women around the world. We could have easily just acknowledged one another and went our merry ways. But we both felt a genuine bond and a kinship and have stayed in each other's lives.

When I talked to Erika about the book, she thought it was important for women to understand the grooming process, as that's where it all begins. Abusers don't lead with abuse, because they know that's a turn off. They lead with honey and spice and everything nice. They use intoxicating words and reel you in with lies, manipulation, deception, and illusions of grandeur. They're like mercenary soldiers. They have no loyalty, and they act with impunity because they know how the system works. They create a pretext years in advance, which absolves them from consequences at the point of reckoning. Understanding the grooming phase is the first step in prevention. Rely on your intuition and trust your instincts; they're crucial to your personal safety. If something or someone seems too good to be true, read the fine print. Grooming is the entrapment process, and once you get caught, it's hard to get out.

Erika's indoctrination was based on Devin's time with me. He created an image and persona of an anti-Corine. That image and persona had to be embraced wholeheartedly. I was promiscuous, confrontational, and deceitful. So, Erika had to be predictable,

Chapter Thirty-Six: Déjà Vu

understated, and controllable. Predators tend to study their victims and perfect their methods over time. They watch and they wait, then when the opportunity presents itself, they pounce. Devin fed Ericka a steady diet of lies mixed with an intoxicating dose of love bombing and charisma. Unbeknownst to her, she fell into the trap, beguiled by his kind words and relentless desire to build trust.

I was twenty-one when I was first groomed, and, like Erika, I discovered the plot much too late.

Predators don't just pounce once; they tend to follow a pattern. Devin was abusive to his college girlfriend before me, to the woman he dated after me, and to Erika as well. Abusers generally come with a playbook, and not all plays are the same. Abusers come in all shapes, sizes, and socio-economic backgrounds. They use stealth and reconnaissance to carry out their missions. What may feel like love may be part of a covert operation. What you may think of as a favor may be the initial step toward extracting something later.

Be on guard! Grooming is a full contact sport.

If this sounds intriguing, you'll learn more about it as part of The Unvirtuous Cycle.

Chapter Thirty-Seven
Red Flags and Risk Factors

As I said earlier, I'm not a doctor, and I don't give specific diagnoses. I don't prescribe medicine or drug treatments. I don't provide psychological profiles, counseling, or analysis. I'm just a mom, one who has been through a cycle of pain, trauma, disillusionment, and reawakening. So, in that sense, I know of what I speak.

This chapter could be called "Lessons Learned," or "The Fifteen Deadly Sins," but those titles sounded a bit too prescriptive. Instead, I entitled it "Red Flags" because the chapter serves as a warning sign. Like a stop sign or blinking red lights along the highway, red flags are intended to get your attention. They advise you to stop, slowdown, detour, or pull over. In the game of life, or relationships, there are no absolutes. There is no one right answer, no one size fits all solution for confronting or escaping abuse. Everyone must make their own decisions, but if you've experienced one or more of the following, be careful! If one or more of the following are present in your current relationship, a light bulb should go off in your head.

Read the signs carefully and be honest, and if you need to stop and pull over, do so!

1. Your core values don't align. If your core values don't align around what I call the "Five Fs": family, faith, finances, fun, and the future, be careful. Sometimes opposites attract, but sometimes opposites attack. If one partner wants a family and the other doesn't, those positions don't

naturally attract. If you're a believer and your partner isn't, those positions don't naturally attract. If you're working three jobs and your partner shops online all day, those positions don't naturally attract. If you hate Las Vegas and your partner is an obsessive gambler, those positions don't naturally attract. If you're saving for a house and your partner is living for today, those positions don't naturally attract. Opposite positions aren't always fatal, and no two people agree on everything, but if you find yourselves locked in conflict at every turnstile, then be careful. Life tends to bring bumps in the road, sometimes they just slow you down, and sometimes they can throw you in a ditch. People don't readily change their beliefs or easily admit their mistakes. To overcome major differences in core values, the parties have to respect and accept their differences, not try to change them. Generally, there must also be strong counterbalancing forces like excellent communication, loads of trust, and meaningful intimacy. Otherwise, you can bring a horse to water, but you can't make him drink.

2. Your relationship is dependent versus interdependent. Interdependence means reliance and accountability. It means that every player on the team feels valued and affirmed regardless of who scores the touchdown. It means you can rely on me, and I can rely on you. It means that every player on the team is accountable to every other player on the team. This is especially important in dealing with strong willed or controlling personalities. If mutual respect and accountability are absent, then the whole relationship could be a house of cards. It doesn't always mean disaster, but it's a gap in the fence that should be

Chapter Thirty-Seven: Red Flags and Risk Factors

tended to. Otherwise, an unhealthy power imbalance could arise where one party views the other as less worthy and attempts to exert unusual control.

3. Your partner tries to gaslight you. Two people can agree to disagree on the same set of facts or have a different take on the same situation. But if a partner tries to "gaslight" you; if your partner tries to deny reality; that's a form of manipulation and psychological control. Your partner is trying to spin the truth in order to introduce doubt and lower your self-confidence and self-esteem. It's a form of covert operations; the Russians call it "active measures." Gaslighting is dangerous; it's not something to dismiss or take lightly.

4. Your partner lies incessantly. Lying is not violence, neither is gaslighting, but they could be precursors. If your partner is constantly lying to you about their actions, intentions, and whereabouts, it's a major sign of disrespect. When people don't respect you, they don't tend to value you or your wellbeing. We all fall short sometimes, but it's one thing to say I'm a pilot and quite another to say I own an airline. All lies aren't equal, some are harmless embellishments, and others represent a detachment from reality. Be especially careful about the latter.

5. Your partner tries to blame shift. Under Newton's law, "for every action there is a reaction," blame shifting can be another form of psychological warfare: "You made me hit you. If you hadn't pushed my buttons, I wouldn't have had to drop kick you on the floor." Really? This is such a pernicious tactic; it can lead to all sorts of dysfunctional behavior. A related issue is, "whataboutism!" "Yes, I cheated with my secretary, but what about you? You spent

too much money at the mall." It's a way of creating a false equivalency. If either of these techniques are predominant in your relationship, you should be careful.

6. Your partner berates you at home and in public. I was always told not to cry over spilled milk. And if your partner berates you constantly, incessantly, over the smallest infractions, it might not be the infraction. It might be your partner. Be careful! They could be a ticking time bomb.

7. Your partner tries to isolate you. If your partner tries to isolate you from your family, friends, or other associations, you should be careful. That's what predators do. They try to separate their prey from the herd. Isolating a partner is one of the main precursors to a phenomenon known as "trauma bonding." It's not a strategy for winning friends and influencing people; it's a strategy for dividing and conquering.

8. Your partner disrupts your place of work. When a partner exhibits belligerent and destructive behavior at your workplace, it represents a significant level of disregard and lack of self-control. Most of us have an inherent desire to be respected by our co-workers. So, when a partner crosses that boundary and brings any form of toxicity to your place of employment, the potential for future violence rises and all bets are off.

9. You find yourself in a state of denial. If your partner headbutts you and body slams you on the floor, and you find yourself making excuses for such behavior, you are in a state of denial. You are trespassing on dangerous ground. You should be careful. Denial is part of the predator's playbook. You have become an accomplice in your own victimization. You are witnessing against yourself. You are

Chapter Thirty-Seven: Red Flags and Risk Factors

gaslighting yourself. You begin to lie to your family and friends and the people who want to help you. It's an injustice to yourself and all those who love you.

10. You have a never-ending feeling of unease. If your partner is prone to unexpected rage, leaving you in a perpetual state of uncertainty, shame, embarrassment, lack of confidence, or fear, you should be careful. Unless you work for the mob, this is not normal in a healthy, loving relationship. Your body is trying to tell you something. Listen!

11. Your partner has a history of abuse. Everyone makes mistakes; I've certainly made my share. But if your partner has a history of past abuse; if he beat his prior girlfriend, and the one before that, and the one before that; the abuse is not an accident, it's a pattern. Predator's prey on the weak, that's what they do. It's part of their DNA. And if your partner has a prior history, be careful. You might be the sequel.

12. Your partner threatens to kill you! Everybody says things they don't mean or later regret, especially in the heat of battle. But if your partner threatens to kill you, take it seriously. It might not be rage; it might be prophecy. Make sure you read the signs carefully. Mistakes in this area could be costly. Don't be afraid to get a second opinion.

13. Your partner gets violent. If your partner grabs you by the hair, slaps you, punches you in the face, and throws you down a flight of stairs, it's not love; it's a lack of self-control and an expression of vile intent. If they hit you once, it could be an accident. If they hit you twice, it's a small sample size but probably not a mistake. If they hit you as part of a recurring cycle, it's not something you did, and it's not something that you can fix. It's who they are. The only

solution is to seek help, separate, press charges, or all of the above.

14. Your partner is quick to apologize but slow to change. Your partner beats you badly or as part of a recurring pattern. He is quick to apologize and bring you perfume, flowers, and jewelry but is unwilling to change or seek help. It's a form of self-righteousness or righteous indignation. In other words, he doesn't really think he was wrong. The flowers are to smooth the waters. But when it comes to domestic violence, actions speak louder than words. If your partner is unwilling to address their violent, destructive, abusive behavior, whatever else they are willing to do is a form of manipulation.

15. You are staying for reasons other than love and respect. Your partner beats you, but you are staying for the children, or for financial security, or social status. I've been down that road before. Be careful, the cost could be much higher than you think. All of the above can serve as enablers for future cycles of your own abuse, or worse.

I don't want to be too preachy, but be aware of another enabler: "nostalgia." It can be such a gut punch. The feeling that, "our relationship was so good in the beginning." The desire to return to the good ole days is incredibly alluring. It can keep you hanging on for far too long. Live in the present and look toward the future. The definition of insanity is doing the same thing over and over and expecting a different result. Remember the movie, *Mr. and Mrs. Smith* with Angelina Jolie and Brad Pitt?

There was a scene where Brad asks her to reflect back to the beginning, when things were good. Angie refuses, she stays in the moment. She refuses to be drawn in by nostalgia. She refuses to

Chapter Thirty-Seven: Red Flags and Risk Factors

go backward in time. She responds with a classic: "It's hard, cold math." She lets Brad know that it's over and proceeds with her plan. Sometimes, that's what life demands: hard cold math

Chapter Thirty-Eight
I'm Just not that Cool!

It's three weeks later, or thereabouts. My alarm went off at three-thirty a.m., and I jumped out of bed full of excitement! Today was the day Leesa and I were heading to Las Vegas to film the promo reel for *Outside the League*. She sent me a text message to make sure I was awake.

An hour later she came rolling around the corner, and I opened the back door and loaded my luggage inside. She flashed her million-dollar smile, and I noticed her perfectly curled hair and batting eyelashes. Margot Robbie is who comes to mind. We looked like matching bookends most of the time. So much so, every trip we took, someone would always ask if we were sisters. I guess when you're around someone day in and day out, you tend to converge or diverge. We had the exact same style, so I always considered it a compliment.

We landed at the airport in Las Vegas and took a cab to the Aria Resort and Casino. The hotel had only been open for a month, and we were happy to check out the newest digs on the strip. We walked up to the front desk to check in, and were met by one of my closest friends, Damion Hall, of the legendary R&B group GUY.

Damion flashed that smile like only he could, picked me up, and hugged me tight. I was so happy to see him. It had been almost a year since we had seen one another. Damion had recently been reunited with his son Sergio, who I loved to death. Sergio lived in Vegas, so it was perfect timing for Damion to join us for the shoot and festivities.

We gathered the film crew for a production meeting and went over the schedule. Our crew was predominantly from Los Angeles, extremely talented, and fun to be around. They always brought out the best in me, which was important, especially when I had to perform on camera. I sometimes got nervous and wanted to make sure everyone knew what needed to happen.

The first night, we were filming the birthday party for Jerome Bettis, beginning with dinner at Tao Asian Bistro in the Venetian Hotel. The restaurant was fabulous, and expensive. We had a private dining room overlooking the dance floor, and as usual, Deral had everything planned to perfection. Nothing but the best. I knew it was going to be a big night, with opportunities for a lot of amazing footage.

Leesa hired a professional makeup artist named Moe from the Aria salon, and we booked Moe and her team for the entire weekend. The first night of filming our camera crew was on fire! They captured amazing footage of Vegas and the night's festivities. They made me look good, which made me happy.

The next day was a whirlwind. We had two interviews to film with marquee athletes and a birthday bash for Heinz Ward. We started the day off with an exclusive interview with Darel Boykin, it was terrific. We went back to the room for a respite, then Leesa called my name.

"Yo, Blondie. LET'S GO!" I depended on her to keep the trains running. We ran downstairs to get my hair and makeup done, and they completely outdid themselves. I was feeling great!

Generally, I did most everything off the cuff. I felt that I did my best work when it was authentic, especially when hosting an interview. But the next shoot required me to use a script, so I was quiet and super focused. When we got back to the suite, I set the script on the bed and got dressed. The entire production crew was

Chapter Thirty-Eight: I'm Just Not That Cool!

downstairs waiting in the lobby. In addition, Damion Hall, his son Sergio, and a couple of athletes were also there, chopping it up.

Leesa and I came down the elevator, and as soon as the door opened, I realized I had left the script. I grabbed the room key out of Leesa's hand and rode the elevator back up, walked into the room, and got a glimpse of my reflection in the mirror. I've always been a humble person, but I looked real good if I did say so myself! I was definitely feeling good. I had worked hard in the gym for months to get my body right. My hair was platinum blonde with loose curls cascading down my shoulders. My makeup was flawless. My ears, wrists, and fingers were blinging with diamonds. I had on an all-black bodysuit with six-inch black Chinese Laundry stilettos. This was a far cry from being beat up in the bathroom or being kicked in the tailbone. I looked like I had just stepped out of a fashion magazine. I gave myself a big smile and said, "Go get 'em."

As I entered the elevator, I hit the lobby button with my right index finger while strategically holding my cell phone and tightly clutching the script a COACH® wrist purse with my left hand. The elevator floor was marble, so slippery, especially with heels.

The door opened and the entire production team was waiting. As I walked off the marble floor onto the plush casino, I developed a strut, a red-carpet swag. I should have stopped there, but I took two more steps and my right ankle buckled underneath. I tried with great effort to catch my balance, but everything started moving in slow motion. I stumbled like a newborn filly, then *BAM!* Just like that, I hit the floor face down on my stomach! My cell phone went sliding across the floor, and the script flew all over kingdom come. My purse was sprawled on the floor, as were my arms and legs. The whole thing was a hot mess. I looked like a chimpanzee on skates! All that was missing was an organ grinder and a banana peel. It was so embarrassing. And if that wasn't enough, I got a rug burn on my chin.

I tried to get up, but all I remember is everyone doubled over laughing. With that, I became the night's entertainment. No comic was needed. Damion Hall literally crawling on all fours, with tears of laughter rolling down his cheeks tried with everything he had to pull me up, but he couldn't stop laughing. Leesa walked over and rescued me, and like a smart aleck said, "That was quite an entrance, girlfriend!" Thank God I wasn't injured and had a sense of humor!

It wasn't like the donut that I had to carry around and sit on for six months, but it certainly was a rough night. Everybody was Chris Rock. They didn't let me live it down.

It was on that fateful night, on the casino floor of the Aria, that I just had to realize, I was just not that cool!

This was a valuable lesson. Humility is like a sixth sense; it allows you to see within yourself.

Several weeks passed since we wore out our welcome in Las Vegas. In the interim, Bernie Madoff pleaded guilty to running the largest Ponzi scheme in American history in early March 2009, to the tune of about $60 billion. That's what I call playing fast and loose with the numbers.

I was on the road again. Weeks earlier, I had received an invitation to an event hosted by former MLB player Torii Hunter that was going to be held at the Wild Horse Pass Hotel and Casino in Chandler Arizona. The invitation was most fortuitous because I had been preparing for an upcoming charity golf event that the Hard Hittin' Radio Foundation was hosting at the same location. So, it was the perfect opportunity for us to attend and check out the new hotel and golf course in advance.

Chapter Thirty-Eight: I'm Just Not That Cool!

For me, it also turned out to be the place where I met two of the most wonderful families: the Spivey's and Lassiter's.

Tabitha Spivey was the gorgeous wife of World Series champion second baseman, Junior Spivey, and Ericka Lassiter was the equally stunning wife of veteran NFL defensive back Kwamie Lassiter. Both women were hugely talented and successful in their own rights. They were smart and knew how to do business. Both families would later prove to be highly influential in my life.

Mark and I were scheduled to co-hosts for the upcoming event. Mark knew everyone, so I was able to meet some amazing people in Scottsdale. In addition, my very best male friend, fourteen-year NFL veteran wide receiver, Michael Westbrook lived nearby. For those of you who follow college football, you may remember that Michael went to the University of Colorado and is the guy who caught the last second Hail Mary pass to beat Michigan. I first met Michael when I interviewed him for the *Outside the League* concept. He is a world champion in Brazilian jujitsu and owns a dojo in Gilbert, Arizona. The interview was fabulous, and our on-camera chemistry was amazing. So much so that we brought him on as my co-host of *Life Beyond the League*, the successor series to *Outside the League*. Whenever I came to Arizona, I most looked forward to seeing the Westbrook family.

The night before we left for Scottsdale, Leesa and I went to the tanning salon to get our spray tans. We both used tanning beds multiple days a week, but there was nothing like the glow of a freshly airbrushed spray tan. For those who don't know, you need a minimum of seven hours to let the tan properly set. We had twenty-four hours before the event. The problem is, however, after more than twelve hours, the tan starts to stick. Leesa and I laughed when we saw each other the next morning at the airport. We were way too dark, with a tinge of "Oompa Loompa" orange! I was wearing my traditional all black bebe® sweatsuit with the blinged-out rhinestones on the back, and Leesa was wearing her signature pink bling sweat jacket and black yoga pants. Our hair and makeup were on point, so despite the horrible residue and smell of our fake tans, we were ready for Freddy.

We landed in Phoenix, and it was almost a hundred degrees. It was low forties back home, so we had more than a little sticker shock. We hailed a taxi outside the terminal to a friend from Eugene's condo. He also offered the use of his car so that we could save additional money.

It was *so* hot. We arrived at the condo and were near delirious from thirst. We retrieved the keys off the counter and went looking for his red convertible. The heat was scorching, and Leesa was cussing up a storm. We crisscrossed the parking lot, looking for a "frickin'" red convertible car that was nowhere in sight. We had been dragging our luggage the whole time, so we were at our wits' end. Then, out of nowhere, I heard, "You have got to be kidding me!" I whipped my head around, and there was Leesa standing underneath a tree at the far end of the parking lot. I didn't have the best vision, but I guessed there was a red convertible somewhere underneath the corrosive pile of bird crap on top!

Never in my life had I ever seen anything so disgusting and foul. The car was saturated in dried bird poop. There wasn't a trace of red paint anywhere. And neither of us could decipher the supposed color of the soft top. The windows were also saturated with dried poop, it was impossible to see inside.

We stood there for a moment in complete silence. At some point, I asked the obvious yet dreaded question, "How are we going to open the doors?" We both started laughing. It was the only thing we could do. We were standing in the middle of the desert with sweatsuits on, with melting, sticky, spray tans. We were expecting Ashton Kutcher to jump out any minute and say, "You've been punked!"

Chapter Thirty-Eight: I'm Just Not That Cool!

I happened to have some napkins in my tote bag that I got from the airport. We wrapped the napkins around the door handles on both sides, opened the doors, and slung our luggage in the back seat. Somehow, Leesa managed to get the car started, googled the nearest car wash, and plugged it into her GPS. I was about to die of heat stroke, so we turn on the air conditioner, and out came this POOF of sand and dust! It blew out with such ferocity that our faces were completely covered with sand and dirt! The only thing you could see were the whites of our eyes. I looked at Leesa with her lips pursed shut and didn't know whether to laugh or cry. She took the sleeve of her jacket and furiously wiped her mouth. I took off my jacket and did the same. All we wanted to do was get to the hotel and shower.

The front window was hopeless. It was a bird crapping pile of a mess. There was no way possible to see the road. So, we rolled down the windows, Leesa poked her head out, and we started our adventure. Her entire left arm and shoulder were hanging out of the convertible. We looked like a couple of crazy women with no business behind the wheel.

As we pulled into the car wash, there were several cars ahead of us. There had to be at least fifteen workers prewashing cars as they pulled in. The look on those poor guys' faces when they saw us was priceless! They looked the other way, not wanting to even acknowledge us. We had to be the talk of the town… for a week… or the year! I learned later that my friend hadn't driven the car in three years… and it showed.

We finally made it to Chandler for the big event, parked the car, lugged our bags to our hotel suite, and started getting ready. I think that was the longest shower I had ever taken in my life.

We were met in the lobby by Mark and Michael, and after taking pictures on the red carpet, we started meeting former teammates and acquaintances of theirs. It was a great opportunity for Westbrook to reconnect with the fraternity of athletes and for me to meet their wives. We were going to interview several of them for our pilot of *Life Beyond the League*.

I remember Leesa and I walking into the nightclub at the casino following several of the guys. Everywhere we turned we were shaking hands with someone new.

I looked across the room and saw two ladies I had been dying to meet. Mark had been telling me about them for weeks. Ericka Lassiter was the President of the Off the Field Wives Association, the group of NFL wives who did charity events and a killer fashion show at the Super Bowl. Tabitha Spivey was an up-and-coming actress and someone I was going to interview in the coming weeks.

The night was fabulous, kind of a "who's who" in Arizona professional sports. We had great food, met a ton of people, and listened to the smooth sounds of Brian McKnight.

The event was a home run, and a great success. The irony was that most of the people there had no sense of the extent of my abuse, and even fewer could have known how they were helping me to regain my voice and rebuild my confidence. The people in Chandler reignited the competitive fire in me, and for that I am eternally grateful.

No one is an island. We all need friends, and sometimes we need help! I certainly did.

Chapter Thirty-Nine
My First Love

Because my mom was the head cheerleading and dance team coach at WHS, she had to fundraise to help support both teams. In the 1980s, competing at multiple competitions and having numerous costumes was extremely expensive. Our high school didn't provide much of a budget for the programs; however, they allowed as many fundraising opportunities as the community would bear. One of the most successful ways to support both teams were school dances. Generally, the dances were a huge hit amongst all demographics. We lived in a city that was centered around the University of Oregon and, as such, there weren't many options for high school students.

When I came of age, Mom enlisted me in the fundraising fight. It was the first dance of the year, and my job was to collect the money at the front door and stamp the students' hands as they entered. I was in eighth grade and attended Cascade Middle School. I was definitely one of the most popular girls at the school, partly because I could invite friends to the high school functions. During football season, I always had my posse meet me at the stadium to hang out and watch the games. On this occasion, I remember asking if my best friend, Shoni, could help. My family loved Shoni, and although we attended rival middle schools, we both attended Willamette High School the following year. Shoni's parents said yes, and we were so excited!

It was a Friday night, and we walked into the school cafeteria ten minutes before the football game ended. It was a special night because the Willamette Wolverine's won. We knew that all of the students would be filing in soon. I ran into the bathroom to touch up my lip gloss and eyeliner, while Shoni turned off the lights to set the mood. We had the biggest smiles on our faces, and we were already dancing to the DJ's jam "Paul Revere" by the Beastie Boys.

The cheerleaders got to the dance and ran into the kitchen to change out of their uniforms. It always seemed like a covert operation when they went from one event to the next. The music was bumping, the strobe lights were flashing, and the line was wrapped around the building. Everyone was in place. Shoni opened the doors, and we began taking money and stamping hands. Students were piling in, and we were stacking the cash box.

Then, out of the blue, someone asked, "Are you Rick's sister?" I looked up from the cash box and saw the most piercing blue eyes that I had ever seen.

"Yes, I'm Corine," I said with hesitation.

He flashed this huge smile and said, "I thought so, I'm Jason."

I smiled back, slightly embarrassed, and said, "Hello, Jason." I took his money, and Shoni stamped his hand. Jason walked into the darkness of the dance, and I followed him with my eyes. My heart was racing, and my palms were sweaty. He was the cutest boy I had ever seen.

I looked at Shoni and said, "I can't believe he knew who I was."

She started laughing and said, "But did you see his friend?" I didn't know who she was talking about, but I knew then I was going to love high school!

After about an hour, we were relieved of our front door duties. We put the cash box away and looked for my parents. They were chaperoning as always and told us that we could hang out. My brother Rick was a senior, and the starting quarterback. I decided to embarrass him a little bit and jump in the middle of the dance floor between him and his girlfriend Tana. She was a

Chapter Thirty-Nine: My First Love

cheerleader on the varsity squad, and I was sort of obsessed with her, in a good way. She was the funniest and prettiest girl in the school. My brother was also the student body president and a 4.0 student. Yeah, no pressure there.

Shoni and I already knew many of the upperclassmen because Rick had his friends at the house all the time. It was honestly pretty normal for us to show off around my brother's friends, we were both extremely talented and the furthest from shy, at least around them. My brother tolerated my behavior at the dance mainly because I was his pride and joy. We were extremely close, and he was absolutely my favorite person in the world.

After a couple songs played, we went to get something to drink at the concessions. We were having a blast, and I never saw it coming.

I ordered a root beer, and once we had our drinks, Shoni and I turned around and practically ran over Jason and his friend. I jumped back, hoping not to spill my drink. He was smiling ear to ear. He started saying something, but I just stared at his lips, mesmerized. Shoni was already talking to his friend Kevin, so we just stood off to the side and made small talk.

I was wondering why Jason was talking to me and not out dancing with one of the high school girls. I kept thinking to myself, *Does he know I'm an eighth grader?*

Kevin introduced himself and was an absolute doll. He was a star wrestler on the high school team. I remembered hearing my dad and brother talk about him.

Jason asked if we wanted to dance, and Shoni and I raced to the dance floor faster than Wile E. Coyote. My cousin Darlene took notice. She was two grades above me and on the Varsity cheerleading squad. Darlene and I were almost inseparable; she was more like a sister than a cousin.

Darlene was on the dance floor with her boyfriend Dan, who I knew really well. He attended all our family functions and played football for my dad. Apparently, Jason and Dan were close friends, and we found ourselves dancing side by side.

Darlene leaned in close, cupped her hands around my ear, and asked, "How do you know Jason Waterman?"

I responded, "I don't." We both burst out laughing!

Jason took it as a good sign, and we danced together the entire night, as did Shoni and Kevin. Nearing the end of the night, Jason grabbed my hand and led me to the front of the cafeteria. He asked me to wait there and said he would be right back. Several minutes later, he handed me a piece of paper with his name and telephone number on it. I folded it up and put it in my jeans pocket. I was feeling really nervous but also excited at the same time.

We were dripping with sweat from dancing, and Jason asked if I wanted to step outside. Just then, we were interrupted by a chaperone who was looking for my mom. I told her I would go look for her and Jason came along. We found my mother by the dance floor and relayed the message. Instantly, Jason pulled me on the dance floor as "Waiting" by Foreigner started playing. We danced close together the entire song. He was five foot eleven, and I was only five foot three. When I looked up, he seemed seven feet.

OH MY GOD, is he going to do it? Is he going to kiss me right here in front of everyone? I was definitely starting to get nervous. But, as soon as his lips touched mine, I was lost in the moment. I'm not exactly sure how long it lasted, but it was a moment that I will never forget. We continued to dance to the last slow song of the night and kissed and kissed some more. I had no idea who was watching, but I was willing to take the heat.

The song was over, and the lights came on. Jason hugged me and said, "Call me when you get home." We were still holding

Chapter Thirty-Nine: My First Love

hands and I asked if he was sure. He said, "I'll wait by the phone." When I turned around, there was Kevin and Shoni. Then the guys took off and Shoni and I looked like we had just won the lottery. It had been an equally amazing night for her too.

Jason Waterman and I were boyfriend and girlfriend for the next three years. Despite our two-year age difference, he was the best part of my teenage memories. Jason was from the North Island in Hamilton, New Zealand. His parents Ronda and Marshall were like my second parents. His brother Shawn was my age, and we graduated together. Our families loved each other, and we were inseparable.

When I met Jason, he was coming off a tragic accident from a year earlier. He had been walking across an intersection after school and was hit by a semi-truck. It had broken just about every major bone in his body. He was lucky to be alive. Jason had been in a wheelchair, on crutches, and had just vanquished his cane when we met. He managed to maintain a straight A grade point average, was a member of the debate team, and became a starter on the Varsity Football team in his junior year.

Jason was my first love and my first everything. We attended proms, dances, games, and other school functions together. We went camping and hiking and spent countless hours doing family things together. We even lost our virginity together.

We had our own friends, but I can't remember more than once in three years when we were a week apart. We had the same heart. We respected everyone, and we believed in each other. Jason spent summers working at Camp Easter Seal as a counselor. He had a heart for disabled people, but he was also a huge prankster. He developed quite the reputation for pulling off practical jokes and showed no mercy on anyone, disabled or not! I was fortunate to work one summer at the camp and saw a completely different side of Jason, his best side.

At the beginning of my senior year in high school, Jason did the most selfless thing. He took me on one last memorable date, unbeknownst to me. He made it a huge deal. We went to dinner at Johnny Oceans Diner, which was a 50s style place that had really great food. Then, we went to the drive-in to see the Kiefer Sutherland vampire flick called the *Lost Boys*. Then, we went to my parents' house, sat outside for about an hour, and just talked. It was a great evening. I knew I was being set up for something, I just didn't know what.

Finally, at the end of the night, Jason broke off our relationship. He felt that I needed to be present for my last year in high school; it was such a special time, a time you'll never get it back. Jason was on the Rugby team at the University of Oregon, and I know he needed to do grown man things too.

He ended the evening by telling me to never settle for less. I was completely heartbroken, but as time passed, I realized that he was right.

We didn't talk for almost a year, but when I made the University of Oregon cheerleading squad, Jason was ecstatic. He used to come down to say hello during the games and even took a picture or two with me in my uniform. I showed up for a few of his rugby games as well. But after attending a couple of rugby parties, I realized that I would never be able to keep up! I always carried a torch for Jason, even as an adult. I think, somehow, I always held on to hope that maybe it would happen for us again.

One of the saddest days of my life was the day Jason passed. He took his own life, back home in New Zealand, the place he loved most. A part of my soul died that day. My heart was literally torn in two for his parents, Ronda and Marshall, his brother Shawn, and for his children. I sobbed like a baby, crying until there were no tears left. I was able to speak at his funeral, as did my dad. We loved him; I still love him. Jason had been suffering because of a devastating break up. He was hurting deeply inside. Having been the victim of severe emotional and mental abuse, I know firsthand how depression can wreak havoc.

"People don't fake being depressed; they fake being okay." This quote resonated with me, in part because it took me over a decade to admit to my trauma.

Jason was such a charismatic and loving person. No one recognized his pain. No one really knows the true state of someone's mental health. We must do better in recognizing the warning signs. We must be willing to have those uncomfortable conversations with our loved ones. If we don't, the risk of suicide is far greater than most people realize.

Sometimes, I can literally feel Jason's presence, as though we were back at that dance.

I miss him.

Chapter Forty

Preseason

I was sitting in the rocking recliner at Julie Kaanapu's house, talking to her husband TK. It was a Sunday afternoon, and we were about to watch the NFL late game.

I was reading comments on a social media post I'd made about my favorite team the San Francisco Forty-Niners. I received a friend request and was surprised to see the name. I hadn't seen him since his playing days at University of Oregon. He was one of the most elite athletes to ever play at Oregon. If you were an Oregon Duck fan, you most assuredly loved him. If you were a fan of any other team anywhere else, you undoubtedly loathed him.

I called out to TK and asked, "Hey, bro, do you know Keith Lewis?"

Without hesitation he said, "We've crossed paths over the years. He's a cool cat."

So, I accepted Keith's friend request and said, "Yeah, I think so too."

TK and I began talking about Keith's football career at Oregon and in the NFL. He had earned a starting position with the Forty-Niners and had a really good seven-year run. From what I gathered; Keith had just retired. He was unexpectedly released from San Francisco and ended his career with the Arizona Cardinals. During his career, Keith was a force to be reckoned with and well respected around the league.

He sent me an inbox message shortly after we connected, and we talked back and forth for a few days and finally exchanged phone numbers. I remember thinking it was kind of ironic because although I had known him since he was eighteen, I had only spoken to him a handful of times. He was actually dating one of my cheerleaders during the time when I was married and pregnant with my second child Jaden. Considering how many of his teammates came over for Sunday dinners after church, it was surprising I didn't know him better. I was ten years older than Keith but newly single for the first time in years.

I had been working hard on *Life Beyond the League* (LBTL) for about six months before Keith asked to come out and visit. I had just gotten a new production team of highly touted producers and former professional athletes together to take the production to a new level. We changed the brand from *Outside the League* to LBTL, and we were ready to get if off the ground.

Keith and I had talked every day for six months and really got to know each other. He referred many of his friends from the NFL to me for possible interviews. He even had his friend, the recording artist "Logic," produce our musical intro. Keith and I really wanted to make sure there was a connection and genuine interest before he came to Eugene. It was preseason and a good time for going public.

I called Haley from her room and told her that the guy I had been talking to in Sacramento was coming for the weekend. It was a Friday.

Haley was on the varsity cheerleading squad at Springfield High School and had a game that night. She was the captain of the State Championship team and the National Champion cheerleading squad. My dad was the head football coach at Springfield, and my brother Rick was the offensive coordinator. It was such a blessing for Haley to have her grandpa and uncle on campus and to be part of a great cheerleading program.

Janet Fryback was the legendary cheerleading coach at Springfield, and her husband Jim was the head basketball coach.

Chapter Forty: Preseason

Their daughters Jamie and Jenny were both on my cheerleading squad at Oregon. Needless to say, we had a similar upbringing, and I knew that Janet would be a great example for Haley. They loved her and coached with an iron fist. I loved that, too, as my parenting and coaching style were exactly the same. The Fryback's were a huge part of our family's life. We had a mutual love and respect for one another.

When I told Haley that I was bringing Keith and his best friend "Bones" to the game, she was happy but, like any teenager, more concerned with her own plans.

Jaden and Haley were ten years apart, which always challenged me to be creative. Sometimes it required parting the Red Sea in order to have a family outing. Haley had a full schedule that weekend, so we agreed to meet at Chuck E. Cheese on Sunday.

I was so excited when Keith finally landed. I drove to pick him up in my little BMW, and he looked huge inside my little car, but he was so beyond cute. I could hardly keep my eyes on the road. It had been a decade since I had seen him in person. He told me that he had been so intimidated by me in college, and even though we had been talking for months, he had to have a drink before seeing me again. That had us laughing, which broke any remaining tension or nerves.

We dropped his suitcase off at the house and headed to The Sidebar, a favorite hang out in Eugene, to meet Bones and his friend Dusty. It was a brand-new hot spot, managed by Leesa. I was eager for them to finally meet! We parked and walked through the door hand in hand. Leesa spotted us and came running over.

She gave Keith a huge hug, then wagged her finger jokingly and said, "You hurt her and you're dealing with me!"

Keith assured her that wasn't going to happen. He grabbed me by my waist, pulled me in close, and planted a big kiss on my lips. We were standing right in the middle of the packed bar the first time we kissed.

We hooked up with Keith's boys and their girlfriends Kat and Lisa, who were already at a table. Kat and Lisa were sisters, and I connected with them immediately despite the obvious age difference.

Keith showed me more public affection than I'd had in a lifetime. He treated me like a queen, and by the end of the night, he made it clear to everyone that this was for real.

The following morning, Bones came to pick us up in his flashy, black, lifted truck. It was a struggle for me to get inside. We rolled down the highway listening to some Tupac Shakur. Bones was a cool guy; he rode quads and motorcycles. Deep down inside, he was a pirate at heart.

We parked his truck at the most famous establishment in Eugene, The Cooler. The bar and restaurant was just down the street from Autzen Stadium. It was a prime location on game days and always packed with tailgaters gearing up for the day's festivities. It was also a hotbed of rumors. If there was going to be any gossip about Keith and I, this was where it would surface. So, I decided to let Keith take the wheel on the entrance. Like the night before, he opened the door for me and the three of us walked in, only this time Keith had his arm around my shoulders. He immediately herded me up the steps to the upper level to look at the wall of fame.

Encased in a mounted frame was his official San Francisco Forty-Niner jersey, autographed to the owner, his good buddy Jonis. I took out my cell phone and had Bones take a picture of us in front of the jersey. I had been in The Cooler countless times before, but this time had a different feeling, we were being treated like royalty. Within five minutes, we were both bombarded with fans and friends wanting pictures and Keith's autograph.

Chapter Forty: Preseason

Later, as we were walking hand in hand to the stadium, and Keith commented, "I've never been with a woman who got the same amount of attention as me." We both started to laugh, knowing that walking into the game together was about to become a spectacle.

We entered the stadium and encountered people we hadn't seen in forever. We visited various tailgate parties, taking pictures and reminiscing with former teammates. We watched the football team go through their pregame walkthrough and watched the Oregon cheerleaders nail their pregame routines. By kick off, we were exhausted. We ended up leaving at half time and went back to The Cooler, where we gobbled down some food, grabbed a few drinks, and watched the rest of the game on the big screen televisions. Once the game was over, the bar quickly filled up with proud Duck fans.

We enjoyed every minute of the day together, despite the minor drama caused by one of Keith's ex-girlfriends. She, along with some of her intoxicated friends, had plenty of disrespectful things to say. But that's life.

We realized that we had a few haters in our midst and decided to leave in order to avoid any additional drama. I was impressed by how well he handled the drunk guys directly hitting on me, and he was equally impressed with how well I dismissed the flirtatious groupies. I got a firsthand look at the obstacles I would face being in a committed relationship with him. It wasn't anything I couldn't handle, but I didn't know at that point just how difficult a challenge it would prove to be.

We left the festivities with complete confidence in each other and our future together.

Sunday came fast, and we made our way to Chuck E. Cheese for Keith to meet my kids. We had a very eventful weekend together, but this was a true testament.

Haley walked in with her best friend Georgina and Jaden in tow. We already had a table, with sodas and a giant pepperoni pizza on the way. Keith stood up to greet Haley and Georgina. And within seconds, he felt a tug and Jaden's desire to play arcade games. Having played in the NFL, Keith knew how to read defenses, so he picked Jaden up like a sack of potatoes and off they went! It was cute. It also gave me time to connect with Haley and hear all about her weekend.

Ten minutes later, Keith and Jaden ("JJ") came back to the table with a stream of winning tickets. JJ was grinning from ear to ear; Keith had passed the first test.

JJ was in the second grade and too young to understand what Keith was doing in our lives. Haley, on the other hand knew exactly what was happening. The great thing about Keith and Haley is that both are absolutely hilarious. It didn't take long for Haley to start regaling us with stories. She had the entire table laughing, and we had to stop eating so we could finally catch our breath. No one could hold a candle to Haley when it came to telling stories; the hand gestures, faces, and animation were priceless.

Everyone got along great, and nothing felt forced. By the time we got home, I was feeling totally optimistic. I got Jaden bathed and ready for bed, then spent some down time with Haley in her room. Keith was in the bonus room relaxing while I attended to my domestic duties. One thing he had to understand was that I was always going to be a mom first. It was good for him to see that side of me before he went back to Sacramento. I wasn't going to always be able to take entire weekends away from my kids. I was fortunate enough to have my parents watch the kids whenever I

Chapter Forty: Preseason

needed. They were such hands-on grandparents, and my kids loved them.

Monday morning, four a.m. came faster than usual. I woke up so I could get Keith to the airport by five a.m. When I came out of the bathroom, he was gone. I walked into the kitchen, then the living room, then to the garage. He was nowhere to be found, until I noticed a light upstairs in the loft. I went upstairs and I couldn't believe it. Keith was checking on the kids. He made sure Haley knew that I would be right back, then leaned over and kissed JJ on the top of the head. He had only met my kids the day before but wanted to make sure they were okay before he left. Fatherly instincts? Check!

I was so moved, I choked up. He was quiet when we got in the car. I thought it was because it was super early, but he said, "I don't want to leave." I remember feeling nauseous, not knowing when I would see him again. Neither of us were ready for the weekend to end.

I pulled up to the curb, Keith got his luggage out of the trunk, I walked around the car to the passenger side, and we embraced with a lingering hug. Our body language was heavy. I had deeply loved a couple of men in my life, but standing on the curb that morning, I felt that I had found my soulmate.

Five months passed, and Keith was coming out to see me and the kids as often as possible. In that time, he created a close bond with my brother and parents. Rick and Keith acted like brothers. They both had a love for football, which served as an easy common denominator for their relationship. They were both stellar multi-sport athletes growing up, so they could relate on a different level. Sports just scratched the surface with them, though. It was their sheer passion for poker that solidified their connection. Rick and Keith would be out all hours of the night playing in various tournaments. I loved that they had so much in common, but I didn't share their passion for gambling.

My dad absolutely loved Keith and, even more, loved how he treated me. Dad was calling him son well before we were even engaged. Keith became family practically overnight. My mom loved teasing him. It was always fun to see the two of them together, because Keith was a total Mama's boy. His mom Gianna was his world.

All of my cousins, aunts, and uncles welcomed him with open arms. They loved is gregarious nature, but mostly everyone saw the genuine love and bond he had with me and the kids.

Haley was dedicated to cheerleading and had huge goals: to cheer and obtain her degree from Oregon State University, the enemy. She had very little free time. So, when Keith came to visit, she couldn't be around as much as we would have liked. We knew her goals went well beyond college because of her drive and determination. We embraced her hustle and gave her the space to accomplish the things that were important in her life. Keith supported Haley the best he could from Sacramento, but he knew how delicate high school could be for a teenager. He struggled to be there for her from a long distance.

Jaden was an entirely different story. When Keith came into town, the first thing he did was drive to Irving Elementary to pick up JJ. He didn't just wait in the car but went to his classroom. I knew when they came home, I wouldn't even see him for at least an hour. They were either shooting hoops outside or upstairs playing video games. They built such a strong bond, and the fact that our last names were Lewis made it easy for people to assume that Keith was the biological father.

Chapter Forty: Preseason

Keith called one day from Sacramento, and he sounded really upset. Something had come up and he had to miss Haley's concert, which was a major production at Springfield High School. The music department at SHS was far beyond the typical high school. Mrs. Swartout put on a major highlight show, an extravaganza. So much so, that people from the community came to the concert whether they had family involved or not. Keith's best friend Bones came in his place. Bones was "Uncle Bones" at this point, and Haley and JJ loved him, as did all of my immediate family.

Bones called Keith before the concert. Jaden was sitting on his lap and kept saying, "Let me talk to my Keithy!" They talked on the speaker phone, and I could hear the disappointment in Keith's voice.

After the concert was over and we got everyone into the car, I called Keith on the way home. He said, "I'm not missing another concert again. I'm not missing anything "my kids" do again!"

Chapter Forty-One
Rule of Thumb

May 12, 2011, Bones pulled up to my house in his giant Dodge truck. I threw my suitcase in the truck bed, and we began an eight-hour trip to Sacramento. I was so excited; we were going to move Keith up to Eugene. This was the start of our lives together as a family.

Bones and I had a great start to our friendship, but the trip solidified our genuine admiration and respect for one another. We both learned a lot about each other and even more when we pulled to up to Keith's house and saw a hundred and ten-pound Pitbull! We jumped out of the truck, and out came this muscular dog with a massive head. He looked like one of the hounds of Hades, only bigger. The dog was staring at us like breakfast; he had big, piercing eyes and teeth to match. The closer we got to the house, the more the dog began to assert himself! Bones and I looked at each other and said, "Oh, h— no!"

Just then, Keith came to the rescue. He took control of Zeus, but it was several minutes before I could process.

After being introduced to some of Keith's friends and his big brother Gary, I started to feel like maybe Zeus wasn't going to eat me.

We spent most of the night packing. Keith gave away just about everything because my house was fully furnished, then he rented a small U-Haul for some furniture and his clothes. We managed to pack all of the big screen TV's, his gorgeous wet bar, and all of his sports memorabilia for the mancave. Unfortunately, the one thing we couldn't manage was the pool table, which went to his father. It was bittersweet for Keith, saying goodbye to his parents, brothers, extended family, and friends. One value we shared was our unwavering love and devotion to our families. He left everything that he loved to pursue a new life with me, Haley, and Jaden.

We had a long but entertaining drive back to Oregon. I had built a bond of trust with Zeus, and we became quite attached to one another, but the true test would be the kids. My parents weren't the least bit amused about having a hundred-pound Pitbull living with their grandchildren.

It was Jaden's eighth birthday. So, when we arrived, we quickly unloaded everything into the house and hosted a skating party at Skateworld for JJ and ten friends. I hadn't seen JJ that happy since Christmas.

Haley just wanted me to be happy. She knew how far I had come from the trauma of her father. We had been through a lot together in her seventeen years, and she was glad we had some structure again.

When I reflect back, it still amazes me. This twenty-nine-year-old man came into my life holding his head high with nothing but confidence in who I was as a woman. He didn't think twice about me having two children us being ten years apart. It didn't faze Keith that I had been through debilitating trauma in one marriage and another unsuccessful marriage in a twenty-year span. He said to me time and time again, "That is your past, and it has nothing to do with your present. I'm only concerned with what you do today moving forward." He took on an instant family and showed his love with his actions. I jokingly said that Keith fell in love with the kids before he fell in love with me!

As the months turned into years, I came to realize that I genuinely never really knew what being in love was until our time

Chapter Forty-One: Rule of Thumb

together. Keith and I began building a great family foundation, and the kids started referring to him as Dad. Haley called him Pops, and Jaden called him Daddy most of the time. It was incredibly special because even my ex-husband Shawn referred to Keith as Dad, at least when talking to Jaden. There were some strained moments in my relationship with Shawn, so the fact that he and Keith had mutual respect for one another, as Jaden's two dads, was good for everyone.

Over the next two years, Keith and I experienced some cloud-topping highs and some sobering lows.

Keith was contacted by his former position coach in the NFL about coming out of retirement to play a short season with the Las Vegas Locomotives in the United Football League. The Locos head coach and GM was former NFL legend Jim Fassel. They enticed Keith with the understanding that he would play in four games and transition back into the National Football League. The Philadelphia Eagles were very interested right away in giving Keith a workout. Keith and I decided that he should accept the opportunity.

Within a few weeks, he signed a contract and we prepared to move to Henderson, Nevada for the six-week season. My parents believed that I needed to invest the time in Keith's comeback and make the temporary move with him. Immediately, my dad began training Keith several days a week on the football field. He knew the stakes were high and that Keith needed to be in shape upon arrival.

Before long, we landed in Las Vegas, and Keith was in the best shape of his life.

I loved watching Keith play again as he dominated opponents. The Locos were stacked with former NFL players and Division one standouts. Everyone believed they could have competed against any team in the NFL.

The Las Vegas Locomotives were heads above the other teams in the United Football League, and the guys were having a blast!

My dear friend and mentor Kwamie Lassiter was Keith's DB coach. It meant so much to me that Keith got to know him and play for him. I always talked about the Lassiters and Spiveys, so it was special for me when they built a bond.

The first game of the season was at Sam Boyd Stadium, where UNLV played. I loved getting to know the other wives and girlfriends. All of us were extremely optimistic about the future for our men. I was equally excited when my "family," Damion Hall and his son Sergio, came to the game to watch Keith play. We had an absolute blast watching him annihilate guys on the field. He even got a "pick" in the second half. Damion was cheering Keith on like they had known each other their entire lives, and when Damion is in your corner, he is a hundred percent all in.

Game two was in Omaha, Nebraska, and game three was in Sacramento. Both of our families were so excited to come together and watch Keith play! Jaden drove down from Eugene with my parents, and I was happy to finally introduce my parents and JJ to Keith's family and friends. Everyone got along great.

It was all good, right until the moment Keith got hurt in the last three minutes of the game. He broke his hand and suffered a compound fracture of his right thumb. I was absolutely numb inside. My heart ached for him. Not because of the pain but because I knew he was done playing football. The injury could end his playing career. He had to be ready for his NFL tryout within two weeks, and he was heading into surgery the following day.

The next several months were increasingly difficult in our relationship. The injury was a huge setback, and Keith was uncertain about what to do. He was incredibly helpful with the kids and helped JJ dominate in multiple sports, including winning first

CHAPTER FORTY-ONE: RULE OF THUMB

place in a Tae-kwon-do tournament. He also helped JJ with homework, resulting in a straight A+ average in school. And Keith was immensely proud of Haley's success as a cheerleader at Oregon State. He also supported my brother by coaching the defensive backs and special teams. But Keith was bored, restless. I tried to get him to go back to school or get a job to stay occupied. But after life in the NFL, it takes a while to readjust. So, that's what we did, held tight and readjusted.

Chapter Forty-Two
Destination Weddings

My television concept was well underway, but the "yes, maybe, maybe next month" aspect of production didn't sit well with Keith. We had an amazing show, but it seemed like one bad turn begat another, and our funding eventually dried up. I knew logically that Keith understood the vagaries of film and television, but when our production team decided to put "LBTL" off for another calendar year, he reached his breaking point.

In the interim, he and I had gotten engaged, and I was working on a new project called, "Destination Weddings." Yep! It was exactly as it sounds. It was a reality television series depicting the dreams and drama of planning destination weddings. The series was being produced by a world-renowned reality television producer who wanted to use our wedding for the pilot.

Our wedding was scheduled for April 19th, 2014, in Lake Tahoe, the day before my forty-fourth birthday. We had an absolutely spectacular wedding and reception planned, with a red-carpet entrance and musical performances by GUY. All of our closest friends and family members were coming. We had marquee professional athletes in the wedding and in attendance. Everyone had purchased their plane tickets, and we were provided lodging at the resort. We had the venues booked, and the wedding planner was able to secure a film permit for the entire casino and resort. We had signed contracts with caterers, potential sponsors, and an expression of interest from a syndicated network. Finally, things were looking up. Our investor cut a huge check, and we were about six weeks away from being married and producing a pilot!

Two weeks before the wedding, I was finalizing the last details. All of the accommodations for the guests and production crew in Tahoe were paid. My wedding dress and the dresses of the bridesmaids and tuxedos for groomsmen were ready to be picked up on April 15th, Tax Day. We had the itineraries and scheduled pickups for all of the participants flying in. And Leesa and I were out shopping in Eugene, trying to help Mom pick out shoes for her dress.

We stopped by the MAC counter on our way out to grab eyelashes. The more glamorous the better! I received a text message from Keith, asking, "When will you be home?" I responded and got another message that read, "We need to talk."

The smile on my face disappeared, and my face went blank. My heart started beating faster, and I remember hearing a buzzing sound in my ears. I handed my phone to Leesa so she could read the message for confirmation.

I wasn't sure if I was overreacting, and I certainly didn't want to alarm my mom. Also, Keith's mom, Gianna, who I loved so much, was battling her third bout of breast cancer. So, the first thing that ran through my mind was something was wrong with Gianna.

Once we got into Leesa's car, I remembered that we had just spoken the night before and she was feeling good. The closer we got to the house, the faster my heart was beating. My mind was playing tricks on me; I was feeling anxious.

As soon as we pulled up to the house, Bones pulled up right behind us. The front door was open, and Zeus was out in the front yard.

I walked into the house with four shopping bags, and the look on Keith's face said it all.

He had been drinking. I don't know what came over me, but I just knew. My worry turned to extreme anger. I literally dropped

Chapter Forty-Two: Destination Weddings

all of the bags in the middle of the living room and yelled, "Say it! Just say it!"

At this point, Leesa was standing behind me, and Bones was standing in the doorway, confused.

Keith looked at the two of them and said, "She and I need to talk." I stormed into the bedroom and sat on the edge of the bed. Keith sat close to me and grabbed my hands. I looked him straight in the eyes and never even blinked.

His eyes began to fill up with tears and he simply said, "I can't do this. I'm not ready."

I said, "What do you mean you're not ready? You wait two weeks before our wedding and drop a bomb on me!" I thought he was going to tell me we needed to push it back a few months. But he went into the garage and brought out a duffle bag and suitcase. He had already packed his clothes. He wasn't just cancelling the wedding, he was leaving. This wasn't a postponement; it was a breakup. He walked out to his truck and threw the bags into the back.

Bones, Leesa, and I were in disbelief.

He was gone.

The wedding was cancelled.

My girlfriends were calling everyone: The hotel, production crew, wedding planner, guests, and family members. We had scheduled opposing bachelor and bachelorette parties that night, so it was a logistical nightmare. I couldn't have gotten through a single minute if not for my girlfriends, friends, and family.

I agonized over how to tell Jaden that we were no longer a family. My heart broke as I told my child that Keith wasn't coming back.

He messaged me several times over the next few days. Once he began to sober up, he said that he regretted making a rash decision. That never seemed to last long. Keith was all over the place emotionally. Regardless, I loved him.

As days turned into weeks, I reverted back to the place I knew all too well. I started feeling the effects of post-traumatic stress. Everything that I thought I had put in the past all came roaring back. All of the work I had done to pull myself out of the darkness seemed meaningless. The self-doubt, the self-loathing, and self-hate all came creeping back into my soul. I couldn't look in the mirror without feeling pure disdain for my own reflection.

"Who do you think you are? Why are you even alive? You are utterly useless!" These were the lies I told myself behind closed doors. In public, I was all smiles. Holding my head high, "you win some, you lose some." That was the outward woman. Inside, I was dying all over again.

My closest friends had to pull me from the abyss. Julie Kaanapu, Jeni Stapleton, Shawna Peterson, Leesa Wilder, Mike Dorman, and Michael Westbrook took away the shovel to stop me from digging. They forced me to keep looking forward and didn't let me slip any deeper than I already had begun to slide.

Keith cancelled the wedding April 2nd, and on April 11th, I was flying out to Albuquerque, New Mexico to meet with producers to host a new pilot. Leesa Wilder and Michael Westbrook were right by my side for four days in New Mexico as we talked and negotiated our way through. We had a production deal signed within two days and were scheduled to begin filming on May 16th. I left Albuquerque with a fresh new perspective, certainly more alive than on April 2nd.

Keith and I went back and forth for a while but, inevitably, our seven-year relationship ended, and we went our separate ways. There was absolutely no animosity between our families, and I

Chapter Forty-Two: Destination Weddings

continued to have a very special relationship with his mother. I leaned on her during some of the most challenging times and never stopped feeling like I was a daughter. Keith's dad, brothers, cousins, aunts, and uncles always treated me and the kids like family. My brother Rick continues to call Keith his brother-in-law, and my parents love him like a son. My cousins, aunts, and uncles still consider Keith family. Haley and Jaden still call him Pops and Dad, and they have a deeply loving relationship. Keith remains one of my most trusted friends and confidants.

My last name of Lewis is not the result of marriage, but what's in our name is nothing but love.

This was another hard lesson, but bridges are for crossing, not burning.

Chapter Forty-Three
I Broke the Internet?

It was a busy morning; I was working hard in the kitchen preparing a soul food dinner. Later that evening, we were having friends over to watch the 2015 National Championship game between Oregon and Ohio State. There was nothing like college football, but having "The Ducks" in the big game was extra special, like having Christmas twice! The guests arrived about an hour before the game and brought an abundance of drinks.

I was sipping on Sangria, while Keith had a Coors Light. Yep, Keith and I were back together again. This was part of the Texas two-step we did for several years. Keith began unloading my world-famous Sahoyu Marinated Chicken off the grill. I stole the recipe from TK, but that didn't stop anyone from loading their plates with chicken, mac-n-cheese, greens, corn on the cob, potato salad, and cornbread. As a group, we were no strangers to overindulging, particularly on special occasions.

About thirty minutes into the game, my phone began blowing up, including lots of notifications from my Twitter account. It was clearly annoying, and even Keith was distracted by the constant pinging. I was focused on the game, but as soon as a commercial came on, I decided to investigate. As I clicked on my Twitter account, there were hundreds of notifications, and more were rolling in. Within three minutes, hundreds of notifications became thousands! I was absolutely clueless. Several minutes later, my Facebook and Instagram accounts were following suit. Next, my text messages were blowing up, and before I knew it, my phone was inundated with people inquiring about a photo of me that was all over the internet! My initial reaction was panic because I couldn't imagine what picture could be causing so much attention. Especially during the biggest college football game of the year. After several minutes, I finally saw what was causing the stir.

It was a tweet by Darnell Dockett, an NFL player for the Arizona Cardinals, that caused a picture of me to go viral! It was a tweet I had posted weeks earlier with a picture of me coaching the Oregon cheerleaders on the sidelines. Darnell retweeted out the picture with the caption, "Hmmm Oregon is cheating." He was implying that if the Ohio State players saw me on the sidelines, they would become distracted from the game. It was hilarious. Darnell was a friend and a former teammate of Keith's. The picture was five years old, but by the time it surfaced on social media, it was being reposted all over websites and sports affiliate pages everywhere. The picture was featured on Barstool Sports Instagram page, and ultimately Playboy… hmm?

The photo trended well into the following day, going viral, not just nationally but around the world. I received messages from athletes, coaches, former cheerleaders, radio networks, and television producers. It was a zoo. Throughout the month, there were articles being written about me and stories about how I "Broke the Internet." It was a whirlwind of publicity, and the picture opened many doors. Ultimately, I had Darnell Dockett to thank. I went on several radio shows and was even contacted by the Howard Stern Show. I declined the Howard Stern show, but I did do a number of interviews.

My favorite was with "The Playboy Morning Show," which had upwards of a million viewers. I was skyped into a segment with Andrea Lowell, a former Playboy Playmate, and another host. I was extremely impressed by Andrea's professionalism and authenticity. It's not always the case that females, famous or otherwise, show such support for other women. In that way,

Chapter Forty-Three: I Broke the Internet?

Andrea reminded me of myself. I could feel her warmth. She was fun, witty, and brilliant. I liked her vibe, especially the subtle hint of feminism. More than anything, I was inspired by our conversation. The interview motivated me to be more intentional about uplifting women.

No slap against men, but it's fair to say that 2015 created a stir inside of me; it became a passion of mine to support, encourage, and inspire women more actively and on a worldwide basis if possible.

It was a great interview, and, equally as important, we were able to keep our clothes on the entire time.

Part Five
Empowerment

Chapter Forty-Four
Fly the Friendly Skies

In January 2015, us ladies got some good news. The state of California outlawed the practice of "Revenge Porn." As most of you know, revenge porn represents the distribution of sexually explicit material without an individual's consent. Typically, pictures are taken or given to an intimate partner on a "for-your-eyes-only" basis when the relationship is good. Then, after a breakup or things go sour, the partner seeks revenge by putting the pictures out on social media. If you remember, the "C" in MICE is <u>coercion</u>. In essence, revenge porn is a non-violent means of coercion and represents a clear betrayal of the relationship.

During the same period, one of my closest home girls, Shawna Peterson, reached out to me. She knew how hard I had been working on LBTL and that the production was at a standstill. Her then husband, Robert, was heavily involved with assisting me with various productions and business ventures. She knew that I was working tirelessly to keep the sports show alive and had firsthand knowledge of my history with television and radio projects. She had even flown to Albuquerque to watch me on the set of *The Producer*.

She and I grew increasingly close when we discovered how much we had in common. Shawna had been through an incredibly painful divorce from her first husband and experienced deep emotional trauma. She was an exceptional mother and moved mountains to take care of her kids, forsaking the counseling and attention that she needed and deserved.

Shawna had a difficult time watching me struggle near the end of LBTL. I was feeling defeated and trying to decide on my next move. I was considering a few opportunities in Canada, but the start dates were likely a year away.

Shawna sat in my living room one day, while I was exhausted from the hurry up and wait life of productions. She asked me if I had ever considered becoming a flight attendant. She had been both a flight attendant and a gate agent, spending the better part of twenty years in the aviation industry, and loved it. She thought I might also enjoy the change of pace. She reminded me that I had spent a lot of time on the road, something my family had grown accustomed to, and that I enjoyed meeting people.

I spent several weeks thinking about it and decided to make the change.

It turned out that Shawna was right. I got a job with a major airline as a flight attendant and loved it. It was completely different from anything I had ever done, and I met countless people from all over the world. I flew nationwide and vacationed overseas. It was quite liberating knowing that I could fly anywhere in the world at any time for free. My family was entitled to the same benefits and privileges, and I was always extremely generous, which improved my poll numbers at home.

In August of 2018, I flew from Portland to Los Angeles to meet my boyfriend, who was flying in from Texas. We hadn't seen each other for about six weeks. We were looking forward to a mini vacation together in Honolulu. I was doing a cheerleading camp in Wailea, and he would be addressing the football team and meeting the athletic director.

We were planning a joint football/cheerleading camp together in the next few months on the North Shore. My boyfriend was a fourteen-year veteran quarterback in the NFL and a former Pro Bowler. He had an extremely successful personal training company

Chapter Forty-Four: Fly the Friendly Skies

where he groomed future quarterbacks for starting positions in both high school and college.

I walked off my flight and down the jet bridge into the terminal, took a seat at the bar, and waited for his flight to arrive. He texted me as soon as he landed. I was so excited to see him, I knocked over my glass of wine. He walked right over where I was sitting and gave me a huge, lingering hug. We had about an hour before our flight to Honolulu, so we both had a drink and quickly caught up on the morning events.

After an uneventful flight, we walked outside the Honolulu International airport and tried to catch an Uber to the hotel. It was pouring down rain and unbelievably humid. We were both tired and couldn't wait to get changed and get something to eat. This was the first "real" vacation we had taken together after being a couple for about a year. I flew into Austin every week or two to see him, and he came to Eugene twice to see me and my kids. We got along great and had so much in common. Although we grew up considerably different, we had similar core values. Our love for our kids and our love for sports, music, and entertainment kept our long-distance relationship alive. We were both cut from the same cloth when it came to allowing people to be themselves and never passing judgement. And neither one of us could throw stones at anyone else's glass house, given some of the mistakes we had made. We were both the first to admit any wrongdoings in our past. We were also the first to praise those who grew from bad choices.

He was easy to talk to, and I trusted him implicitly.

The first two days in Oahu were wonderfully relaxed. We spent time walking around the city and exploring beautiful Waikiki Beach. The next morning, we decided to get a rental car so we could drive out to the North Shore for our camp the next day.

That night, we enjoyed a great show and a Hawaiian family style dinner at Germaine's Luau.

We both loved live performances, so the fire and Tahitian dancers were our favorite part of the Luau. We were ultimately there for the football and cheerleading camps, but it was his first time in Hawaii, so we did the more traditional things. He and I were always on the go, so we agreed to just plan as we went along. We didn't want to have any obligations other than our scheduled business.

The morning of the cheerleading camp, we woke up early and spent a little quality time together. It was a two-hour drive to the high school, so we were on a tight schedule, but we were both looking forward to seeing the sights and scenery along Oahu's coastline.

Despite the fun we were having, something seemed off. We never ever argued during our entire relationship, and I could only think of one time I had even been upset with him. But something was different, and I was feeling increasingly frustrated. I finally just came out and said, "Alright, what's the deal?"

Out of nowhere, he said the most horrible thing a man can say to a woman, something to the effect of, "I'm no longer attracted to you. I hate how your skin feels, and it's embarrassing."

We had been together for over a year, and he'd never complained. Then, two hours before I had to teach a cheerleading camp, this was what he said?

I was in just about the best shape of my life. I was rocking a string bikini at forty-six and giving the twenty somethings a run for their money. But all the years of tanning beds and sun exposure had taken a toll on my skin. I was doing a series of chemical peels and laser treatments to try to reverse the damage, and I was extremely insecure about this, so I always had a deep spray tan and

Chapter Forty-Four: Fly the Friendly Skies

airbrushed my makeup. I worked hard at looking my best, but sometimes too much is never enough.

I looked at myself in the full-length mirror, and despite what was fresh in my mind, I looked better than good, and I knew it!

After an hour had passed, I gathered my things to bring to the camp. We got to the high school and walked into a mad rush of kids racing toward us. They gave us a big Hawaiian group hug. It was the sweetest thing I had ever experienced in my thirty years of conducting camps. And given what was said earlier, it was exactly what the doctor ordered.

My boyfriend had never really participated in a cheerleading camp before, but to his credit, he was a huge help and a big hit with the kids. He gave them an amazing pep talk and inspirational speech. He even spotted some of the elite stunts so the kids could try advanced pyramids and stunt combinations. While I was teaching the dance routines on the big stage, I looked over at my boyfriend, and he was genuinely impressed. He had a huge smile on his face, and it was a bittersweet moment. I tried to act like it didn't bother me, but my soul was crushed. We had a full tour planned across the island chain. Unfortunately, that got short circuited. When I got back home to Eugene, I scheduled an appointment with Dr. Blake Sampson, a brilliant dermatologist and surgeon. After a complete body scan and several biopsies, he determined that I had an extreme form of skin cancer. Over ninety percent of my body was covered in squamous cell carcinoma and basal cell carcinoma. My diagnosis was lousy. Dr. Sampson was so kind and patient. He scheduled surgery to remove cancer on my left thigh and left tricep. He explained that my health was at risk and my entire body needed to undergo an Efudex treatment, which is a topical Chemotherapy drug.

There was no time to put it off.

I wanted to tell my boyfriend and sent him a heartfelt text. He called me back right away, and before I could mention the diagnosis and treatment, he let me know that he wanted to part ways.

Although Efudex would be the most painful procedure I would endure in my life, my surgeon was right. It changed my life. By day fourteen of the chemotherapy treatments, I looked like I had been in a house fire. I could no longer open my mouth or turn my head left or right. My skin went from fire engine red to a canvas of blisters and open wounds. Layers of skin fell, from my forehead to my ribcage. Mentally and emotionally, I was pushed to the limit. This was trauma of an entirely different type and challenged me in ways I could not foresee. By day thirty, I looked like the Pink Panther, but I continued to endure. By day sixty, I had brand new, beautiful, cancer-free skin. I regained my confidence, and my skin looked better than when I was twenty.

Regarding my boyfriend, it was a wakeup call. He showed his true colors, but after thirty minutes of crying, I never thought about or spoke to him again. As Mya Angelou says, "When someone shows you who they are, believe them the first time."

My testimony as a skin cancer survivor became an additional building block toward regaining my voice and advocacy. I was amazed at how similar the word survivor translated between victims of abuse and medically diagnosed victims. To be a survivor is to be a warrior. It's finding the strength to overcome life-threatening challenges and potentially deadly obstacles. It means continuously learning how to love your body and battle the thoughts of self-doubt that can plague your mind. No one chooses to be a victim of sexual assault, domestic violence, or cancer. No one wishes to find their strength as a result of battling to stay alive. No survivor wants to live with the scars of the fight of their life.

Chapter Forty-Four: Fly the Friendly Skies

The truth is—what other choice do you have? Either you rise up, stand tall, and begin putting one foot in front of the other, or you surrender the initiative and die a slow, mentally debilitating death.

Survivors choose power because it's our second chance at life. Sometimes we get a mulligan, a do over, in order to get it right and be an example for someone else. I'm a victim turned survivor. I have become a warrior, and I know exactly who I am, where I'm going, and where I want to be. I'm a woman who lives with great pride and great humility. I have overcome many regrets.

I'm a beautifully flawed woman, but I am fierce.

Chapter Forty-Five
The Sound of Music

In January 2018, Larry Nassar received a prison sentence of 175 years after the testimony of more than a hundred and fifty sexual assault victims. In case you don't remember, Nassar was the team doctor of the United States women's national gymnastics team for eighteen years, which gave him access to hundreds of girls, whom he sexually abused. The man's a pig, and I don't understand why they didn't round up to a hundred and eighty or two hundred years.

Although I was still with the airlines, I had stepped outside of the box and created a professional cheerleading company called P3: Pure Pro Productions. In the middle of 2018, I refocused the company to cater to European cheerleaders who aspired to cheer and dance in the United States.

P3's services include elite dance and cheerleading camps, choreography, private coaching, and assistance with college and professional recruitment. I was blessed to start my company with my daughter Haley, who was a former cheerleader at Oregon State and an NFL cheerleader for the San Francisco Forty-Niners. We were also fortunate to team up with an incredibly talented dancer, gymnast, and recording artist from Texas, Torre Blake. In 2018, we were able to partner with a highly respected European football company called Europe's Elite and make our first foray into Europe.

I was excited to work with the owners Alonzo and Evan, who were both American and had played college football for the

University of Colorado. We had several mutual friends and acquaintances, so it was easy to connect and build trust.

Alonzo lived in Austria with his wife and children, and Evan lived in Switzerland with his family. They orchestrated football camps all over Europe and brought professional and collegiate football players and coaches from America to participate in their camps. Providing cheerleading camps alongside their football camps had been a desire of theirs for years.

Romeo Bandison, a mutual friend of ours, was from the Netherlands. He played football at Oregon and coached at the University of Colorado. Alonzo wanted Europe's Elite to bring in an American style cheerleading program, and Romeo referred him to me. Shortly thereafter, I received an Instagram message from Alonzo, and we were off and running. Within two weeks, we were planning our first joint cheerleading and football camp at a site in Vienna, Austria.

Recruiting cheerleaders and dancers to a camp is a challenging and time-consuming proposition. Social media became our indispensable lifeline in reaching out to various organizations. The time change between the two countries served as another obstacle, along with the language barrier. I never thought about such mundane things as needing to translate our marketing and sign-up materials from English into German or Swiss German. The entire process was frustrating and fascinating at the same time. We also had to learn some of the cultural and procedural differences between cheerleading in Europe versus the United States. In Europe, cheerleading tends to be more competition oriented, where in the U.S., cheerleading mostly happens around game-day performances. In Europe, cheerleading is more stunt oriented, whereas in the U.S. we're more dance oriented. I quickly learned

Chapter Forty-Five: The Sound of Music

the differences and embraced the challenges. I remember continually telling myself, "Goosfraba, goosfraba," an anger management technique.

Haley and I got to the Eugene airport at five a.m., eagerly awaiting our flight to O'Hare Airport in Chicago. We'd triple checked our bags before we left the house, and I must have asked Haley three times if she had the converter for our chargers. Everything had to be considered. There wouldn't be time to go shopping once we landed in Austria. Everything had to run like clockwork.

Torre was flying in from Austin, Texas, and this was our first time meeting in person. The plan was for us to meet in Chicago, then make our way to Frankfurt Germany together.

Haley and I made our way to the gate and decided to meet Torre there. I was upgrading our tickets to business class when I turned around and saw this beautiful girl walk into the seating area. I waved, and Haley gave her a big hug.

Torre was even more stunning in person, along with a magnetic smile to match. We had been working together over the phone for weeks, but I was excited to finally meet her in person.

Haley and Torre were both twenty-four and had a passion for art. Beyond their intelligence, athleticism, and personal drive, they bonded together in a way that was rare. By the time we landed in Germany, you would've thought they were lifelong friends. Sometimes putting three people together in a pressure situation can be awkward, and sometimes it creates diamonds. The three of us never missed a beat.

We landed in Frankfurt, and I was surprisingly well rested considering the three-hour flight to Chicago and nine-hour flight to Germany. I watched hours of movies on the plane, and they fed us like royalty. United Airlines had a fabulous business class, and the crew's service was divine.

Once we got off the plane and made our way into the terminal, Haley and I headed to the currency exchange to obtain enough Euros for the week. I had been warned not to use the ATM machines because the transaction cost was extremely high. Our next mission was to find the bus station and make our way to Vienna. We had never been to Europe, and, in fact, it was the first time Haley had ever been outside the U.S. Torre studied abroad, so she had experience traveling in Europe. And you know what they say, "In the land of the blind, the one-eyed man is king." Thus, Torre took the lead. I'm not sure we would have made it without her.

But before we ventured out, Haley had I doubled over with laughter, as she went to use the bathroom and didn't have the correct change for the stall. Haley came storming out of the bathroom exasperated, "Are you telling me I have to pay to pee?" Torre and I both tried to quiet her, but Haley intended to make a point and wanted everyone to know, "A sister's about to get a bladder infection in here!" Comedic timing is one of Haley's best qualities. Between her forthrightness and my constantly having to say, "Sorry, I'm an American," every time I had a question, Torre was wondering what she had gotten herself into!

We walked to the bus station with luggage in tow. The buses were quite nice, but I had no clue about the distance between Germany and our destination in Austria. We had all agreed that it would be fun to see the countryside, and because of our American orientation, we didn't even consider taking the train. Fortunately for Haley, she can sleep anywhere and under any circumstance. Torre and I were awake the entire ride to Vienna. What a mistake!

Chapter Forty-Five: The Sound of Music

Other than taking incriminating pictures of Haley sleeping in order to post to our Instagram and Facebook accounts, we sat through seven hours and four hundred miles of absolute boredom... and hunger.

We traveled nineteen hours in total, one day before our camp, but chalked it up to lessons learned and vowed to never take a bus in Europe ever again.

Finally, we pulled into the station in Vienna and were greeted by Alonzo and several of the other coaches. Luckily, we only had a few miles to drive to the sports complex where we were staying. Our lodging was all inclusive, which was convenient because we were only yards away from the camp location. We had expected to stay in a nearby hotel, but after the first night at the complex, we were happy to be in the mix with everyone else.

Seeing football in a foreign country was incredibly fun. Half of the coaches were from the United States and had played in the NFL. The other half either played college football, in the Canadian Football League, or in NFL Europe. The coaches were a talented group of guys and were really good about including the three of us in all the group activities.

During a break from their coaching duties, most of the guys took the time to learn an advanced hip hop routine from Torre, and some joined in Haley's yoga sessions. Meanwhile, I spent the majority of my time scouting out locations for future pop-up clinics and connecting with head football coaches from European professional teams about the possibility of working with their cheerleaders.

The highlight of the trip was our visit to the city of Vienna. We walked for hours and hours through the cathedrals, shops, and farmers markets. The restaurants were everything I expected and more. I enjoyed trying new foods, drinking shots of espresso, and indulging in decadent desserts. I definitely didn't worry about my calorie intake. I worked out and exercised so much, I burned through everything I ate.

The most memorable experience was taking the train to Salzburg to visit the Sound of Music tour. The rolling green hills and romantic scenery were absolutely breathtaking.

I purchased our tickets for the tour, but before we boarded the bus, we toasted with individual bottles of champagne. I bought a few bottles from the beverage girl at every stop. We had fun taking pictures along the way, especially where there were famous movie props. As part of the tour, they played the soundtrack of the Sound of Music the entire trip. Haley and Torre sang backup the whole way and recorded it on their social media. They could have starred in a Broadway play. Both sounded beautiful and captured the attention and admiration of everyone on the bus.

It was time to leave, and the morning was somber. We had fully enjoyed our time in Austria and built a strong foundation for P3. We'd developed solid friendships and relationships with all of the coaches and trainers, including the head trainer, who was from Spain. I learned so much from him about professional athletics in Europe. He agreed to be available for any future European cheerleading camps, and I hoped to provide that opportunity.

We knew that we would be back at some point in the future, but we also knew it wouldn't be the same. It's hard to duplicate your first impression of anything, especially when the experience was so raw and positive and authentic.

CHAPTER FORTY-FIVE: THE SOUND OF MUSIC

Everyone bunched in tight together for breakfast. Then, one by one, people started sharing stories, mostly at the expense of someone else. We took pictures and posted them on social media. Finally, we said our goodbyes, gave our last hugs, then headed for the train station for the long trip home.

The three of us wouldn't have long to reminisce, for as soon as we got home, we began gearing up for a camp in Switzerland!

Chapter Forty-Six
The Tower of Babel

Several weeks after leaving Austria, I began working with Noemi Riekeles, an acquaintance of Evan, Alonzo, and Jessica Haefelfinger in Sissach, Switzerland.

Jessica was an intelligent and gorgeous woman with crystal blue eyes, jet-black hair, and a glowing smile. We hit it off instantly, mostly because our personalities were similar. Jessi was from Newport Beach, California and had been heavily involved in cheerleading when she lived in the states. After studying abroad, she met her husband and built a new life in Switzerland.

When we first met, Noemi had created an elite cheerleading program and was coaching a competitive cheerleading team in Switzerland. She was also a member of the Swiss All-Girl National Team. Jessi was an assistant cheer coach with Noemi and dance choreographer for the Basel team. Both Jessi and Noemi had contacted some of the Swiss team owners to see if there was any interest in having P3 go to Switzerland and conduct a pro style cheer and dance camp. After receiving positive feedback from teams in both Germany and Switzerland, it was on!

Jessi worked hard at getting the teams signed up, and I spent several weeks building the website, along with my web designer and cousin Bobby Gibson. Torre was instrumental in updating the company logo and putting together a beautiful marketing flier.

With both of them hard at work, Haley and I worked up different levels of choreography for the various age groups, along with a full array of advanced partner stunts and multi style dance routines. Noeme and her husband were nationally recognized partner stunt coaches, which was the icing on the cake. This dynamic duo, along with Haley's stunting expertise, made for a formidable trio. In addition, Haley also shined in advanced sassy pom routines, Torre was a master hip hop dancer and instructor, and I specialized in choreography and advanced pro style dance. Consequently, we were able to offer a full menu of dance, cheer, and stunts.

One of the best perks of being a flight attendant was free global travel, but there were a few hitches. Because we were going to work, I purchased our tickets instead of flying on my employee benefit. I did the same thing for our trip to Austria. We didn't want to take any chances of missing our flight. My family had no such qualms and took full advantage of the privilege whenever possible.

Haley and I left Eugene at three a.m. and drove to the Portland airport. We parked my car in the employee parking lot, caught a bus to the terminal, and printed our boarding passes for a flight to Newark, New Jersey.

We boarded the plane to Newark and slept the entire four-and-a-half-hour flight. Finally, we landed in Zurich at seven-forty a.m. the next morning right on schedule.

Once we made it through customs, we did what all American tourists do: take pictures. We took loads of pictures, videoed ourselves in front of the Zurich Welcome sign, and posted to social media. We vowed to document our adventures through Switzerland much better than we had in Germany and Austria.

We proceeded to the currency exchange to load up on Euros, but luckily, I love to talk. When I told the currency clerk how excited we were to be in Switzerland, she made it known in no uncertain terms that we were better off using her currency, the Swiss Franc! Who knew? I thought everyone in Europe used the

Chapter Forty-Six: The Tower of Babel

Euro. This was one of many lessons I would learn about living the Swiss life.

Torre had friends in Spain, so she'd gone out a week earlier to do some sightseeing. After the excitement wore off, we realized that we were on our own. It was a little scary, because in Zurich there were even fewer people speaking English than in Austria. We had to pay close attention in order to catch the right train to Sissach. But Haley and I were both incredibly resourceful, and street smart. You could drop us in any community in America, and we could find our way. Unfortunately, I never learned a second language, which is quite possibly my biggest regret, and Haley's broken Spanish was absolutely worthless in Switzerland. We knew nothing more than "Gruezi:" hello! And "Ciao:" goodbye! I pulled up my Google translator app, and we headed inside the train station to purchase our tickets.

As soon as we stepped off the train, we ran straight for the bathrooms. Much to our surprise, there was no charge to use the ladies' room in Switzerland. We actually gave each other a high five. Sometimes it's the little things in life that make you happy.

We boarded the train and agreed that the trip was going surprisingly well. We were just hoping it wasn't the calm before the storm. A few minutes later, I received a text message from Jessi saying, "I'm here!" We walked around the corner into the parking lot, and there stood this stunningly beautiful woman, who was an even more spectacular person. We climbed into her SUV and headed to the Airbnb. It was an apartment just around the corner from Jessi's house and owned by her best friend Monica. We were pleasantly surprised at how new and modern everything was. I could have easily lived there forever and made it my home.

Once Haley and I were unpacked, we began to bombard Jessi with questions about Sissach. She hinted that her in-laws owned the town. Owned the town? Really? It was incredible, but they really did. They ran every aspect of this incredible little town in Switzerland. It sounded like a Hallmark movie.

After about an hour, there was a knock at the door. I looked out the window and there was Torre, flowing in like a cool Spanish breeze. Now the gang was back together again.

Torre made her entrance, and Haley sang a little off the cuff number to welcome her arrival. Those two together never missed a beat.

It was only eleven in the morning, so we spent most of the day getting to know Jessi and going over the first day of activities. The camp was being held at a multi-sport facility in the city of Basel, about an hour away.

I had no idea how close we were to the border of Italy. As soon as I found out, I yelled, "Let's get Italian. I'm starving!" The girls agreed, and Jessi knew the perfect restaurant, "The Restaurant Sternen."

We walked inside, and the smell of fresh garlic bread and pasta filled the air. Seating was by reservation only, but we mentioned Jessi's name and were seated right away. We each ordered a glass of wine and a steady supply of bread. I have always been a huge fan of Italian food, so the thought of eating lasagna sixty miles from Italy made me euphoric. We ate too much bread and drank a couple bottles of wine, all before our main entree. I told the girls they may have to call the "Oompa Loompas" to roll me out like Violet in *Willy Wonka*. I ate far more than necessary, and I loved every bite!

The following morning, we woke early. Our internal clocks were completely off-kilter. International travel is brutal when vacationing, let alone after ten hours of hardcore dancing, stunting,

Chapter Forty-Six: The Tower of Babel

and coaching. My body was unusually tired, but strangely my mind was wide awake.

A half hour before we loaded the car for Basel, Noeme and her husband showed up full of energy and life. They walked in and it felt like I already knew them. That's the fun thing about cheerleading—no matter where you are, there is a sisterhood and brotherhood unlike any other sport on earth. The dynamic between them and us was fascinating.

In developing choreography, I generally follow a standard process: First, I consider the purpose of the performance and the audience. Next, I consider the venue and amount of time allotted. Third, I select the music and break it down by eight-count. And finally, I incorporate the music and develop the moves. In Europe, I also had to consider a new dynamic: language!

As Jessi, Noeme, and her husband began speaking, it was eye popping. I was once again reminded that English was not the primary language. Jessi was from the United States but spoke Swiss German. Noeme spoke Swiss German, but her husband's primary language was German, or High-German. They explained that none of the kids spoke English, so they would have to translate. I quickly learned that Swiss German and German are not the same. The Swiss speak Swiss German, and Germans speak High-German.

So, when I addressed the group at the beginning of the camp, Noeme and her husband began translating in two different languages. It was both hilarious and a little frightening. It sounded like the Tower of Babel. Fortunately, as a dancer, as long as you can count to eight, that's all that's truly necessary.

It was exhausting, but I grew so much as a choreographer and coach because I was forced to perform outside of my comfort zone. The cheerleaders and dancers were so sweet and tried so hard to communicate with us. The more I threw at them, the harder they worked. I was so proud of Haley as she commanded the large group segment for the pom routine. She had a way about her that made people want to follow no matter what language they spoke. Haley is a gifted communicator and inherently high energy. She got the best out of people, regardless of the obstacles. Torre was killing it as well, teaching her master hip hop routine. She was new to teaching but not even a trained spymaster would have known. Torre was a natural born dancer and instructor. The three of us captured the hearts of these talented cheerleaders, and we were invited to come back for the European Nationals in Belgium.

The week was ending, and Jessi organized a fun performance for us in Saint-Louis… France, that is, not the Missouri "show-me" state. Saint-Louis is located at the border of both Germany and Switzerland, just north of Basel. It is absolutely gorgeous: the architecture, waterways, scenery, and people.

Neome performed with the Gladiators Cheerleaders Basel squad, and they were absolutely amazing. After the buzz died down a little, Torre got up and sang an extraordinary song from her new album. Not to be outdone, Haley got up and performed one of her original rap songs. The audience loved it all. The crowd was so amazing. It became clear to me why Switzerland is surrounded by France, Italy, Germany, and Austria but is never attacked: the country and the people are too beautiful.

Mission accomplished! Our effort to build a solid name for ourselves overseas was well under way. The camp was a huge success, and we planned to return in the spring and complete an entire European tour through Germany, Sweden, Poland, Switzerland, Austria, Amsterdam, England, and Spain. We were fired up when we boarded the plane.

The flight from Zurich to New York was seven hours and forty minutes. I watched multiple movies and consumed several

Chapter Forty-Six: The Tower of Babel

glasses of Chardonnay. Haley stayed up just long enough to eat and down a glass or two of Vino. I had never been more envious in my life; that girl could sleep anywhere and never missed an opportunity to do so.

Chapter Forty-Seven
Moonshot to Asia

The excitement of our European tour got me to thinking about Asia. I'd never been, but in the past, I'd had several close calls. In early 1993 we had been invited by the Universal Cheerleaders Association to travel to Japan for the inaugural World Cheerleading Championships. Willamette High School would be appearing as an exhibition squad from the United States. Mom and I had been so excited to receive the opportunity and accepted without hesitation. I was living in Portland at the time and just starting my second trimester of pregnancy. I had been having some preterm complications, so my OBGYN advised me against overseas travel. However, my complications would not stop me from choreographing a fabulous routine! I spent hours coming up with the perfect music, splicing songs together, and adding all the bells and whistles. Once the performance track was put together, it was time to work on the routine. I had so much fun putting everything together, it was a killer act, metaphorically speaking. But little did I know, in a few short weeks, I would be in Emanuel Hospital fighting for my unborn daughter's life.

My mom's sister, Valerie, stepped into the breach and accompanied Mom to Japan. Aunt Val had been around cheerleading and dance most of her life. Both of her daughters Laurel and Darlene were also cheerleaders and dancers. Laurel was a cheerleader at Centralia High School under my mom and a cast member in some of the school musicals. She was a gifted singer and a natural born performer. Darlene was on the dance team and Varsity cheerleading squad under my mom at Willamette High

School. She was just as talented as her big sister and one heck of a softball player. All of my cousins, male and female, had my parents as a coach and teacher at one point in their lives. Like I said, we were much more like siblings than cousins.

When my mom and Aunt Val returned from Japan, they were walking on cloud nine. They shared the stories of their adventures; the food, the culture, the pageantry. Japan has such a rich culture and deep traditions. They had a blast! And the cheerleading squad proudly represented the state of Oregon and the United States with a phenomenal performance. East met West, and it was a huge success! This would have been the first trip to Asia, but as fate would have it, it wouldn't be the last time I would be denied overseas travel.

In 2005, we were fortunate to receive another opportunity to travel to Japan, this time to Kakegawa, Eugene's sister city. Based on an audition tape, the University of Oregon cheerleading squad was invited to perform for the Emperor of Japan! Naturally, we used our 2005 winning routine from the USA nationals. It was an all-expenses paid ten-day trip for sixteen of our most elite cheerleaders. Our squad performed at various venues in the city of Kakegawa, including three schools. The primary purpose of the trip was to help celebrate the opening of the new stadium built to hold the Japanese National Championships. The winners would advance to the Japanese Olympic Team. As promised, the Emperor of Japan was in attendance. Our squad was accompanied by a brilliant Japanese marching band. They even played the Oregon Fight Song! It was such an unforgettable experience.

During that time, we were blessed to have a full-time interpreter on our squad. This was especially important when they took a bullet train from Kakegawa to Tokyo for an afternoon of shopping. Everyone treated them like royalty! Some of that was made possible by having Maki Nakayama on our squad. Maki was

Chapter Forty-Seven: Moonshot to Asia

a Japanese exchange student and a rookie, but she was sensational. Maki went on to become a cheerleader in the NFL for the Washington Redskins (as they were formerly called) and is currently a cheerleading coach and performance judge in Japan. I would have loved to have been on that trip too, but, unfortunately, I was the junior woman on the Oregon A-team and had to hold down the fort at home. We had another twenty-six cheerleaders on the squad to cover other university games and events. I did the choreography, and Mom did a fabulous job with the squad. Once again, she enlisted my Aunt Valerie to be her assistant!

In 2012, I was presented with another amazing opportunity, this time to be a presenter in Macau, China for an award show much like the ESPY awards. I was thrilled with the invitation, but the timing was off. I had previously committed to film for our trailer for *Life Beyond the League* and had to decline. This was so heart wrenching because China is such a tremendous and fast-growing sports market. I'm told that NBA China is worth about $5 billion dollars and rising.

Finally, I had another opportunity to get to China that came completely out of the blue. A former University of Oregon basketball player and NBA veteran approached me in 2019 with the prospect of building a cheerleading program throughout China, alongside the USA Basketball Academy. We were researching Chinese culture, basket operations, and developing a proposal for an official upcoming meeting with the Director of USA Basketball Academy. Then, like a tsunami, the COVID Pandemic hit, and once again, my foray into Asia was put on hold. It was like being left at the altar. Perhaps, that's an overstatement, but I was starting to get a phobia. It kept feeling like the one that got away, water flowing between my fingertips.

India is another country I've never been to but have been fascinated with all my life. The country is thousands of years old, has a rich tradition in culture, dance, and strong female leaders. That is a trip I would truly cherish.

One thing is certain, I have a strong desire to help fight violence against women and deliver a message of women's empowerment worldwide. If successful, this will undoubtedly take me to Asia! As somebody once said, "Anything worthwhile, is worth waiting and working for."

Chapter Forty-Eight
The Lassiter Effect

I first met Kwamie Lassiter at the Wild Horse Pass Hotel and Casino event in Chandler Arizona. Kwamie was a former NFL player with the Dallas Cowboys and the Arizona Cardinals. I was introduced to Kwamie by my co-host at Hard Hittin' Radio, Mark McMillian. I was just beginning to film the pilot for our sports show *Outside the League* with my cohost Michael Westbrook. Kwamie had his own sports radio show on Voice America Sports called Kwamie Lassiter Sports Talk. He had a fun and charismatic personality and was larger than life! I quickly noticed his ability to capture an audience no matter how big or small. Kwamie was the guy in the room everyone gravitated toward, and the more I got to know him, the more I realized why he earned the respect of so many professional athletes.

Although Kwamie was gregarious and had a constant smile on his face, he was deadly serious when it came to business. Mark set up a few business meetings for us in Arizona to discuss projects with Kwamie, who had an uncanny ability to quickly see both the risks and strategic potential of projects of all sorts. He was the former President of the Arizona chapter of the NFL Players Association and was generous with introductions. If the idea was well thought out and had potential, he was the first person to help. I was fortunate enough to have him as an advisor and mentor. At the time, I had two major projects in the hopper, and that's exactly what he did. Help!

After a little more than a decade of troubleshooting projects, we decided to do a joint venture between my production company,

P3, and The Kwamie Lassiter Foundation. The project was spearheaded by Michael Westbrook and involved conducting cheerleading and football camps across the U.S. and Europe. I had just come back from Switzerland when Kwamie agreed to our plan: to start with ten camps in the United States, followed by a tour in Canada, then a third run in Europe.

I had just been in Chandler with my girlfriend, Stephanie Vaughan, working on the project at Westbrooks house with Mark and Kwamie. Tabitha Spivey came by to show her support and love as well. I was so excited; it felt like ten minutes before lift-off. We had an excellent plan, and everyone was bought in.

I was flying on a four-day trip three weeks later, and I had just landed in Dallas and had multiple text messages from Westbrook telling me NOT to get on social media. They read; "Call me ASAP and DO NOT get on your social media before we speak." This made me want to look all the more, but I knew Westbrook well enough to just do as asked. Finally, I got to my room at the Magnolia Hotel in downtown Dallas and changed out of my uniform into workout clothes. My anxiety was through the roof, and I felt completely nauseous. I took a deep breath, closed my eyes, and verbally spoke out loud, "Whatever this is, I can do this." I had no idea what Westbrook was about to tell me, but I knew it had to be serious.

As I was dialing Michael's number, a text message came through from Mark that read, "I can't believe he's gone. I don't know what to do." My heart stopped, and time stood completely still. I started to feel lightheaded, so I grabbed for the edge of the couch, put the television on mute, and tried to catch my breath. I knew right then. No name was needed. I could feel the pain. My body began to shake uncontrollably. I didn't respond to Mark right

Chapter Forty-Eight: The Lassiter Effect

away. I needed Michael to say it first; it wasn't real until I heard it from him.

The phone rang one time; Westbrook answered by simply saying, "Corine." The tears were falling so fast down my cheeks and into my mouth. Michael's strong voice wasn't the same. He was reserved and quiet. His pause felt like an eternity. "I'm so sorry. Kwamie is gone."

I screamed out "Why? Why, Michael... Why Kwamie?" I just couldn't comprehend it. I guess the shock to my mind was too great. I was utterly traumatized with grief. I spoke with Michael at length, then with Tabitha. No one could make sense of his death. He was young; he was healthy. He was in the gym working out and had a heart attack. The level of respect, gratitude, and admiration I had for him is hard to convey in words. I was absolutely gutted by the loss. My heart ached for his beautiful wife Ericka and all of his sons, friends, and teammates. There are just some people who are not replaceable. No matter how hard you try to move on, their memory and spirit never leave you. For me that person was Kwamie Lassiter.

I had a difficult time recovering from the loss, and I put my cheerleading projects on hold.

Several months later, I began working on a unique project with Westbrook called "The American Dolls." We decided to build a professional cheerleading squad that traveled globally for games, performances, fundraising events, and noteworthy causes. We began fielding interest about becoming the first cheerleading squad to perform for major league baseball. As the planning progressed, so did the global pandemic. Another one bites the dust. COVID-19 reared its ugly head again. We didn't think the opportunity was gone forever, but it was gone for now.

The last several years have been unbelievably difficult due to COVID and other geopolitical factors. Many people lost hope, others rose up and pushed harder.

Cheerleading is my passion, and women's empowerment is my advocacy. Some say you can't do both. At this writing, the jury is still out, but I'm still playing. The American philosopher Lewis Gordon said, "There is nothing more powerful than the made-up mind." My mind is made up.

Chapter Forty-Nine
Strangers in the Night

One thing I loved about being a flight attendant was traveling to different cities several days a week. I began to build strong bonds with our crew, and we were like family. The airline industry is like a brother-sisterhood, an extended family.

It was 2020, and I was on the third day of a four-day trip. We were all ready for a little R&R and some alone time, and I was looking forward to a day off. The crew was staying at a hotel at Love Field in Dallas. Despite being a hard-core Forty Niners fan, Dallas was always one of my favorite overnight stays. The hotel had an amazing gym, and the rooms were new and modern.

We collected our hotel room keys at the desk, and I told my captain that I was going to lay low. The crew were going to grab a bite to eat together, but I decided to take a salad upstairs and stay in for the night. I told the other flight attendant that there was a new episode of *The Bachelor* airing that night and I had to see it. We laughed, and on the way up the elevator, we made a quick bet on which bachelorette was going to get sent home. The elevator opened, we said our goodbyes, and went our separate ways.

On most overnights, unless I was visiting with family or my boyfriend, I went out to eat with the crew. So, this particular night was a rarity. I made my way to my room with way too much in my hands. I had my cell phone and readers in one hand, my hotel key in the other hand, and a turkey salad perfectly tucked under my arm so as not to pop the plastic lid. Simultaneously, I was dragging my crew bag. Talk about multi-tasking. I must have looked a mess. I opened the hotel door with my elbow, propped the door open with my bag, and maneuvered my way to the kitchen and set the salad down. I threw my phone and glasses on the bed and exhaled loudly, "Lord Jesus!" The hotel room echoed loudly, as the heavy hotel door slammed behind me.

My stomach was growling like an ally cat. I was ravenous! I took off my credentials and all of my jewelry, set everything on the desk next to the telephone, hung my uniform in the closet, set my suitcase on the suitcase holder, began my face washing ritual, then changed into more comfortable clothes. I plugged my phone into my charger, turned on the big screen television, crawled into bed, and prepared to eat my salad and binge watch the TLC channel. All I wanted to see was who got sent home.

Several hours had passed, and I was struggling to stay awake. I didn't want to miss *The Bachelor*, so I propped myself up and began texting back and forth to friends and family.

Finally, it was time. *The Bachelor* came on, and it didn't disappoint. The episode had its usual complement of twists and turns and fake drama. Then, after the show was over, I called my kids to say goodnight. Dallas was two hours ahead of Eugene, and differences in time zones was a never-ending battle. We had a five a.m. call time in the morning, and I was wiped out! I always got up two hours before call time in order to avoid being in a rush, which meant I had to get some sleep.

I can't think of a single night in five years where I turned my television off to go to sleep. Even when my boyfriend stayed on layovers, the television was always on. I got undressed, brushed my teeth, and set my alarm for three different settings, then crawled into bed and turned off the television. The pillow felt so good. I had a smile on my face, and I went off to sleep without a care in the world. Then, suddenly, I was jolted awake. I looked at the clock and it was two a.m. Then I heard a boisterous voice in the next

Chapter Forty-Nine: Strangers in the Night

room. I thought *How rude. At this time of night? What jerk!* It was disconcerting, and I started to get upset.

Moments later, my worst nightmare became a reality. There, in the pitch blackness, was a strange man standing in my hotel room. My panic level went to warp nine. He turned on the bathroom light, and I heard him mumbling to himself. I jumped out of bed and ran naked across the room to grab the phone. The bathroom light illuminated a portion of the room, so I could see the numbers. The girl at the front desk answered and I began screaming at the top of my lungs, "There's a man in my room! Please help me! Please!" As I yelled into the phone, I turned my attention to the startled intruder. He came into the bedroom, and I yelled, "GET OUT! GET OUT! LEAVE!" He just stood there staring. I jumped up and drop-kicked him in the face. The intruder fell back against the wall, and I followed up with a reverse round house to the jaw, a brutal knee kick to the groin, a fierce left-right combination, then I ended things with a vicious elbow strike to his throat and a savage palm strike to the nose. The intruder folded like a two-dollar bill. He was down for the count, lying in a pool of blood, anguished, and in pain... NOT!

What really happened was I stood my ground, yelling, screaming, crying, and shaking. I was hoping that the hotel staff would come busting through the door at any moment. The stranger looked confused, yet he didn't move. I continued to yell and plead for help. Every bit of my 1990 rape came flooding back. My body was paralyzed with fear and shock. I didn't know if this man had a weapon, but I was terrified. Nevertheless, I wasn't going out like before. He was not going to assault me without a fight! Not tonight! I would not be the one! I grabbed the cordless phone and rushed toward him with a vengeance. He grabbed the door handle and quickly left. I raced to the door and flipped the dead bolt shut.

Shortly thereafter, I received a call from the front desk apologizing profusely. The clerk had given the intruder a duplicate key to my room by mistake. The man had been out drinking and misplaced his room key. She was beside herself with remorse for the mistake. I was in a very bad state mentally, but somehow in that moment, I just wanted to pray for her. I pulled myself together and comforted her. She'd made an honest mistake, and I didn't want her to lose her job. It was a dangerous situation, but I didn't report it. Trying to get her fired or reprimanded wouldn't have changed a thing. I told her to always double and triple check when it came to handing out keys. She knew she was wrong. I could tell it wasn't a mistake she took lightly.

I thought, *Wow! How's that for a wakeup call?* Needless to say, I didn't go back to sleep after that. My alarm was nearing the three a.m. mark, so I decided to shower and get ready for our flight home to Portland. When I met the crew in the lobby a couple hours later, a clerk at the front desk was updating my captain and first officer about the incident. They were both incredibly worried, but I assured them that I was okay. None of them knew I had been raped in a hotel room at nineteen. They had no idea of the trauma that haunted me.

Later, I had time to think about what I could have done differently. I was so preoccupied with getting inside, I didn't lock the dead bolt. If I had, when the man tried to use the key, the dead bolt would have alerted us both and probably none of that would have happened. There is a first and last time for everything. And that was the last time I haven't locked a door in years.

Believe it or not, I grew leaps and bounds from this experience.

In reflection, I also realized that I wasn't the same girl who was assaulted years ago. I wasn't Muhammad Ali, but I yelled! I

Chapter Forty-Nine: Strangers in the Night

screamed! I made a call for help! And I made it clear that I was ready to fight.

I had evolved, and I was confident in who I had become.

Chapter Fifty

Spotters Up

I was preparing for a midnight redeye from Portland to Dallas. I worked predominantly the first-class cabin of the airplane, and after I had done all of my safety checks, and the captain had our initial crew briefing, it was time to do my personal primping in the forward lavatory. I had the privilege of greeting every passenger who boarded the aircraft. Greeting everyone with a big smile was the highlight of the job. I took it seriously and was extremely professional, but I also liked to entertain the passengers and have fun, especially on long haul flights. I played a game or two of trivia and made jokes to relax the passengers when it was appropriate.

This flight to Dallas would prove to be most memorable and meaningful. After all the passengers were boarded and we completed our pre-departure announcements, I checked on the first-class cabin one last time. It was complete darkness outside, and all of the cabin lights were off. I could barely see my hand in front of my face. As we taxied out to the runway, there was a remnant of light coming from a seat. Before takeoff, I always went over my brace-for-impact commands in my seat. I was looking down, reciting them in my head. We were building speed for takeoff, and I caught a glimpse of a woman sitting in 2A. She had tears running down her face. Instantly, my heart sank. I concluded from experience that she was probably afraid to fly. I made a concerted effort to ease the minds of passengers like this. We got the release signal from the captain, and I glanced at my twelve first class passengers. There were two distinct scenarios.

On the left side of the cabin was a group of six women who were ready to party hard. They were on their way to a friend's bachelorette party. These women were having a blast and had absolutely no intention of sleeping the three and a half hours to Texas. They requested mimosas, chocolates, and anything else I could provide! As I was taking food and beverage orders, I noticed the woman who was crying in 2A. She had her head against the window with her eyes closed. I remember thinking she must be cold, given the way she was clenching the blanket. I stepped into my galley and began to get their meals prepped, and I heard someone fumbling with the lavatory door, so I pulled aside my curtain and saw it was the woman from 2A. I had forgotten to unlock the door, so I unlocked the latch and told her I was sorry. She could barely respond. I didn't let too many things bother me when it came to serving passengers, but I had a feeling she was having a tough day.

I had served two rounds of drinks and the meals. The party girls had me hopping. I knew there would be little chance of me getting in a quick nap. I triple checked on the passengers, then decided to make myself a cup of peppermint tea with honey. I don't know what caused me to turn around, but I saw the passenger in 2A, streaming tears once again. I couldn't let it go unnoticed, so I decided to kneel in close. I asked if she was okay. She looked at me with profound sorrow, grabbed both of my hands, and cupped them in hers. I immediately realized that she wasn't holding a blanket, she was holding an American Flag. It was given to her by the military in remembrance of her son. A tear came tumbling down my cheek. I was sorry for her loss and honored that she shared her story with me.

I was summoned by the girls across the aisle who were in need of more champagne. I flashed a smile, gave them a nod, and got them a glass of bubbly, then walked into my galley, closed the

Chapter Fifty: Spotters Up

curtain, and leaned my back against the wall. I began taking big deep breaths. I could feel my heart rate accelerating. I realized on that red eye to Dallas that my job meant much more than getting people from point A to point B. I had human beings on board. Not everyone is flying on vacation, and not everyone is okay. I spent the remaining three hours consoling my passenger in 2A and graciously servicing the party girls getting ripped.

This was a metaphor for life—the best of times for some, and the worst of times for others. I had to find a way to make certain that all of them had a memorable experience. I had to treat both needs with integrity and grace. I genuinely love people. All people. This day, that flight solidified my desire to make a difference in people's lives. I wanted to make an impact on humanity and use my gift of compassion for the greater good. I needed to do something more profound in my life. Something bigger than myself.

A few days later, I received a call from my Crew Chief. He wanted to congratulate me on a job well done on the Dallas red eye. The lady in 2A called the airline and told them that I had helped her. She said before the flight she didn't care whether she lived or died. But after talking with me about her son, she had a renewed perspective. I couldn't have received a more meaningful compliment. I was glad I was able to help. Sometimes, we all just need a little help to get us over the hump.

One of the last flights I worked before the COVID Pandemic hit was from Los Angeles to Seattle. I remember watching this stunning blonde woman board with several small children all under the age of seven. She was disheveled and completely overwhelmed. She was the first passenger on the flight, so I took the time to assist her before the gate agents boarded the rest of the plane. She was out of breath and kept apologizing for needing help. I assured her that it was my pleasure, and I was available whenever she needed me.

During the flight, I checked on her often. I was able to see the entire cabin from first-class. She was occupying four seats and had an infant on her lap. She spent most of the flight trying to keep her children entertained while frantically texting on the phone. The other flight attendant and I stepped into the aft galley in the back of the plane and noticed that she was under great stress. I walked up and asked if she needed anything. I'll never forget the look in her eyes. She said, "I think I'm beyond help." I told her that I understood being in difficult circumstances and I was willing to listen if she needed someone to talk to. I walked back to the galley and a few minutes later, she came up with her infant in tow. She asked the other flight attendant if she could hold the baby while she used the bathroom. We both smiled and played with the adorable little boy.

When she came out of the lavatory, she asked if I was willing to talk. I said, "Absolutely!" She was a little hesitant at first, but she got the story out. She started telling me that she was being abused by her husband. She turned around to look behind her, to make sure no one else was looking, then lifted her shirt and showed us the black and blue bruises all over her back. She lifted her long blonde hair, and the back of her neck was swollen and bruised and completely discolored. It was a deep purple and greenish mix. It looked like bruises on top of bruises. She said that they were supposed to be going to Seattle as a family, but when they got to the airport, her husband threw all of her luggage out of the car on the sidewalk. He took her wallet and keys and punched her in the back of the head and forced her and the kids out of the car. Fortunately, she had her passport and the kids' plane tickets in the bottom of her purse. Her husband had all of her cash, credit cards, and her ticket when he drove off. She didn't realize it until

Chapter Fifty: Spotters Up

she got to security. Apparently, a wonderful couple at the check-in counter saw the entire incident outside and offered to buy her a ticket.

By the time we were ready for descent, the woman had confided in me about the severity of the abuse. She knew no one in Seattle except her husband's brother. This poor woman had her children and no money. She had been extremely battered, and her children were afraid as well. They wouldn't even look up at us because of the terror they had witnessed. Abuse not only affects the wife, but it affects the kids too. They had little self-confidence; their self-esteem was shaken. The only family she had was in Hawaii.

I wasn't sure how I could get her and her children to Honolulu, but that was my mission. We asked her to remain seated when we landed so the other passengers could exit the aircraft. We told her we would consult with our captain and figure out the next steps.

When everyone deplaned and the captain and first officer came out of the flight deck, we introduced them to the woman and explained the situation. My captain could hardly stomach the story and what he saw in the children. He walked them all out to the gate agent, bought them food, then spoke with an airline supervisor. We happened to have a couple hour layover at the SEA/TAC airport, so there was time to work through the issue. By the time all was said and done, the airline found a way to get her and her children on the next flight out to Honolulu. She contacted her sister in Oahu, who took them in with open arms.

I was emotionally exhausted that day and running on adrenaline the entire flight. I could see myself in her body and remembered the feeling of fear and insecurity. Seeing her helpless and defeated made me want to fight for her even harder. I couldn't explain how I knew that she was in distress. There is something inside someone who has been victimized that can sense the trauma in another. The signs were all there, but I felt an awakening in my spirit. Something told me to reach out. Having been down that road, somehow, I knew she needed help.

Before we departed, I looked in her eyes and told her that I would be praying for her. We hugged, and the captain took it from there.

I never saw her or heard from her again. But I know she's out there somewhere, safe, and I know we did the right thing. It was also great to work for a company who really does value the welfare of their customers, particularly in such a time of need. No one deserves to live in fear. The truth of the matter is that anyone can be a target, especially if they misread the signs, become isolated, and don't fully appreciate the fact that they have value.

The last four-day trip I worked ended with an overnight stay in Vancouver, British Columbia. I was working with a high energy, charismatic flight attendant named Keri, and it didn't take us long to build a strong rapport. She was a very open person, and I talk too much, just ask my dad. We had only flown together once before, but I believe this trip was meant to be. She had just separated from her husband, and they had a beautiful little girl. Her husband had been extremely emotionally and physically abusive for many years; she said she tried everything to make things better. She thought if she just tried harder, maybe he would change. If she worked more trips, maybe he would appreciate her more. If she gave in to his every demand and neglected her own desires in the process, maybe they could make it.

Like so many battered women, she believed that despite being a successful flight attendant and talented writer, she couldn't live without him. But prior to the trip, all that changed. Her husband had hit her for the last time, and she had finally left and taken the appropriate steps to separate. He was served with a restraining

CHAPTER FIFTY: SPOTTERS UP

order, she moved her money, and secured a safe place to live. She was severely traumatized by the relationship, but, against all odds, she was still in love. It's hard to digest, to listen to someone who has been living in danger talk about their abuser with remorse. I know because I was that person for a while. But instead of judgement, I listened and tried to identify with everything she was saying. The more she spoke about her husband, the more I could see the power he exerted over her. But, given the steps that she had taken, it was also clear that she had turned the corner.

When you live with extended abuse, you can build what's known as a "trauma bond" with the abuser. You begin to buy into your abuser's manipulation, and your life becomes a ball of confusion. Reality becomes a cloudy haze of half-truths and lies. It generally occurs with the presence of several factors: a severe power imbalance, either real or perceived, a recurring cycle of abuse and rewarding behavior, isolation from family and friends, and credible threats of death or violence to you or loved one. Another related phenomenon discussed briefly prior is called the Stockholm Syndrome. It occurs when a victim bonds and identifies with their perpetrator or abuser. The term originated in the 1970s when four people were taken hostage during a bank robbery in Stockholm, Sweden. After being released, the hostages defended their captors and refused to testify against them in court. Neither of these phenomena mean you're crazy, and neither phenomenon are irreversible.

When we got to the hotel in Canada, the crew decided to meet downstairs for dinner. There was a beautiful steakhouse called Chopped in the lower level. I walked in first and got a big round booth in the corner. I strategically placed myself so that I could see every television in the bar and watch the full array of games. Keri came in and we ordered a glass of wine. We were joined later by the captain and first officer. After an hour had passed, I picked up the phone and glanced at my social media. I started scrolling through stories and saw a picture of a high school friend. She had been brutally beaten in the face. Her eyes were swollen shut, and she was completely unrecognizable had I not noticed her name.

I was sick to my stomach. Without hesitation, I sent her a direct message. I asked her if she was okay and if she needed help. She messaged me right back and said something to the effect that she would be fine. After a few messages back and forth, she finally opened up and allowed me to call for help. I explained to her I was out of the country, but I would be making phone calls on her behalf. She understood and I called the first person I knew who would come through. I dialed a family friend and business partner Rob Ward.

Rob was a deputy sheriff in Multnomah County for twenty-five years, and he continued to work with kids in the Portland area after retirement. I took a screenshot of Lauren's picture and sent it to him. Rob was in Portland, and my girlfriend was in Eugene. Rob picked up the phone and called our mutual friend Robert Crumley, who was living in Eugene. We got on a three-way together to troubleshoot. While we were putting together a plan of action, we patched in a friend of mine named Rodney Stearns. Rodney is a former medic in the US Army and worked as paramedic in both Portland and Los Angeles. He created a multimedia software application called Sobrdrive, which provides real-time notification to a user's self-identified network in the event of intoxication or other high stress situations. The APP can be downloaded to your phone and activated by voice or touch. Once activated, the program will issue PANIC alerts, provide GPS location, and produce real-time video of your surroundings, all of which can be critical in keeping a victim safe or saving their life.

I messaged my girlfriend and told her to meet Robert at a local convenience store. Robert picked her up, checked her and her son

Chapter Fifty: Spotters Up

into a hotel under his name, and downloaded the Sobrdrive app to her phone. She had gotten away from her abusive husband but had no money or access to her bank account. Robert and I pitched in and took care of the hotel. All I cared about was that she was safe.

When I got back to my hotel room that night, she called me from her hotel room in Eugene. We hadn't spoken in twenty years, but it felt like only yesterday. She began to open up about some of the violent abuse that she had endured. She told me the story of how her husband had dragged her body behind his car. I let her know that we were family and that my friends had her back. She knew that getting a restraining order was the right next move. She and her children were in danger. I explained to her how I understood; that I had been down that road before. She was exhausted. I could hear it in her voice. She was also very scared, but ready. The following morning, I received a text message from her thanking me. I was relieved to hear from her and felt confident she would take the right steps to stay safe.

My crew didn't know who I was talking to at dinner the night before, but they knew the nature of what I was doing. I explained to them my passion for this work. I told them about my advocacy and desire to fight against abuse. I had fully taken my power back that night in British Columbia. There was not a second thought about what God had planned for the remainder of my life. I had work to do. I was determined to do everything I could to raise awareness about abuse. Numerous scenarios ran through my mind. How could I best help? Start a foundation? Fight for victims' rights? Write a book? Do all of the above?

I talked with Keri about what we had been through and how we could change lives. I shared my goals, and she sang me a couple of original songs that she had written of her past abuse. She sang acapella, and I was overcome with emotion. I didn't expect her to have such a beautiful singing voice, but the lyrics, the level of pain pouring into my soul was debilitating. It was difficult and simultaneously therapeutic.

My final four-day trip as a flight attendant proved to be the most profound.

Keri left her husband, relocated, and is happily raising her daughter in a safe and secure environment.

The truth really does make you free.

Sometimes we bite off a little more than we can chew, but just like at the gym, sometimes all you need is a spotter to help you get over the hump. I was glad that I was able to be that spotter for a couple of beautiful women during my time as a flight attendant. I felt fulfilled and transformed. The victim had become a spotter. How ironic was that.

Chapter Fifty-One
An Intervention

Twenty minutes before the kickoff of Super Bowl LV (fifty-five) between the Rams and Bengals, I received a text message from a close friend who was a former NFL player. The text started something like, "C, I have a close friend who needs your help. She is going through some serious issues with her husband. I know you help women with domestic violence. He played college ball for Alabama and retired from the league. She is in trouble. Can you please talk to her?" I texted him back and said I would be more than happy to help. Within five minutes, I was text messaging back and forth with this terrified woman. She followed me on Instagram, and I followed her back. It was helpful to put a face with a name.

She was a published cover model in Arizona, with long black hair and green eyes. She was in amazing shape and had the face of an angel. As I began to scroll down her Instagram page, I was reminded that abuse has no specific identity. Here was this young, vivacious woman fighting for her sanity and safety. She was a wife and mother of two children. She had been abused for some time, but that afternoon he had pushed her head into a wall so hard that she was knocked out for over thirty minutes. As I listened to her story, I completely forgot about the Super Bowl. I was so frustrated to hear the terror and fear engulfing her life. He had taken her money and car keys; she was trapped, a hostage in plain sight. She lived in Phoenix, so it was difficult for me to quickly get her the help that she needed. We exchanged text after text, and with each successive round, I could feel the pain as though she was part of my own soul. She was so down and despondent, broken, an empty shell of herself. I was getting nauseous as I listened to her describe the name calling, the verbal abuse, and the accusations of infidelity. He was out of control. The accusations were made up; they were a smokescreen to justify all the physical abuse. How else could he explain the brutality of giving his wife a vicious concussion.

She repeatedly denied any cheating on her part, and I felt, without a doubt, that she was telling the truth. Her explanations and the desperation in her messages were proof positive. I knew how it felt to have to defend yourself against absurdities and conspiracies to the point of losing your sanity. She texted me saying: "I have nothing. No money, he has control of everything. I try hard every day and it doesn't matter; he still thinks I'm a bad person. I try, OMG, I try! I've been put outside in the cold naked so many times I can't count. My mind is traumatized! Like OMG, I would say you have no idea, but I know you do." I could feel the heat of my body radiate.

I responded back in the only way I knew, with truth: "Men like your husband and my ex-husband are damaged narcissistic sociopaths. They can't be fixed by good works or submission. They're master manipulators. They are actually extremely insecure but try to turn that insecurity on you. They gaslight us to the point that we are so psychologically mind-screwed; we can't tell up from down." It's psychological warfare. Keep them in a state of fear and terror. Isolate them from their friends and family, and keep them under threat. Keep them totally financially dependent, mentally despondent, and devoid of all hope. If it's done long enough and deep enough, an abuser can get you to undermine yourself. Suicide looks like a welcome relief. I was furious for her, but more upset

Chapter Fifty-One: An Intervention

that I didn't have the right resources in place to help further. I reached out immediately to Rodney Stearns to get her the App. I knew she needed a safety valve, especially since she was planning to leave. Once again, the SOBRDRIVE App has a PANIC feature which sends an alert, contemporaneous audio and video, and GPS location to a preselected group of contacts. My biggest fear was that her husband would return to the house while she was packing and beat her again. I called a couple friends in Scottsdale to see if they could assist. There were two people who I knew with access to hotels. My first concern was getting her to a safe location.

Because it was Super Bowl Sunday, it was hectic and difficult to convey the sense of urgency to my friends. One was in Las Vegas, the other had family in town. There wasn't a lot I could do other than listen. I sent her the phone number and website link for the National Domestic Violence hotline. I let her know that I was once in her shoes, that she wasn't alone, and that I was there to help.

She had finally gotten in touch with her parents. They knew what was happening and were expecting to see her the next day. She told me about her dad's reaction to the physical abuse and it broke my heart. Her father wanted her to have her husband arrested. She, like me, told her dad that she would leave him the next day. It was like reliving my final night with my ex-husband. She didn't want to infuriate him any further for fear of retribution. I wanted to interject. I knew it wasn't the right answer, but I understood her fear. Every word she spoke sounded like a recollection of my own experience. I could commiserate with her stories and rationale. She sounded like the same wounded, insecure, and scared girl that was me twenty years prior.

I never spoke to her again, and I don't know how the situation ended. But it bothered me. A few weeks after my conversation with this beautiful soul, I started thinking about ways to be more intentional and began working on some tools. You read earlier about the Red Flags. Later, I will provide a few more.

Chapter Fifty-Two
On Bended Knee

I stepped outside into the bright sunlight. It was one of those rare Oregon days with February snow. I was trying to decide whether to walk, or more like hobble, down to the mailbox. I was roughly eight weeks into my recovery from spinal fusion surgery. For those of you who are curious, I had to have emergency spine surgery. In doctor terms, I had a lateral discectomy, posterior laminectomy, and fusion of my L4 and L5 vertebrae. From there, my neurosurgeon took bone marrow from my hip for a bone graft for the fusion, then he implanted a screw in my hip and titanium rods in my back to stabilize my spine. In other words, I was in pretty bad shape. The doctors can't point to a specific cause but believe it's probably the result of a combination of cheerleading, dance, weightlifting, the fall on my booty, and God knows what else! But at this point, I'm as good as new money. In fact, I work out five to six days a week and think of myself as the bionic woman.

Anyway, I was hoping for some fresh air, but not at the risk of slipping and injuring the newly fused vertebrae. So, wisdom prevailed. I turned around to go back in the house, when I got a series of text messages from Haley. I saw the first of four pictures. The first being a photo of her boyfriend Marcus on bended knee in one inch of snow with a ring in his hand and an effervescent Haley. She looked happier than I had ever seen her! I glanced at the other photos and the answer was a resounding, "YES!" I was absolutely ecstatic and, of course, I immediately posted to my social media. I was so happy, and, within minutes, I was inundated with tons of well wishes.

Haley called and blurted out, "This is going to be a huge year for us, Mom! I'm getting married and you'll be a GiGi!"

A what? A GiGi! That's the name they'd decided on instead of Grandma. I thought it was absolutely adorable! I took to the name instantly; it had pizzazz. I even became GiGi to their new Chiweenie puppy, "Raider." It was as though time stopped for just a few moments. Visions flashed through my head of Haley being born and episodic moments of her growing up. I also pictured her walking down the aisle to join the love of her life. What I wasn't prepared for was the thought of her dad entering my mind. I wondered whether Devin would react the same way or would even care?

Haley had spoken many times about breaking generational curses and finding a man who treated her like my dad treated my mom. Despite several guys she'd dated before Marcus, Haley always knew what she deserved and how she wanted to be valued. I never worried about Marcus. He was raised by a strong and fabulous mother. She instilled in her son all the qualities a mother would want in a son-in-law. He was a true Southern gentleman from South Carolina, and his solid upbringing was transparent.

Initially, they decided on a July wedding, but with the pandemic wreaking havoc in 2020, countless weddings had been pushed back a year. People were hot to trot; 2021 was like a dam breaking. There were weddings everywhere you looked, including Haley's stepparents Keith and Amy Lewis. Yes, Keith eventually found his soul mate. Amy is someone I've known for decades, and we have been able to build a genuine relationship of mutual trust and respect. Amy cares deeply about my children and embraces them with love and kindness. I consider her a friend, and I love her like a sister. Nevertheless, the postponements created a run on

Chapter Fifty-Two: On Bended Knee

locations, ministers, churches, and booze. Even people who married in 2020 had their actual wedding ceremony in 2021.

Given the circumstances, Haley decided to move her wedding up a month. We all knew that a June wedding in Oregon was dicey. You could never truly count on the weather; plus, the pandemic was still turning our state upside down when it came to group gatherings; and Jaden's high school graduation was tentatively scheduled on June 12th, but the in-person celebration was still iffy. With all that in mind, Haley decided on a wedding date of June 13th, making the logistics tight.

The day Haley got engaged, she wasted no time in calling her Bridal party. One of the first calls was to her little sister Kaitlyn. I spoke with Erika Ramos shortly after their conversation, and we were both excited to have our daughters together for this special occasion. Erika and I discussed whether Devin would be invited. At that point, Haley had decided that he would not. And with Erika's restraining order still in place, it was for the best. Haley made clear from the beginning that her grandpa, my dad, would be walking her down the aisle. That was an honor Dad had earned. He had been the most consistent man in her life, and he was the rock that mattered.

With the wedding only four months away, Haley and I began to do what we do best... plan! Within a day, we had decided on the venue. Notwithstanding the restraints of the pandemic, we took a chance on a beautiful four-thousand square foot house in Beaverton, Oregon. It was sweet. And although I was the mother of the bride, Haley asked me to also be the wedding planner. I had carte blanche to do whatever. And that's exactly what I did. The first task was to call Rob Ward and pull him out of retirement. It was an inside joke, but while Rob was a Multnomah County Deputy Sheriff for twenty-five years, he also owned a successful production company. He had recently retired from both, but I knew I could rely on him for this.

Rob was one of the four mainstays of guys in my core group since my time with Devin. Daryl, Flash, and Michael were the others. Flash was from Olympia, Washington; the others were from Los Angeles. They were my foundation, my inner circle. They were the group of guys I leaned on when things got tight. Michael was a basketball player, and the other three all played football together at Oregon. I was an Oregon cheerleader, so the circle was complete. For nearly three decades, we had remained a close-knit group; they knew virtually everything about my life. The good, the bad, the drama, and the trauma. Not once did one of these guys let me down, judge me, or let me fall into the abyss. But not once did they sugar coat things either. If I asked a question, I got an answer, and rest assured, it was the stone-cold truth. That's why I trusted them.

Within a month or so, Rob and I had booked the various vendors for the ceremony and reception. But one of the remaining tasks I passed to Haley; it was the invitation list. I gave her my list that included family, friends, and coaches, and she collected names from others. By the time the list was compiled, including the wedding party and pastor, we were at about one hundred people. As time passed, we discovered there were many people who had conflicting graduations. It was disappointing, but we knew that was a distinct possibility. With the final number at around eighty, we continued planning with a vengeance. It seemed like every time we turned around someone stepped up to help or contribute in some way or another.

Things were coming together, and I could see the light at the end of the tunnel.

Two weeks before the wedding, I received a call from Haley. She let me know that Devin and his wife would be attending. It

Chapter Fifty-Two: On Bended Knee

changed the dynamic of the wedding. My initial reaction was concern. I knew there were many people who would be uncomfortable in his presence. I was, specifically, concerned for Erika and Kaitlyn. Next on the list was Devin's mother, they had been estranged for more than a decade because of a family dispute.

The first thing I did was call Rob. I knew it was going to be a serious issue with my core group. They were Devin's college roommates, teammates, and longtime friends. They were also quality men who didn't condone Devin's behavior toward me or Erika and her daughter. After a long discussion with Rob, he decided to call one of the guys to meet for lunch. After much debate, they felt it warranted a group video chat. One thing about our inner circle, we kept family business private. There was never a need to preface something. Secrecy was always understood... omertà, was an immutable code.

We all got on the conference call later that day. After a couple hours of debate, we agreed that the wedding had to be about Haley. The guys were prepared to put their difference with Devin aside and yet take whatever precautions necessary to handle any drama. The one issue that was not up for discussion was the role of my dad. The guys spoke to him personally to let him know they had his back. They understood the mental anguish that Devin had caused and, being fathers themselves, it was business and personal.

I woke up at four a.m. as usual to go to the gym. The last six months had been centered around physical therapy and regaining my strength and flexibility. Recovering from spine surgery was excruciating, but I was no stranger to challenges and dedicated myself to making it happen. One person who always stayed true was Julie. This particular morning, she picked me up and we hit the gym, ready to annihilate the stress of the week.

It was hotter than normal for early June. So much so I didn't have on a jacket. It had been in the high nineties all week, which caused me to realize that I may need a tent for the ceremony. The wedding and reception were both being held outside, and I knew it could get really warm in the afternoon. Later, I called the party rental company in Portland and made sure they had a tent available. What I didn't bank on was a weather forecast two days before the wedding that called for scattered showers all day long!

I pulled up to the house in Beaverton the night before the wedding. We drove up with a truck loaded with wedding decorations, the bridal gowns, tuxedos, and more. We had the Airbnb booked for five days, but we only had a few hours to put everything together. It was already getting late because Jaden had high school graduation earlier in the day. It was ninety degrees and beautiful in Eugene, but the weather in Beaverton was a different story.

Nevertheless, it was exciting. I was meeting Marcus's mom and her sister for the first time. They flew in from Charleston, South Carolina, and it was the first time they had been to the Pacific Northwest. I walked through the front door and was greeted by Rob, who had been there for a few hours, along with Marcus, and his brother. They were working diligently to get the furniture, tent, dance floor, and bar set up before dark. That was the plan, just before it started raining, then a full-blown deluge. It was like the famous quote from Mike Tyson, "Everybody has a plan until they get punched in the mouth." The forecast for the next day called for showers. There went the plan. To say the least, I was a little uneasy.

Haley, Jaden, Rob, and I went inside set up for the reception. It was midnight before we called it quits. The wedding decor was flawless. The downstair area looked absolutely beautiful. It was decorated in black and white, with a Napa Valley feel. Gorgeous

Chapter Fifty-Two: On Bended Knee

long stem white roses, mason jars and white candles, black organza table runners, wine barrels, and bistro pedestal tables. We had the six-foot bar stocked full of alcohol and various nonalcoholic beverages. There was nothing more that we could do but pray.

Between the powerhouse entertainment by DJ Playtime, the Hawaiian Food, and load of spirits, I felt the wedding reception would be a runaway success.

The delivery of the wedding cake and food from the caterer were not due until noon the next day, but the rain was blowing sideways into the tent, drenching the dance floor, farm benches, and birch arbor. The only x-factor had been the weather, and it turned out to be a huge crap shoot.

Chapter Fifty-Three
The Wedding Crashers

The morning of the wedding, I woke up earlier than anticipated. I looked at my cell phone and it was 5:15am. I had little more than four hours of sleep, but I was feeling invigorated. I walked down the hall to the bathroom, trying to be as quiet as possible as I took my shower and got dressed in my workout clothes. I then proceeded down the long spiral staircase to admire our work. I was confident it would be well received by all the guests.

Shortly after I got downstairs, the Best Man walked into the living room, eager to help. As I stared out the windows, he was a calming presence. I think he knew I was stressing about the torrential downpour we were witnessing. We walked outside to assess the situation, and without hesitation, the Best Man began grabbing towels from inside and drying the dance floor and benches. There wasn't a dry spot under heaven. After a few minutes, Daryl pulled up and immediately jumped in to help. Within an hour, the guys had all of the furniture and props dry and perfectly placed. They were invaluable to the success of the wedding… and to my sanity.

I had received several text messages from Erika Ramos over a three-day period before the wedding. She was incredibly sick with pneumonia, possibly COVID induced. She was struggling to decide whether to have Kaitlyn and her husband Tony come to the wedding. We knew how excited Haley and Kaitlyn were to share the special day together. In the end, regretfully, Erika had to make the difficult decision to stay in Seattle. She and her family had been on vacation in New York a couple of weeks before, and out of nowhere she was hit hard and admitted into the hospital. What mattered most was Erika's health. I had been looking forward to spending the day with her and Tony, but there was no question she made the right decision.

One by one, the members of the wedding party began to arrive. Once everyone was present, I had the unenviable task of informing Haley about Kaitlyn. No doubt, Haley was disappointed to not have her sister present, but she and the wedding party were looking fabulous. The vibe was fun and light, and everyone was excited.

It was raining cats and dogs, guests were arriving, and the parking became precarious. But like true gentleman, Keith Lewis, the Groomsmen, the four guys from my inner circle, and Haley's God Brothers began running out in their suits to park cars for all the female guests. It was a bit of a madhouse for about fifteen minutes, but once the guests were seated for the ceremony, the real drama began to unfold.

The Minister, Joshua Stroud, told me that Haley needed to speak with me upstairs. When I walked through the door, she was a vision of beauty, but the look on her face was one I knew all too well. Her body language spoke volumes. She asked for my parents to come upstairs as well. Tears began welling up in her eyes. She was visibly nervous. Haley began explaining why she waited until this moment to say something.

I bluntly blurted out, "You're going to have your dad walk you down the aisle with your grandpa?" She confirmed my question with tears falling from her eyes. I told her not to mess up her makeup. I looked at my dad and could see his heart was broken, but we shook it off and just rolled with the punches. My parents went downstairs to get into place, and Joshua Stroud and the

Chapter Fifty-Three: The Wedding Crashers

bridesmaids came back into the suite. I said out loud, "Can we pray?" and Joshua led us in prayer. I could feel God enter the room, and my mind was divinely prepared.

Amy and I made our way outside to the front row under the tent. Mama Pearl was seated in the row next to my mom, and as I looked around, everyone was there: Becca, TK and Julie, Leesa, Shawna, Erica Winger, Andiel Brown, Darlene, Jamie and Janet Fryback, Johny "Flash" Taylor, and Pastor CoCo. The whole gang, plus family.

We were waiting for Keith to reappear so that we could start. It was taking him a little longer than expected. We had no clue what was happening.

Keith had been keeping an eye on events unfolding in front of the house. Devin showed up twenty minutes before the ceremony with his wife and a few friends in tow. He approached the front door and was met by my inner circle, all of whom were college friends and teammates. Devin received an icy reception as he made his way into the house. Flash let him know that he was about as welcome as Sasquatch. The guys had no clue that Haley had just announced to my family that Devin would be accompanying her and my dad down the aisle. The closer Devin got to the front door, the more pushback he received. The four of them had no issue letting him know there was a level of decorum they expected before he could enter.

Meanwhile, Daryl and Rob asked Devin's wife to take a seat so we could start. Devin's wife came at Daryl like a prize fighter.

This was a mistake. Everyone knows that Daryl isn't a confrontational dude, but if he feels disrespected, the flip side is true as well. Daryl would open up a can of "whoop—" on you quick. She didn't realize who she was dealing with. But in short order, she found out. And she learned more about her husband than she bargained for. Devin began to puff out his chest like King Kong and attempted to boast about "throwing" the wedding. Devin had no idea that Rob coordinated the wedding with me, and he shut down that nonsense quickly. Once Rob pulled off the covers, Devin changed his tune. At that point, there was no doubt who was running the show!

Then, after a heated exchange, it was finally brought to light that Devin was part of the ceremony. Flash, being an honorable man, said he was unaware of the change and apologized for trying to throw Devin off the property. But that didn't stop him from standing his ground.

It was an intense interlude, to say the least, but the guys did exactly what they set out to do. They established a red line, which wasn't to be crossed. I don't think Devin saw that coming. He was a master manipulator of women, but these guys weren't looking for a date.

Once the guys allowed Devin through, the bridal party moved into place. Haley was happy and excited to meet Marcus under the beautiful birch arbor, and the ceremony was absolutely stunning.

Haley and Marcus wrote their own vows, and there wasn't a dry eye in the tent. Joshua Stroud did a magnificent job officiating and, despite the earlier drama, all seemed forgotten. It was so beautiful. Everyone felt the sincerity of Haley and Marcus' love. It was one of the proudest moments in my life. My daughter was truly happy.

Once they were pronounced husband and wife, everyone made their way to the lower level of the house. It was still raining heavily, but everyone was laughing and in good spirits! The bartender was inundated with requests and, Hayward, the caterer, was serving his amazing Hawaiian cuisine.

CHAPTER FIFTY-THREE: THE WEDDING CRASHERS

It was exactly as I had hoped. Good food, good drinks, good vibes, and good people!

I looked across the room and caught a glimpse of Devin. My eyes saw nothing but red. I had to take a deep breath, whispering, "Goosfraba, goosfraba." Haley had asked me to be cordial. I had to put my sword away, metaphorically speaking. For her sake, I agreed to be civil.

Deep inside, I knew that I would have to be the bigger person. I walked over to Devin and his wife and said, "Hello," and extended my hand. Devin replied in a deadpan fashion. We shook hands, and I looked across the table and said, "Hello." The music was loud, so I had to concentrate hard to understand his wife's reply. She introduced herself as Devin's wife. It was a bit amusing, and I had to force myself to keep from laughing. We quickly reached a point of "nothing else to say." I told them to, "enjoy the party" and retreated.

At this point, I still had no idea about what happened between Devin and the guys before the ceremony.

Devin and his wife were both dressed beautifully and looked great together, but they had permanent evil scowls on their faces. It made them seem unhappy and unapproachable. I don't know if they thought that they were going to intimidate people, but they couldn't have been more out of place. All the other guests were having a blast, eating, drinking, grooving to the music, and reminiscing about the good old times. We were there to celebrate and enjoy one another. I guess they were there for something other than that.

Once everyone had an opportunity to eat, the guests grabbed their champagne glasses, and it was time to toast the bride and groom. I grabbed the microphone from DJ Playtime and stood in front of the room. Before I began my remarks, I called up several key people to join me. I announced Haley's uncle and Godfather Rick Raish, Haley's Godfather Johnny "Flash" Taylor, her Godmother Darlene Watson, her Stepfather Keith Lewis, and Godbrothers Keith Allen and Andiel Brown. It was an arsenal of power. I felt an extreme sense of confidence. I'm not sure what came over me, but I took a deep breath, and called Devin up to stand with me. There are moments in our lives that make no sense, this was one of those for me. I guess there is nothing I wouldn't do for my daughter.

I heard a resounding, "WOW" from the back of the room as Devin approached. It was Pastor Joshua; he knew better than most how much I struggled with Devin's invite. About an hour earlier, I had thanked Josh for showing me the will of God. He knew it took every ounce of strength I had to rise above the years of pain and anger. The moment was not mine, and it was not Devin's. Once I took myself out of the equation and made it about Marcus and Haley, everything began to flow.

One by one, the microphone was passed between the people I called upon to speak and others who wanted to contribute. Everyone had their own blessings, words of encouragement, and advice for the newlyweds. Some messages to the happy couple were fun and entertaining, others were sentimental and emotional. I remember looking out into the sea of faces and thinking how blessed Haley and Marcus were to have the magnitude of genuine love and support.

I caught the eye of Erica Winger and Leesa Wilder when Devin was making his speech. They looked totally perplexed as he announced how he was solely responsible for Haley's intellectual qualities because of the time he spent helping her with her homework. He congratulated himself for Haley graduating from Oregon State University and reminded everyone of his own genius.

Chapter Fifty-Three: The Wedding Crashers

It was all I could do to hold back the laughter and absurdity of his comments. After he finished taking a bow, I couldn't help but turn my head and blurt out, "You have got to be kidding!" I had a complete disgusted grin on my face. Even Devin had to laugh. It was actually a comedic moment between us, and it eased some of the tension in the room. Devin knew that everyone was calling BS on his self-congratulations, except his wife. Nevertheless, there was no doubt that Devin was happy for and proud of Haley.

The festivities continued with the toss of the bridal bouquet, garter toss, and cutting of the cake. The reception was going off without a hitch. The same couldn't be said for Devin. He believed he could just waltz in with a basket of tall tales, plead his case, and miraculously make a decade of physical abuse just disappear. He was like a bad comic trying to tell one last joke before he got booed off the stage and ushered out of the building.

The rain let up as guests began departing. Many people had to make the several hours drive back to Eugene. People were running in and out of the house changing into comfy clothes for the trip home. I loved that, because although we had all been dressed for the occasion, it showed how close we were collectively.

The last year had been a whirlwind for everyone, the whole world having to navigate through the pandemic. Spending more than a year fighting an uphill battle for a multitude of reasons proved damaging for many. The wedding brought so much joy and relief to everyone. Seeing the faces of loved ones without masks and finally getting to hug one another felt so liberating.

That's why the little hiccups just didn't matter. There is something to be said for embracing important moments in your life and taking nothing for granted. My daughter and son-in-law exemplified love and compassion on their wedding day. They knew the challenges of bringing together people with deep wounds and a dangerous history. But instead of focusing on the events of the past, they decided to focus on the future. Their attitudes were enlightening, and I was deeply grateful. I learned a lot about moving forward and focusing on the things within my control.

Forgiveness is a funny thing. I realized that it wasn't Devin I needed to forgive, it was myself. I had ignored my instincts; I didn't react to the violence quickly enough; I lived in shame and denial and nostalgia. For all of those reasons, I needed to forgive myself. And, on that day, I did.

Chapter Fifty-Four
My Friend's Enemy is My Friend

It was four o'clock in the afternoon, and I was feeling extremely exhausted as I sat on the edge of my bed. But I was determined to push myself twice a day to do my physical therapy. Once I make up my mind about something, in true Taurus fashion, my stubbornness tends to override logic.

I was about to grab my resistance bands when the phone rang. I didn't want to look at the caller ID, but curiosity got the better of me. In bold letters across my iPhone was the name of an old acquaintance from Alberta Calgary. We hadn't spoken much in the last couple of years, so I eagerly picked up and said, "Hey, what's up?"

On the other end of the line, I hear my friend and former business partner say in his Canadian accent, "CORINE!"

We exchanged a few quick jabs, playfully of course, before I told him about my spine surgery, and we did a quick wellness check on each other's families. I'm not even sure exactly how the conversation arose, but he asked me to consider speaking about my experience on a tour throughout Canada. The objective was to bring awareness to sexual assault and domestic violence. He hesitated for just a second and after taking a deep breath asked if I knew about a mutual friend who was incarcerated in Utah.

I couldn't even process what he said, "Anthony is in Prison?" I had no idea! "What the heck happened?"

Anthony was the person who had introduced us about seven years earlier. He was a division one football player in the PAC-10 when I was a cheerleader. He was a stellar athlete and well liked among his peers and the public. In the early 2000s, Anthony and I linked up at his alma mater while I was coaching an away game. We decided to put on a series of football and cheerleading camps together for youth in his state. After his professional football career ended, he started a motivational speaking and fitness training company. He traveled all over the states and into Canada teaching fitness and conducting youth football camps. Anthony was incredibly charismatic and could easily draw in a crowd. His magnetic personality was infectious, and his work ethic was legendary. We did quite a bit of cross promotion together for our individual businesses on social media. I really liked him, and I appreciated what a devoted and dedicated father he seemed to be. Our mutual respect for one another was why he introduced me to his friend in Canada; he felt there was a synergy in our television production. I never had one bad conversation with Anthony in all the years that I was associated with him. I guess that's why hearing that he murdered his wife hit me like a ton of bricks.

I was completely numb. As the story unfolded, it didn't sound like the Anthony I knew. I had to sit down and concentrate. I could feel my skin crawl and my blood pressure rising.

It turned out that the man I revered as an athlete, father, and motivational guru had been beating his wife for some time. He had become insanely jealous and menacing. As many victims of domestic violence do, according to my friend, his wife tried valiantly to make their marriage work. I never had the privilege of meeting her, but from what I was told, she was a loving, devoted wife and mother.

The more I listened, the more my sadness was transformed into anger. Beyond the intimidation and abuse he put her through, the calculated way he killed her made my blood boil! Anthony had given her a safety bracelet to wear for protection. Apparently, this bracelet had a small, built-in utility knife. Anthony repeatedly

Chapter Fifty-Four: My Friend's Enemy Is My Friend

slashed her throat with the blade, virtually decapitating her. She was alone and vulnerable and brutally slain by the man she once loved. How senseless and troubled must one be to take the life of your children's mother?

In that moment, Anthony's enemy became my friend.

When I hung up with my friend, I immediately went online to search for the story. Maybe I needed to see it to believe it, or maybe I couldn't fathom the truth. I found the story, and sure enough it was true.

I looked on his Facebook page, and his posts were still there, including a long video rant about how life was so unfair. He'd posted this sick video days before the murder. Obviously, he was severely unstable. But how did all of his "friends" watch this video and not reach out to help or notify the authorities? Why not encourage him to seek professional help? This post was made only a few days before Anthony murdered his wife. Where was her protection? Who failed her? I could not accept the outcome of her fate. I refused to stand by knowing that someone I once called a friend had defiled his wife in the worst kind of betrayal.

Once again, a torch was lit inside. No more! I will not stay quiet! Not today, not tomorrow, not ever!

This story and others got me thinking about the cycle of abuse that many women face. And like the red flags, which are designed to warn about the signs of abuse, I began creating a tool to help a victim understand where they might be in the cycle. The first step in solving a problem is to admit that you have one. I call this next tool, "The Unvirtuous Cycle."

Part Six
Finding My Purpose

Chapter Fifty-Five
The Unvirtuous Cycle of Abuse

Based on my own experience and discussions with numerous survivors, I have come to the conclusion that abuse doesn't typically happen in a vacuum. It tends to occur over time and as part of a continuum of power and control that I call, "The Unvirtuous Cycle," a pattern of escalating violence that occurs when one partner seeks to exert unhealthy dominance over the other. Of course, no two relationships are the same, and not everyone experiences the same level of abuse. But when dealing with strong-willed, controlling personalities and a significant power imbalance exists, either real or perceived, be careful! An unhealthy and dangerous pattern of behavior could arise, leading to violence.

Grooming and Courtship: This is the initial stage of the relationship. During this phase, you can do no wrong. You're showered with attention, gifts, love, and affection. Everything you do is pure perfection. Things are sweeter than cotton candy. You talk to your partner until three o'clock in the morning, you receive romantic text messages on the ready. There are picnics in the park and spontaneous getaways. Your partner really understands you; they can almost read your thoughts. Everything they do is through the roof and over the top. Your partner acts as your chief benefactor. The whole goal is to gain your trust. There are some troubling signs in the relationship, but you tend to misread them. You mistake "control" for "protectiveness." You see gentle critiques of your family and friends as genuine expressions of concern. Incessant phone calls are mistaken for romantic interest. "Love bombing" is mistaken for love. All the time your partner is wining and dining you, he's trying to pull you away from your tribe. Lions attack the prey that is separated from the herd. Sooner or later, you're lulled into a false sense of security with someone who's infinitely insecure. At this point, return to the "red flags." Take the quiz. If one or more are present, think deeply before proceeding. Set expectations for how you want to be treated and establish clear boundaries.

Trial by Fire: Imagine a wildebeest grazing on the savannas of Africa. A gentle breeze sweeps over the plains. All is well, then suddenly a lion leaps from the brush. This is the trigger stage. It can occur because of the loss of a job, a failed promotion, financial problems, baby mama drama, death of a loved one, a car breaks down, the loss of a gambling bet, or a thousand other life events. As you know, once the lion is triggered, the grits hit the pan! Your partner is transformed. You may see the true face of evil. He comes at you with rage, unbelievable tension, and lies. You're bewildered and terrified, but somehow you get away unharmed. Later, your partner delivers a bucket of apologies. Gifts flow like rainwater. He assures you that it will never happen again.

Be careful! This could be a prelude to your future. You may convince yourself you misread the situation and see it as an outlier. He's just under so much pressure. Plus, you're invested at this point, so you want to believe. You feel something inside, but you ignore your instincts. The episode was a trial balloon, a test. Your partner has successfully moved the goal post, but you continue down the field unaware. This is the frog boiling exercise. You need to turn the temperature down and reset expectations or jump out of the pot if any physical violence occurred.

Chapter Fifty-Five: The Unvirtuous Cycle of Abuse

Danger and Denial: There's another trigger, and your partner crosses the Rubicon. He's filled with rage and takes it out on you. Maybe it's a slap or a punch or he spits in your face or violently rapes you or does all of the above. It's displacement behavior, an act of misdirected anger. He's the man who comes home and kicks the dog because of a bad day at work. A line has been crossed; you both know it. You're ready to leave, but he's unbelievably sorry. His tears flow like water from a firehose. He showers you with more gifts: dinner at your favorite restaurant; a weekend getaway in Cabo; a new couch for the living room. Promises abound. Everything has an explanation; it's all plausible deniability. If you buy it, his behavior changes for a while. He manages the rage with great care. It's intermittent, but it's still there. You're disillusioned, but now you have a child and feel trapped. Fear and disparagement are mixed with moments of great joy and happiness. The cost of leaving has risen, and hope springs eternal. The emotional roller coaster has dulled your senses. Shame and low self-esteem creep in like a dark cloud. Resist these thoughts. Instead, insist on tangible change. Your partner must stop drinking, name calling, gaslighting, blame shifting, marital infidelity. Something has to change. You should seek marital or psychological counseling, establish a family intervention, move in with a friend, at least temporarily, or separate.

Reality and Surrealism: The beatings become more than intermittent. You feel embarrassed, ashamed, isolated, and afraid. It's surreal. You can't believe that this is your life. You wonder how you got here. The world was your oyster, and now this? What happened? You had big plans; everything was ahead of you. But now you're totally invested. How can you uproot the kids? Threats and intimidation have replaced romantic text messages and spontaneous getaways. Violence has become normalized, once a year, once a quarter, once a week. You're walking on eggshells. You can cut the tension with a knife. You've been isolated or partially estranged from your family and friends. They notice, but you can't talk about it. You don't want to make the situation worse. You don't recognize your life, and you can't believe the choices you've made. You can't stay, but you're afraid to go. He said that he would kill you, kill himself, or kill a member of your family. Your partner has everyone fooled; they think he's such a good guy. The demons used to only come only at night or after heavy drinking. Now they're ever-present. Your blood pressure is through the roof. One false move and you pay the price! One wrong word could mean a trip to the hospital. His comings and goings are irregular, but the other women in his life are not. You don't really care, but he won't let you leave. At least, not without one good beating. He's an existential threat, but the police want more evidence. Your love has turned cold. Hate and despair are your primary emotions. The kids feel it, too. They're wondering how this it's going to end. Everything is moving in the wrong direction.

You must document the abuse, establish accountability. You must seek marital or psychological counseling; talk to your pastor; call the police; get a restraining order; press charges; or separate.

Fight or Flight: It's the moment of truth; the reckoning. Your jaw is swollen; your eyes blackened; and your spirit is totally broken. In the words of those young street poets, "you just got served." Sometime later, he loses his job. The drinking escalates. Things are really spiraling out of control. He's threatening to kill you every other day. You can't take it anymore. Something has got to give. You're that wildebeest on the savanna and you've been caught or cornered. Do you have a plan? Where will you go? What will people think? None of that matters now. The only thing that

Chapter Fifty-Five: The Unvirtuous Cycle of Abuse

matters now is survival. Even the kids can't move you. They're in danger too, they just don't know it. You plot and plan; you lie in wait. You're starting to see more clearly. The fog is beginning to lift. It's not a matter of if you're leaving but when and how. You're prepared to face your fears. You're prepared to learn how to swim. There's a thin line between love and hate, but that line has been totally erased. In fact, it's no longer a line but a figure eight. Your soul has hardened. The future is unclear, but you've reached the point of no return. Death and dishonor are one and the same. This is the end of the line. Your relationship has reached the outer limits of sanity. Your options are few: Seek help! Flee! Fight! Press charges! Or all of the above!

Eventually, the nightmare always ends. The only question is how: some people get out, some correct the situation early, some get the help they need, some grow and transform themselves, but unfortunately, too many end in tragedy.

Some of the above may seem too fantastic or overhyped. But let me assure you that while my journey has been unique, it is not unusual. It is not even an outlier. Pick up any local newspaper, any day. Pick up the *New York Times*, the *Washington Post*, the *Hollywood Reporter*, and you'll find violence against some woman somewhere. Millions of women in this country and around the world have their own stories to tell. There was an especially heinous case in India in 2021 where a husband put a Russel's Pit Viper in his wife's bed. Then, two months later, while his wife was recovering at her parents' house, the husband threw a cobra at her while she was sleeping. Fortunately, this sham of a husband was tried and duly convicted of murder.

Abuse is not representative of all relationships, and even in cases where abuse occurs, the above is not reflective of everyone's experience. I get that! But if this is your experience, it's an ominous sign; it's a trauma bond and a potentially dangerous game of Russian roulette. The Unvirtuous Cycle, won't tell you what to do. It's more like a GPS; it tries to show you where you are, and where you might be headed. It tries to tell you that you're not alone, that it's not your fault, that you're not delusional, that you're not imagining things, that you're not stupid, that you're not the cause of your own terror, and that you're not worthless. It also tries to shake you from the trap of complacency and despair and encourages you to seek the safety of the herd.

You don't have to solve this problem alone. Do not allow yourself to be isolated! Observe the signs and notice the patterns. Be prepared to buck the cycle. Violence is not something you have to endure. Relationships are not like a Ferris wheel where you can't get off. If anything, they're more a river boat cruise. If an alligator jumps in the boat, you either throw it overboard or get out of the boat.

Chapter Fifty-Six
Sex Education

As you know by now, my advocacy is centered around the issues of sexual assault and domestic violence. It seems as if, unless an assault ends in death or mayhem, it's not compelling enough to gain media attention or the attention of the public. Someone almost has to die in order to gain political support or for policy makers to act. Why is this the case? What most of those policy makers don't seem to understand is that once you've been a victim of traumatic abuse, a part of you has died already, mentally, spiritually, a little bit every day. The person I was at eighteen is no more, "finito!" The terror I endured during nearly a decade of abuse did kill me, or at least a portion of me. People who remember the early Corine don't realize that I buried her long ago. I had to in order to survive and have the opportunity for rebirth. Transforming myself wasn't an option, it was a necessity; the difference between life and death, spiritually speaking, and maybe even literally.

People see the fear and bruises, but they don't see the internal necrosis, the inner death. I believe the reason why many victims don't come forth or continue to bleed inside is because they don't believe enough people care. They're afraid of the ramifications. They don't believe that they will be protected or that their story will be told. If the situation is not sensational or gruesome or decadent or involves a celebrity, who really cares? If the body is intact, people just seem to move on. In writing this, I wonder if my story will resonate. Will they believe me? Will it break through? Can I have an impact? Will anybody be saved? Sexual assault and domestic abuse are part of a vicious continuum of violence against women, a scourge. I wonder what would happen if instead of sweeping it under the rug, we as a society celebrated survivors and gave them a platform. Would more transparency stem this epidemic of violence? That's the proposition of this book, and it's a question that I have been posing to many of my male friends.

When I asked these questions of Andiel Brown, the Director of the Gospel Choirs & Ensembles at the University of Oregon, a former Ducks football player and close family friend, we had an eye-opening conversation. Andiel told me two stories that I found fascinating. The first occurred during his sophomore year. Andiel was having intimate relations with a young lady who had a boyfriend. They would steal away on occasions and go for food or a movie, then end the evening with oral sex. This was the pattern for six months. Then, one night, she threw a birthday party at her apartment. Andiel showed up, and the place was packed; it was a typical college party with food, music, alcohol, and all the trimmings.

After a while, Andiel took his friend by the hand and lead her to the back room. He sat on the bed, awaiting the normal scenario, but on this night, his friend told him to wait. After forcibly, but not violently, setting her down on the bed, he asked a second time. His friend again said, "Let's wait until after the party." At this point, hormones were raging. Andiel stepped back to cover the door, grabbed her arms, and pleaded his case. This time she was more adamant. After composing himself, Andiel did the right thing and left. The next day, he received a call from her boyfriend, accusing him of attempted rape. Needless to say, Andiel was shocked. The allegation was completely false. The only thing that he could surmise is that someone saw them together and his friend needed an excuse to preserve her relationship with her boyfriend. And, although the allegations were false and no charges were filed,

Chapter Fifty-Six: Sex Education

Andiel learned a valuable lesson: no means no! And when consent is withdrawn, all contact must cease *Immediately*! No physical, mental, or emotional coercion is appropriate at that point. Just take your ball and go home! Live to play another day.

The second story he told me occurred the following year. Andiel hosted a pajama party along with a couple of female friends. His friends were absolutely stunning, and because of the frequency of unwanted attention they received, Andiel's job was to invite athletes to the party but provide force protection as well. The plan was to check on his friends every five to ten minutes to make sure they were okay. Later that night, Andiel said there were a sea of scantily clad women, but he realized that he hadn't seen one of his friends in a while. As proscribed, he went through the house checking. Finally, he arrived outside her room and heard a man's voice inside. He opened the door and found his friend laying on her back with her pajama bottoms down at her knees. There were two men in the bed and two more by the door. She jumped up immediately and gave him a hug. The situation was clear. She was in the process of being gang raped against her will. Sometime later, Andiel asked her why she didn't fight back or yell. The answer was simple: fear and the stigma of being assaulted. She didn't want to be raped, but she was more afraid of people knowing.

Because of Andiel's personal experience and discussions with countless other men and women, he conducted a survey about the topic of sexual <u>consent</u>. He quickly realized how critical it was to establish better communication between consenting adults and developed an App called "Consentsis," which goes through the finer points of consent in a course-like format. It includes a consent quiz and a contract for the parties to sign to eliminate any misunderstanding. The simple point is this: Guys, once again, no means no! And Ladies, you have to say what you mean and mean what you say. As a former division-1 student athlete, Andiel's goal is to significantly reduce the number of Title 9 cases nationwide. I hope he succeeds.

Chapter Fifty-Seven
What Men Can Do

The conversation with Andiel also got me to thinking about how men can help generally. Sexual violence and domestic abuse are not just women's problems; they're family problems, community problems, and societal problems. They don't just impact the victim, they impact the victims' kids, job, church, foster home, public health center, non-profit organization, and governmental policy. So, if you solve the problem at one level, you begin to solve it at all levels. Violence against women happens universally but not to the same degree. This suggest to me that, at some level, violence against women is learned or accepted behavior. If so, then the behavior can be unlearned and rejected. So, to the men out there wishing to help, I have the following suggestions:

1. **Be a Good Samaritan**. Be a good role model for your sons, stepsons, brothers, cousins, and friends. Like father, like son. And birds of a feather flock together. In other words, talk the talk and walk the walk. One of the most important things you can do to influence people, especially friends and family, colleagues, parishioners, teammates, and the public at large is to practice what is preached: "Do unto others as you would have others do unto you."
2. **Apply the Desmond Doss Rule – leave no woman behind!** Don't turn away the woman in need, be she a stranger in the park or the neighbor's wife next door.

Don't let evil persist in the dark. Don't be the man who sees no evil and hears no evil. Be on the right side of history and on the right side of right. Choose the path less traveled. Help the sister-in-law in need; the daughter-in-law; the colleague at work; or the clerk in the grocery store. I can't tell you what to do, but when abuse rears its ugly head, I'm suggesting you do something. Don't let "it's not my business" be your default response.

3. **Man Up!** We all fall short sometimes. None of us are perfect. But if this is your problem, do something about it. Fix it! Be accountable! Take responsibility for your actions and get help. Stop blaming other people for your mistakes. Stop making excuses! Stop gaslighting your partner and lying! In any aspect of life, you can either make progress or make excuses, but you can't do both. Remember: God helps those who help themselves. So, if you need help, get it!

4. **Get in the Game**! Take off your warmup suit and get on the court and start playing. Get in the fight. There are plenty of organizations dedicated to fighting sexual assault and domestic violence. Find one and help out. Help spread awareness. Help pass legislation. Help prosecute offenders! Help protect women's rights. As a corollary, if you're a business or military leader or a team owner, don't permit an environment of sexual harassment to take hold. As a second corollary, don't vote for candidates who have a record of sexual violence or domestic abuse. This applies to whether the candidate is democrat, republican, jew, or gentile. Just don't do it. Don't legitimize abuse.

5. **Support the Golden Rule**! Money talks and all else walks. If you can't join them, fund them. Financially support

Chapter Fifty-Seven: What Men Can Do

those organizations already in the fight. Freedom is not free, and neither is empowerment. Invest in women and women's organizations and watch your community grow.

Chapter Fifty-Eight
Uncle Sam Wants You!

One evening, I was expressing my concerns to a friend about the epidemic of sexual assault in the United States Military. The continual stories of rape, sexual coercion, and sexual harassment of female soldiers was weighing heavily on me. There were also stories of men being raped and hazed in their barracks. Ultimately, I was disgusted by both. How can these women and men, soldiers, America's finest, be mistreated and abused by members of the world's greatest military? They enlisted to serve and protect our country, yet so many were just trying to survive the torment of abuse at the hands of their own officers. I'm sure it happens everywhere, but to me it was appalling, especially the story of twenty-year-old Army soldier Vanessa Guillen, who was murdered on April 22nd, 2020. This story kept me awake at night. She was bludgeoned with a hammer and dismembered by another soldier at Fort Hood in Texas. Her murder haunted me for more than a year.

Specialist Guillen was reported missing after last being seen in a parking lot at Fort Hood. Later, her body was found on June 30th, 2020 by some contractors when they discovered partial human remains along the Leon River. The area had previously been searched by Texas Rangers, police detectives, and cadaver dogs on June 20th after a burn mound was discovered nearby. Investigators believe that her body was buried under concrete and dug up by animals. A few days before, an Army specialist was charged, and he shot himself in the head. Later, the suspect's girlfriend was also arrested for allegedly helping to dismember and dispose of Guillén's body.

This was a horrific crime! And the sadness I felt for this young woman and her family only deepened when I discovered that she had also been a victim of sexual harassment from a different soldier at Fort Hood. Her killer had also been accused of sexual harassment in another unrelated case, but because of a breakdown in communication between his unit and investigative team, he was able to escape charges. Vanessa's family called for an investigation into the culture at Fort Hood after a series of deaths, violent crimes, complaints of sexual harassment, and a suicide occurred on the base.

In December of that year, the Army disciplined fourteen commanders and other leaders at Fort Hood, citing multiple "leadership failures." The investigation found that there was a "permissive environment for sexual assault and sexual harassment at the base." Among those disciplined included a Major General, a Colonel, and a Command Sergeant Major. Afterward, I watched a series of documentaries where, one by one, our beloved soldiers spoke out about the ugly truths of their abuse while in the military. The fear and humiliation of being raped or assaulted, then having to report the assault to the very person who raped them, was frickin' unbelievable. These soldiers, male and female, would try everything possible to escalate their reports up the chain of command, only to suffer significant personal repercussions. No wonder a number left the military or committed suicide. It was gut wrenching.

I was pleased to discover that Defense Secretary Lloyd Austin is supportive of an independent civilian panel's recommendation that prosecution of sexual assaults and sexual harassment cases be removed from the military chain of command. The US Military

Chapter Fifty-Eight: Uncle Sam Wants You!

will now use independent prosecutors to handle sexual assault cases. This is a huge victory for assault victims.

We have the greatest military in the world, not because of our weapons but because of our people. When our soldiers sign up to protect the country, they don't forego their rights as human beings.

The change in policy is exciting, and our military leadership has to get this right. Secretary Austin appears to be headed in the right direction, but political momentum tends to shift over time. We must ensure that our military men and women feel protected from this type of conduct in the future.

In 2017, I was still working as a flight attendant. Although I lived in Eugene Oregon, I was based out of San Diego California. This meant I had to start my day around five a.m., fly from Eugene to San Francisco, and from San Francisco to San Diego. My work duty day generally started around two p.m., so when things worked well, I had plenty of time to get to San Diego and relax. The return trip was the killer. Once we landed back in San Diego, I had to get my hustle on to make the departing flight to San Francisco. Sometimes that meant I had to take my shoes off and skate through the terminal like Walter Payton. I repeated this ritual every week for a little over a year. And believe it or not, I was not alone. It's not unusual for pilots or flight attendants to live in one city or state and fly out of another. It's a testament to the reliability of air travel in this country and the flexibility afforded to airline employees.

One morning, I was lying in bed after a long four-day trip. I turned on the television to relax and escape the hustle and bustle of the week. The first thing I saw was a series of stories about movie mogul Harvey Weinstein. Truthfully, I was so exhausted that I only halfheartedly listened. I gathered that a couple of A-List actresses had come forward regarding unwanted sexual advances, which didn't surprise me considering the prevalence of sexual harassment in Hollywood going back to the days of Shirley Temple and Judy Garland. After all, isn't that where they invented the "casting couch?"

However, as the night progressed, I began to realize just how big the story was. It was all over social media and on every news station. Feeling more rested, I decided to turn up the volume on the television and pay closer attention. I quickly learned that among the accusations, Weinstein had promised to help advance the careers of female actresses in return for sexual favors. Some of the victims alleged that Weinstein forced them to massage him and watch him naked. Really? How gross is that! The allegations were coming from dozens of women spanning almost thirty years. For those of you who don't know, these were not the acts of a benefactor but a predator. This is what happens in prisons. It's a "quid pro quo." You do me a favor and I'll protect you. It's an act of coercion and humiliation. It's what spies do to get terrorists to talk. It's a power move and one of the most psychologically stressful situations one can experience.

I began looking at my social media feeds and saw that the story had gone viral. It shocked me to see the level of vitriol and conflicting opinions. Some of it was incredibly ugly. Some people seemed to suggest that the women deserved what they got or that they brought it on themselves. Others seemed to minimize the impact of rape and sexual abuse. It started becoming all too real for me as a survivor. I began to realize just how uninformed mainstream society was about the level of sexual harassment and flat-out abuse that many women face. It sickened me that even some women were victim shaming other women. As former Secretary of State Madeline Albright once said, "There's a special place in hell for women who don't help other women."

Chapter Fifty-Eight: Uncle Sam Wants You!

One tweet that particularly caught my attention was from actress Alyssa Milano. She was going in hard with support, knowledge, and great wisdom on sexual abuse. She was standing up against Harvey Weinstein and advocating for sexual assault survivors worldwide. I learned one of the most empowering terms I had ever heard, "#MeToo." I began looking into Alyssa's hashtag, and my eyes were opened wide. This was the moment of reckoning. I was moved and inspired by the movement. I felt encouraged and empowered. I felt like I belonged. I felt like I wasn't alone. I was a survivor like millions of other women around the world. I was just like them, #MeToo!!!

Later, I read about a phenomenal woman named Tarana Burke. She was the founder of #MeToo and the *MeToo Movement*. Tarana was a women's rights activist and pioneer in the fight against this scourge. Rape and sexual harassment were not something new but something renewed. But as a result of a powerful group of Hollywood actresses coming together to demand justice and change, #MeToo now had a voice. With Tarana leading the way, women worldwide began speaking their truth and coming forward with their own traumatic stories of rape, humiliation, and abuse. In this moment, we as beautiful queens began to rise up and be heard!

Later, I continued to research #MeToo and sexual assault and found a hero: Civil Rights Attorney Gloria Allred. I read her story and discovered a powerful documentary about her journey. I was so inspired and deeply moved by her intelligence, grace, grit, strength, perseverance, commitment, and personal journey. In my opinion, Gloria is one of the unsung heroes of the women's empowerment movement. In the media, she is sometimes painted as an angry, money-grubbing attorney. She has been criticized relentlessly because she stands up for those of us who fear the media backlash and repercussions that she has had to face. Gloria is not just an attorney but an activist for women's empowerment, the LBGTQ+ community, and for the civil rights of all Americans. She is also a rape survivor. Every victim she represents is always personal at some level. It's because of women like Gloria Allred that the rest of us have some of the opportunities that we have.

If God is still handing out gifts, I for one will take a helping of Gloria's strength, passion, and intellect and apply it to my own advocacy.

By the end of 2017, over one hundred models and actresses had alleged sexual abuse by Weinstein between the late 1970's to 2017. His victims spanned the globe, from Hollywood to New York to London and elsewhere. Weinstein was eventually arrested in 2018 and charged with rape and a number of other offenses. In March 2020, he was found guilty and sentenced to twenty-three years in prison.

I would like to thank each and every attorney, advocate, activist, and supporter of the #MeToo Movement. I am deeply humbled by your strength and courage. And to all the victims and survivors of sexual abuse, I'm here for you, I understand you, and I love you! #MeToo!

Chapter Fifty-Nine
I've Got Your Back

Conforming to myths or popular opinion has never been my forte. I learned early on that you can't believe everything you hear or read, especially on social media. "Do unto others as you would have them do unto you" is the universal truth that we all seek, one without limitations or restraints. Strong-minded individuals are continually learning so they can think for themselves. With freedom comes responsibility. Being your authentic self also entails respect for others to do likewise. Today, there is all the knowledge in the world at our fingertips, but it's wisdom that we need to find. In my view, that wisdom includes a recognition for the fair and equal treatment to members of the LGBTQ+ community. Many people may not realize it, but there is an epidemic of hate, abuse, and violence against this community. Action and empathy must replace violence and discrimination. We must jealously guard the mental health and physical wellbeing of all of our citizens, including those in the LGBTQ+ community. This hit home for me on my fiftieth birthday.

It was April 20th, 2021, and I just turned the big fifty! My cell phone announced the coming-of-age moment with my roaring ringtone "Meant to Be" by TLC. To no surprise, the first call of the day was from Erica Winger. She was right on time to wish me a happy birthday! The call was special enough, but then Erica informed me that she and some of our home girls were taking me to Vegas, baby!

Ten days later, we boarded a flight for a little fun, relaxation, and, yes, shopping! Everyone knows that what happens in Vegas should stay in Vegas, but on this particular trip, we were posting everything to our social media accounts.

We were having an absolute blast!

Erica had everything planned out, but the one special request I had was to visit my favorite store on the strip: VERSACE! In true sisterhood fashion, my girls made sure that my birthday request was fulfilled. After a day of eating, drinking, socializing, and laying poolside under the cabana at the Flamingo, we all got ready and strutted across the street to Caesars Palace. I walked faster and faster the closer we got, like a kid nearing a candy store.

Along the way, I started telling the girls my VERSACE story. As a teenager, I had more than a slight obsession with the VERSACE brand. The clothing and accessories were too expensive for my family to purchase, but it didn't cost much to look in the fashion magazines and dream. The first time I saw a Gianni Versace dress in *Cosmopolitan* magazine, I promised myself that I would fly to Milan one day and see this birthplace of genius. That hasn't happened… yet! But irony is a funny thing; you never know when it will cross your path. There was a male cheerleader on one of our cheerleading squads at the University of Oregon in the mid-1990s.

Turns out, the cheerleader was casually dating a handsome young man from California and invited him to one of our games. Like all friends of the squad, we welcomed this young man and treated him like one of "the crew." Several years later, we discovered that the young man was Andrew Cunanan, the same person who murdered Gianni Versace in 1997. He shot him in the back of the head at point-blank range. Versace was only fifty years old. This resonated with me deeply. I had just turned fifty. I couldn't imagine being cut down at that point in my life given my desire for further accomplishment.

Chapter Fifty-Nine: I've Got Your Back

Cunanan had been obsessed with Versace and claimed they had a personal relationship. Cunanan died eight days later from a gunshot suicide. This felt a little too close to home. I loved VERSACE and cheerleading… one of our cheerleaders brought a friend to a game… that friend later murdered my fashion icon. The term two degrees of separation came to mind. The girls were all shocked, but the mood lightened considerably the moment we entered the VERSACE store and saw all of the beautiful designs.

Throughout my life, I have always loved people from every walk of life and have been fascinated by differences in cultures, lifestyles, and thought processes. Fortunately, being involved with cheerleading and aviation has afforded me the privilege of working closely with many members in LGBTQ+ community. I have known dozens of flight attendants who have either transitioned themselves or have spouses or partners who have. And as I absorbed the lessons of my own struggles with abuse, I learned to become more empathetic of others, especially given the magnitude of violence and hate impacting the LGBTQ+ community. Now, I'm an ally, and I can say that reaching out makes a world of difference. Just as listening is frequently better than speaking, empathy is frequently better than judgement. Being an advocate against sexual violence and domestic abuse requires me to also stand up for the rights of the LGBTQ+ community as well. The Red Flags and The Unvirtuous Cycle were developed for them, too. Simply put, I'm passionate about making a difference in doing what's right.

Chapter Sixty

Romeo and Juliet

On September 21, 2021, I was finishing my workout in the gym. It was six-thirty a.m., and I was on the tail end of my cardio regiment, doing a high interval incline on the treadmill, having to motivate myself to get through the last fifteen minutes. I needed a distraction, so I looked up at two of the televisions that were playing side by side. The one on the right was showing local news. They were reporting about the search for a sexual assault suspect in the Eugene area. My eyes became glued to the pictures and video coming across the screen. As usual, I could feel my skin heating up anytime I was reminded of sex crimes. I glanced at the TV on the left, and there was a report of an autopsy of the missing girl, believed to be Gabby Petito. There was a full man hunt for this beautiful young lady's fiancé, Brain Laundrie', who allegedly abused her repeatedly.

Gabby was only twenty-two years old, close to my daughter's age. I kept a close eye on this case, as did most of America. Social media was trending for weeks with an outpouring of support from millions of Americans trying to help find this missing girl. Gabby was found in Wyoming on September 19, 2021. Law enforcement agencies said they were able to find her as a result of the ongoing focus of TikTok and Instagram users. The coroner's report listed the cause of death as manual strangulation. Since then, Gabby's parents have filed a lawsuit that also lists blunt force trauma to the head as another cause. The recovery of Gabby's body set off another search for her boyfriend, Brian Laundrie. Prior to the discovery of Gabby's body, like a modern-day Romeo and Juliet, Brain had professed his undying love for Gabby.

But in October 2021, investigators found the remains of his body and personal items, including a backpack and notebook in the Carlton Reserve in Florida. The medical examiner said Laundrie's death was caused by suicide from a gunshot wound to the head, and in January 2022, the FBI found written statements by Laundrie claiming responsibility for Gabby's death.

The more I learned about Gabby's case, the more I realized how critical it was to speak out about domestic violence.

That morning, witnessing the two stories being reported side by side on local and national news stations, I made the decision to no longer stay quiet. Sexual assault and domestic violence stories were becoming all too commonplace. I was compelled to speak out. I felt a strong responsibility to raise awareness about the importance of personal safety and abuse prevention. A huge motivating factor for me in writing this book was to do exactly that. It was long overdue for me to tell my story and position myself to be part of the change.

King Solomon said, "There is a time for everything and a season for every activity under the heavens." (Ecclesiastes 3:1).

I feel that THIS IS MY TIME TO SPEAK!

For some reason, Gabby's murder took me back to another era, to a murder that hit close to home many years earlier in Springfield Oregon, which is about five minutes from Eugene where I grew up. In 1998, Kipland Kinkel shot his father in the back of the head at the kitchen table, then waited for his mother to come home from work. He met her in the garage, told her he loved her, then shot her twice in the back of the head, three times in the face, and once in the heart. The next day, Kip proceeded to Thurston High School, where he was a student and his father taught Spanish, and

Chapter Sixty: Romeo and Juliet

unloaded fifty rounds into the school, killing two students and wounding many others.

The tragedy was devastating to our community. And the sickening reality for me and my family was that Kip's sister Kristen was one of our most talented and beloved cheerleaders. Kristen was a brilliant young woman and an elite stunter. She had an unwavering faith in Christ and was an example to everyone who knew her. Kristen's parents, Bill and Faith, were at virtually every home game to watch her cheer. They helped put up the cheerleading tailgate tent, provided food and beverages and support like the other parents. Bill and Faith were devoted, loving parents and fun to be around. Kip attended many of the tailgater parties and games as well. I remember him as being a very nice boy. I never suspected that he had such severe mental and emotional issues.

Our hearts were absolutely heartbroken for the Kinkel family. Kristin was in Honolulu practicing with the nationally ranked Hawaii Pacific cheerleading squad at the time. I was told by a close mutual friend and squad member that she found out about her parents' death on the news. I briefly spoke with Kristin weeks after her parents' funeral. It was no surprise that she was visiting her brother on a regular basis. That was exactly the type of human being she was. Kristin loved her brother unconditionally, despite the heinous nature of the crime.

Kip Kinkel is serving out his life sentence of one hundred and eleven years at an Oregon correctional institution.

As I have become more knowledgeable about abuse, I have come to realize that much of the violence perpetrated against women is by people with insufficient mental health care.

As a society, we have to do a better job of addressing the mental health care needs of our citizens, especially our youth.

Chapter Sixty-One
Finding My Purpose

I continued coaching the University of Oregon cheerleaders twelve more years after my divorce from Devin. I developed new passions and ambitions, and my life was enriched and nourished by new relationships and new momentous experiences. I've traveled the world teaching choreography and experiencing other cultures. I've become a public figure, an advocate, and an influencer. My experience in both radio and television led me to hosting a podcast, and now I'm advocating globally with my story. Where I was once lost, now I am whole. Where I once was blind, now I see.

It took me thirty years after my sexual assault and twenty-three years after my divorce to find revelation. I discovered what I had been missing for over two decades. I wasn't created to be a victim, I was built to be a survivor, an overcomer. I finally found my voice and took back my power. I realized that my testimony was valuable, it is my "raison d'être," reason for being. I discovered that finding my power meant overcoming my vulnerability. Understanding what I had been through meant owning it and turning it into progress, purpose, and power. Like half-time at a football game, life is about adjusting and acknowledging mistakes, determining what you need to do to be better.

For me, that meant that I needed to speak out about what I endured and the lessons that I've learned. Sometimes you have to go back to the source of the pain in order to find your strength. Sometimes you have to reflect on what went wrong in order to do what is right. We can't always choose what happens to us, but we always have the power to choose to try to overcome it.

I began writing my memoir to tell victims of abuse that they were not alone; that they don't have to suffer in silence. I learned that being powerful is more about how many people you help than about how much money you have. Being powerful means knowing how to stand in the truth of who you are. It means knowing how to love yourself and how to protect yourself.

No one has the right to infringe on that power; it's not to be compromised, batted away, or beaten into submission. My truth is that I'm a victim turned survivor, and I walk in that power. I'm determined to try to help others to do the same. The epidemic of sexual violence and domestic abuse has to be stopped. We must come together to raise awareness. We must educate, encourage, and empower women around the world. I've developed a few thoughts in this regard; I call it the CL Way. But, before we get there, let me leave you with one last story…

One day, I was sitting in the living room watching television with my dad as he was scrolling through the channels. He stumbled upon a movie and yelled out, "*Hacksaw Ridge*! Have you seen it?" I thought for a second, then told him no. He sat up and said, "Ahhh, you have to see this!" I could tell by the excitement in his voice it was a rhetorical statement.

Hacksaw Ridge was released in 2016, and the Oscar-winning film tells the real-life story of Private First-Class Desmond Doss. Doss served as a combat medic in World War II; he was awarded the Bronze Star on two separate occasions for his actions in the Philippines and in Guam and was a three-time recipient of the Purple Heart. But the movie covers his incredible heroics in the Battle of Okinawa, for which he won the Medal of Honor.

Chapter Sixty-One: Finding My Purpose

The battle took place in April 1945 on top of a sheer cliff four hundred feet high. The location was nicknamed *Hacksaw Ridge*. The soldiers were asked to secure the location because of its strategic nature, but the mission was thought to be nearly impossible. When Doss's battalion was ordered to retreat, he refused to leave his fallen comrades behind. Facing heavy machine gun, mortar, and artillery fire, Doss repeatedly ran into the kill zone and carried wounded soldiers to the edge of the cliff, then singlehandedly lowered them to safety. Each time he saved a man, Doss prayed out loud, "Lord, please help me get one more." By the end of the night, Doss had rescued seventy-five men.

I have always loved war movies. I binge watched the 2001 HBO series *Band of Brothers* produced by Tom Hanks and Steven Spielberg, and until I saw *Hacksaw Ridge*, the clear front runner was *Saving Private Ryan*. But in *Hacksaw Ridge*, scene after scene, I found myself engrossed in the story of Private Doss. I began to find myself identifying with his heart. Private Doss was a man of great conviction. He enlisted in the Army not to defend his country but to save lives. That was his sole purpose in life. Doss' mission was rooted in faith. As a result, he refused to shoot or even hold a gun. This was infuriating to his fellow infantrymen. They saw him as weak and powerless, possibly a traitor. Doss was considered a pariah. He was beaten and berated and found himself in military confinement awaiting court martial. It was only after his father, a veteran corporal of the United States Army, petitioned the military court that Doss was released back to Company B and allowed to serve as a medic and conscientious objector.

In the Battle of Okinawa, Private Doss endured the pressure and fear of gunfire and remained steadfast, fighting for every living soldier he could find. Throughout the night, Doss searched for the very soldiers who loathed him, who had beaten him. One by one, he lowered soldiers down the four hundred-foot cliff. Before searching for and securing the next soldier, Doss would pray, "Lord, help me get one more." He repeated this plea seventy-five times, and seventy-five times he searched and secured and saved a man's life, even lowering three injured Japanese soldiers to safety.

By the following morning, the miracle was revealed for the entire battalion to see. The man they hated and despised was the very same man responsible for their safety. Private Doss was now their hero. He earned the respect that he greatly deserved. More importantly, Private Doss' character was intact, and his mission was complete.

His story resonated with me deeply. It's one of the reasons I wrote this book. I figured if Desmond Doss could single handedly save seventy-five lives in a combat zone, I could fight to save the lives of one victim at a time. "Lord, help me get one more."

Chapter Sixty-Two
The CL Way

Enduring years of mental, physical, and emotional abuse wasn't easy, but it serves as a personal testament to my faith. I was brought down so low that I could see Antarctica. But I never lost hope. My family and friends wouldn't let me. They carried me when I couldn't walk, they believed in me when I didn't believe in myself. They kept me looking forward when I was mired in the past. As a result, I made it. I ran the gauntlet and finished that horrible part of the race. Now, I'm running a new race; a race to help educate, inspire, encourage, and transform other women who may still be running the gauntlet.

As I said before, I'm not a psychiatrist. I don't have a PhD. I'm just a mom who cares; a mom who has learned a few things and is now guided by a set of principles that I call "the CL Way."

1. **SMILE, *Chin Up*!** This is not a slogan for me but a way of life. It means fortifying myself; being encouraged; knowing that I am worthy, valued, and loved. It represents grit, determination, resiliency, and a fierce resolve. Holding your head high means believing in yourself. The best defense against abuse is to love yourself, to feel good about yourself, and to invest in yourself. Smiling is not an expression of agreement but of encouragement. It is not a sign of weakness but a sign of inner strength, courage, and self-determination. Smiling is not for the crowd; smiling is for you. It's a window into your soul. Psychologists have proven that

smiling promotes self-confidence, a positive mood, creativity, and problem solving. It's a tool given to us all. Use it!

2. **Acknowledge your fears and power up**! Courage is not the absence of fear, courage is acting in spite of your fears. Fear is the body's way of telling the mind to act… change… adapt… grow. Use the impulse of your body to drive <u>positive</u> changes in yourself, your relationships, and your environment in order to step into your power.

3. **Don't separate from your tribe**! Your tribe is your support system: it's your family, your friends, and your faith. It's a ballast against anger, resentment, violence, and disparagement. In times of distress, cleave to your tribe. Don't let yourself be separated from the ones who love you the most, from the values you hold true, and from the things that you know are right. Hyenas seek to separate their prey from the herd. Hateful and insecure people operate in the same manner. Don't be complicit in your own demise!

4. **Spotters up**! A spotter's sole job is the safety and protection of the stunting cheerleader. If the pyramid fails, the spotter is there to catch her fall. In addition to family and friends, spotters come in many forms: hotlines, churches, ministers, marriage and psychological counselors, support groups, police, and more. Utilize life's spotters, they're there to catch your fall and power you to greater heights.

5. **Steal away for a rainy day**! During the harvest, squirrels gather more acorns than needed and put some away for a later season. They know that there may be difficult days ahead. This is a great lesson for anyone who aspires

Chapter Sixty-Two: The CL Way

toward more or finds themselves in a season of uncertainty.

6. **Follow the Aguilera rule**! There are two types of beauty: external and internal. Sometimes God gives us both, but he gives every woman the later. "You are beautiful no matter what they say!" Believe it, and it will be so. Don't let there be any shame in your game. Don't live in guilt! Don't live a lie! And don't live with regret! Life is precious, seize it!

7. **Use the calm before the storm**! If you're sleeping with the enemy, a period of reflection can lead to rejuvenation. It can be a time to renew your strength and build momentum. Get your ducks in a row, and use the time to learn how to swim. Then, if at some point you find yourself in the "Perfect Storm," get out!

8. **Don't be a deer in headlights**! Denial is a form of disinformation, a way of gaslighting yourself. Fast moving cars are a sign of danger. You have to move left or right. Doing nothing could be fatal. It is said that "the definition of insanity is to do the same thing over and over expecting a different result." If this is you, as it was me, you have to change things up! You have to make a move! Do something different! Transform your situation and circumstances!

9. **No targeting**! In football, targeting occurs when one player uses the crown of their helmet to spear another player. The action is considered so heinous that even one infraction gets a player kicked out of the game and fined. And if targeting occurs too often, the player risk suspension or being get kicked out of the league. That should be the rule for relationships. Domestic violence is so heinous, it should never be committed or excused.

Boundaries must be drawn. The player must be held accountable—to their partner, to their kids, to the ones who love you. And recurring domestic violence, like targeting, should receive the harshest penalty.

10. **<u>Overcome and become</u>**! Envision what you can become and commit yourself to the necessary work. If you can see it, you can be it. Whether it's having more education, a new job, a new business, a new look, a new relationship, or a new attitude. The first step is the hardest step. So, step up and step lively into the best version of you.

Chapter Sixty-Three
Audrie and Daisy

I mentioned Rodney Stearns and the SOBRDRIVE App earlier. Rodney is also the founder of a company called "Driven by Safety," which is dedicated to providing mobile applications for shared community safety. In June 2021, Rodney was working with the court system in Los Angeles to provide an alcohol monitoring service called "Check Back" for people who had received a DUI. Until recently, blood alcohol content (BAC) data was only available to law enforcement and the courts. But commercial breathalyzer products have made it possible for individuals to test their own BAC levels, which allows people to make better decisions regarding driving and other shared activities.

Rodney contacted me because he was extremely interested in getting his safety App into the hands of millions of high school and college students nationwide. He explained that one in four women are sexually assaulted in college and that alcohol is the most widely used date-rape drug.

The correlation between sexual assault and alcohol resonated with me deeply, especially since I was raped in college and the perpetrator was drunk.

As I dug deeper into the issue of teenage sexual assault, one particular story caught my attention. It was the story of Daisy Coleman, who was the subject of a Netflix documentary called *Audrie & Daisy*.

The story depicts the life of two teenage girls who pass out while intoxicated at high school parties. While unconscious, they were both sexually assaulted by boys who they thought were friends. Throughout the documentary, the girls undergo extreme victim shaming, harassment, and bullying from their peers and even from adults. Unfortunately, the harassment and cyber bullying becomes too much for one of the girls, Audrie, and she commits suicide. Afterward, Daisy begins an advocacy program against sexual assault. She built a network for other teenager rape victims who were struggling to cope. Daisy's peer-to-peer organization was called *SafeBAE* (Safe Before Anyone Else).

Daisy and her brother Charlie advocated together for sexual assault survivors nationwide. The Huffington Post named Daisy one of the "Thirteen Most Fearless Teens of 2013." So, it was a heart wrenching moment for me when I read that Daisy had also committed suicide on August 4th, 2020. She was just twenty-three years old. The wounds ran so deep for her mother Melinda that she also took her life four months later. Melinda was only fifty-eight. Both died of self-inflicted gunshot wounds.

I wish that stories like these were rare. I wish that it was uncommon to hear about rape and cyber bullying amongst young adults. Unfortunately, the reality is that hate and cruelty are ever-present. Why? What is the common denominator between social media and hate crimes? How has "The Gram" become such a perfect platform for social injustice and vicious abuse? Why does this generation or any other think it is okay to publicly drag a human being through the mud? I get that life is much harder for young adults today than when I grew up. One mistake can become magnified a thousand times or go viral in an instant and live forever. But as part of my advocacy, I want to both challenge and inspire young adults to better themselves and hold their peers accountable. I want to create an open dialogue about body shaming and sexual assault prevention. I'm here to help, and I invite you to take a look at my modified principles of empowerment. They are tailored specifically for you.

Chapter Sixty-Three: Audrie and Daisy

1. **SMILE, *Chin Up*!** This means holding your head high, believing in yourself, and maintaining your grit, determination, resiliency, and fierce resolve both in the real world and online. The best defense against abuse is to love yourself, to believe in yourself, to invest in yourself, and to protect your posse in public spaces.
2. **Power up**! This means to make the necessary changes in your relationships and social media to empower your <u>future</u>. Social media is real but not tangible. Don't let what you do today limit your options in the future. Don't let social media destroy you, deter you, diminish you, or distract you. Stay on the path! Whatever happens online shall pass.
3. **Spotters Up!** Friends don't let friends get raped. If you're going out to party hearty, have a designated spotter! Someone who is not going to let the wolves have their way. This is not a downer or the opposite of fun; it's the opposite of being victimized. It's a means of empowerment and protection, a way of staying safe physically, emotionally, and socially. Running with the crowd shouldn't entail endangering yourself. Remember, it is better to be a live dog than a dead lion.
4. **You are beautiful!** I have coached hundreds if not thousands of young girls over the years, and never have I seen an ugly duckling. You are all beautiful in your own design. No adjustments or further assembly is required. A Chinese philosopher once said, "Once you master yourself, mastering others is easy." I say, "Once you <u>like</u> yourself, that's all the <u>likes</u> you really need."
5. **Overcome and become!** You have your whole life ahead of you. Envision what you can become and let that be your north star. You can live in the moment, but be

guided by your future. Social media is the tail that wags the dog. Be the dog! Have a one-year plan and a five-year plan and make your decisions accordingly.

Chapter Sixty-Four
Roll the Credits

I believe some people come into your life for a season to encourage you, to help you get over a hump, or to teach you some valuable lesson. Others come into your life for a far greater purpose. They touch your inner core and, for better or worse, they make and reshape you. They are tethered to your spirit and create unbreakable or unforgettable bonds. I have been blessed to have had so many fascinating experiences, alongside some dark days. It is absolutely certain that I would not be the woman I am today without both. I am grateful and thankful for being a little wiser and more worldly than when my journey began.

Haley is now thirty years old. She earned her bachelor's degree in speech communications from Oregon State University, was the dance captain of the Oregon State University cheerleading squad, and was an NFL cheerleader for the San Francisco 49ers. She's currently an entrepreneur and an expert in the dance and fitness industry and has earned her five-hundred-hour teacher certification through the prestigious Yoga Alliance. Haley has also recently obtained her yoga therapy license and has begun a new business called ZaZen Yoga. Haley puts on yoga raves that are comprised of yoga, meditation, and ecstatic dance parties (Trans & Dance around the world). Haley is married to a wonderful young man and is fabulous mother to my first grandchild.

Jaden is now twenty years old. He is just finishing his third year of honors college with a 4.0 GPA. Like my traitorous daughter, Jaden has decided to transfer to Oregon State University. This may make things a little awkward at Thanksgiving, but I'll adjust. Jaden is a stellar student with ambitions to become a neural and forensic scientist. Living in Portland has been tremendous for his personal growth. I believe that he will continue to flourish in college, albeit with the enemy, and achieve all of his personal and professional goals in the years to come.

My brother Rick is living his best life as a loving husband to his beautiful wife Joy. He is still coaching football and supporting his little sister's dreams!

My parents just celebrated their fifty-sixth wedding anniversary! They are loving retirement, traveling in their RV, and spoiling their grandkids and great grandson rotten.

My extended family is growing in abundance! All of my cousins have children and most of them are now grandparents. My cousins, aunts, and uncles have lived extremely full and fruitful lives. We all continue to be a close family unit and they continue to be a beacon of support and a great blessing.

Julie Kaanapu is still pushing me hard every morning at the gym. She continues to be my rock and fortress. Julie and TK remain happily married, thriving in their careers, and are incredible examples to their children.

Ericka Dotson is living her dream life! She is running a major department for a global brand and is married to an incredible man, who cherishes her and her daughter deeply. The three of them travel the world together, enjoying life's little splendors. We have an unbreakable bond!

Chapter Sixty-Four: Roll the Credits

Andiel Brown is going on his fourteenth year as the Director of the Gospel Choirs & Ensembles at the University of Oregon. He is actively pursuing his advocacy for human rights, particularly in the area of consent education. Andiel spends much of his time devoted to the needs of others but always makes time for his passions: training, dancing, and quality family time.

Leesa Wilder is currently a successful real estate agent, tearing up the market! She continues to push the limits in all areas of her life. While she is no longer a fitness competitor, she continues to train like one. Leesa has recently become a grandmother and the matriarch of her beautiful family.

Erica Winger has a successful business at the "Spray Tan Queen!" She is a talented aesthetician and highly respected in Lane County. We continue to see each other every week for spray on tans and "Girls Lunch!"

Shawna Peterson continues to thrive in the aviation industry. She is pushing the envelope to build her business as a personal trainer and an eventual gym owner. Shawna excels every day doing what she loves most; being a devoted mother.

Michael Westbrook remains my best friend, mentor, business partner, and confidant. He is an incredibly successful entrepreneur in Arizona. Michael is a devoted, dedicated, and disciplined family man and world traveler, pushing the limits and boundaries in every area of his life. He is continually striving to be better than the day before and is the epitome of "Just do it!"

Mark McMillian is taking entrepreneurship to new heights! He has recently launched his new brand Grillin McMillian, where he teaches BBQ grilling segments and sells his famous BBQ sauces and rubs. He continues to focus on football training camps with his brand Camp 29 and remains a co-host for ESPN Las Vegas!

Keith Lewis is the owner of a successful business called "Once Famous Grill." Once Famous is a stationary food cart located in the highly touted Beer Garden in Eugene. Keith also owns a mobile food truck "Once Famous Grill 2" that caters to statewide events. Keith is ever present in my family's life. We continue to co-parent together and maintain a wonderful friendship. And me, I am currently living my best, unapologetically happy life! Today, I spend my days smiling for all the right reasons. I am the most powerful I've ever been. I am walking into the fullest version of myself. I worked valiantly on this book and have fielded a few requests for speaking engagements. I have also been approached about working alongside a major state law enforcement agency to help bridge the gap between victims and the police. I am considering a number of advocacy platforms, including the possibility of a podcast. My goal is to help empower women generally and victims of sexual assault and domestic abuse specifically. So, stay tuned.

Epilogue

Sometimes people come into your life unexpectedly, or in unexpected ways. Erika Ramos is such a person. It has also been said that "my enemy's enemy is my friend." And while I no longer consider Devin an enemy, I definitely count Erika as a friend. We shared the same nightmare, trauma, and abuse and were victimized by the same predatory behavior by the same predator. We found one another at a difficult point in her life. It's like when you're in the gym and you are all pumped up and you get on the bench press and you've bitten off more than you can chew. These are the times when you need someone to spot you. I needed that during my time with Devin, and later, although we were once pitted against one another, I became a spotter for Erika. When I told her about the book, she wanted to help in some way. Below is her powerful story and testimony. Again, I have changed or deleted some of the names to protect the privacy of the individuals involved. Nevertheless, Erika's story is incredibly instructive and insightful in understanding the psychological and physical aspects of abuse.

EPILOGUE

The Lies That Bind:

"My name is Erika Ramos, and I am writing and sharing these memories of my time with Devin for the purpose of contributing to the memoir of Corine Lewis. I am titling this contribution, "The Lies That Bind," and it is my hope that it will provide additional insight and perspective to the lies and the man who brought Corine and I together.

The year was 2006, it was the year I turned thirty-one. One particular Saturday in June, my friends and I were out welcoming the summer. We had started our night bar hopping at the annual Summer Solstice Festival in Fremont. As the festivities wound down, my girlfriends and I made our way to the Wonder Bar in Seattle. It was a favorite place of ours and held many good memories, and on this night, our favorite band was playing. Like many bars that night, it was packed, and the line was around the block. It helped that my best friend was dating the lead singer (a future contestant on *The Voice*). It also helped that their drummer liked me enough to put me on his guest list. We didn't have to wait in line, and we didn't have to fight for a place to sit. We sang along, sipped on our favorite cocktails, and when the band took a break, we all stepped outside to take in some fresh air. My girlfriend and I said our hellos to our favorite guys in the band and told them how fantastic their show was that night. The excitement in the air was electric and full of flirty fun and laughter.

I didn't notice him. I would never have noticed him. Like any other night, I was never on the lookout for who was looking at me. A night out with my girlfriends was just that—a night out with my girlfriends. We didn't go out to clubs or bars with the goal or intent to meet men. Our goal was to always show up and show out, have a good time with one another, and look good doing so. For us, most of the fun was in getting together and enjoying our girl time. Meeting men was never the objective, because meeting men came easy; at the gym, at the grocery store, our apartment complex, or while out eating or shopping. The idea of meeting a man at a bar

EPILOGUE

was gross. It couldn't be trusted. Men in bars only had one desirable purpose, to buy us drinks and not be creeps about it.

Once the band's break was over and we returned to our table, it wasn't long before a waitress came over and approached me directly. She tried to hand me a Cosmopolitan that I hadn't ordered. She proceeded to tell me over the loud music that the man "over there" had sent it to me. I made no effort to look in his direction and declined the drink and sent her away. Not only was I at my limit but I was also in no mood to engage any man with the obligatory 'thank you for the drink" conversation.

Several minutes later, the waitress returned. This time with a bottle of water. Again, from the same man "over there." Again, I said, "no thank you" and sent her away. I was annoyed at this point. I hated when men tried to interject themself into "our" night and "our" time. My girlfriends and I were having a blast together, and I had no desire to entertain a stranger's gestures. Luckily, the night was almost over, and when the band wrapped up, we stepped outside again to take in the fresh air and continue hanging out and talking with the guys in the band.

Most of the people who had been in the bar were outside as well. Milling about, some smoking, some making plans as to where to go next. From among the crowd, a man tapped me on the shoulder and said, "My boy wants to talk to you." I barely made an effort to look and simply said "no thanks" and turned my attention back to the drummer. He was kind enough to leave me alone, and soon I forgot he was there. As we were preparing to leave, I made my way back to the entrance with the drummer. I was waiting just outside the front door, surrounded by random people, waiting for my girlfriend to return from the restroom.

It was at this time that he finally touched and addressed me directly. All I saw was the arm pulling back into the crowd, followed by, "I've been trying to get your attention all night." I was

EPILOGUE

annoyed, it was the second time a man I didn't know had touched me. Not only did I not appreciate the invasion of my personal space, but I also clearly had my attention on someone else. I ignored it, and the next thing I know he's standing close enough to reach out to hand me his business card. During all this, I didn't have a clear view of him or his face but could see that he was a Black man. I looked at the card and noticed he was in mortgage financing.... just like me. I looked up, still not clearly seeing him, and said, "You're my competition," and laughed.

I would have thrown the card away, but that was a rudeness I didn't want to engage in with a stranger, so I put the card in my back pocket. He then proceeded to yell out, "Call me, maybe we can do business together."

I laughed and said, "I'll think about it." By this time, my girlfriend and the lead singer were coming out, and we all began to leave. We had decided we would go out for a late-night bite to eat.

I didn't think about the stranger again.

To this day, I hate that the reason I picked up the phone and dialed the number on his business card was simply boredom. The one time I can think of an iPhone potentially saving my life. But back in 2006, cell phones couldn't stream. Facebook was a novelty for college students, IG didn't exist, and I didn't know Twitter existed. There was nothing to entertain me. I remember the day was sunny and I couldn't wait for the workday to be over. From my desk, I had a view of Lake Union, and I was ready to go out for happy hour. It was a Friday, and I was wearing jeans.

As a matter of fact, I was wearing the jeans I had worn when the stranger handed me his business card, which I had absentmindedly placed in my back pocket. Now, here I was with his card in my hand. I didn't want to work, and I told myself it would be a "business" call. It would be an interesting way to help pass the next few minutes and make the next hour fly by a little

EPILOGUE

faster. So, I called him. When he answered, I said, "Hello, this is Erika, your competition." The joy and excitement in his voice when he realized who was calling made me smile. I was taken aback by his happiness.

I couldn't recall a time when a man had responded with such enthusiasm. Most men kept their cool. Not him, he said over and over how happy he was that I called him. He said he didn't care if he showed how happy he was. He explained that I had made him a winner because all his friends believed that I would never call. He told me how during the drive home that all his friends clowned him and teased him about how I would never call. And here I was, calling him and making his day.

We spoke for about twenty minutes, covering the basics. Where he lived, what he did for a living. How he liked to spend his free time. What brought him to Seattle that night. He sounded like a "good guy" who would be good to keep as part of my work network. Overall, my guard was down. I had no reason to question anything he said because for me, there was no romantic interest. Not only did I not remember what he looked like, but I wasn't looking for a relationship. And at thirty-one years old, I wasn't interested in trying out a long-distance relationship.

The following week, I received a call from him at work. He asked me for my email address and if he could have my cell phone number. Harmless, I thought, so I shared my contact details, and later that day I received an E-Card from him, and every day afterward. I also received good morning texts. I didn't realize it at the time, but he was grooming me already. I came to look forward to my daily E-cards and texts. He would call me after work. He would entertain me as I drove home. He was always so happy and excited to talk to me.

Devin spoke of his lifestyle, his house, his luxury cars. The now-famous people he grew up with in Los Angeles. The famous

EPILOGUE

athletes he played with, the musicians and celebrities he knew and was "cool" with through his music label. He was a man of action. A man who didn't waste time. He was committed to his career, building a legacy, and giving back to the community. He was a man who knew what he wanted and went after it.

Devin spoke of his upbringing and how accomplished and well respected his family was back home. He spoke of his daughter and all he did to support her and be there for her despite the divorce. Devin also spoke of his impending move to Georgia. More than anything, he spoke of his desire to get to know me better and see if we could be more. He was persistent in his declaration of wanting me in his life. I was the one he had been waiting for.

Gradually, his daily commute call became a nightly call. I often had networking events or happy hours with friends, so talking to him after work wasn't really an option. At first, I would ignore his evening calls or keep the calls short, but the more he reinforced what an ambitious, hardworking man he was who knew what he wanted, I began to view him differently. His joy on the phone was contagious, and being given a happy boost after a call became a want.

Now my guard was up. All the time spent on calls and emails, I was invested, and now there was a reason for me to confirm all he had been saying. Devin _____. A quick Google search, a novelty in 2006 for me, only produced a LinkedIn profile and Sacramento Attack Arena Football "career" stats from 1992. I wasn't a big football fan, but those stats didn't suggest anything resembling a football "career." This search result, prompted by the name on his business card, would later prove to be the FIRST red flag. I didn't know it at the time, but it was one of hundreds of lies Devin would tell me about who he was and what he had done in his life. In 2006, at barely six feet tall and overweight at two hundred pounds, you would never have guessed that at one time he was a highly recruited football player, one of the few facts he told. The lie was that he was in the NFL and played for the Raiders.

When I didn't find that fact online, I chalked it up to that data not being uploaded in Google. Just like his University of Oregon stats were nowhere to be found on Google. Plus, who would lie about playing in the NFL or being a star football player at the University of Oregon? And with that thought, I gave him the benefit of the doubt... Unfortunately for me at that time, I wanted to believe him. He made me smile when we spoke, he entertained me and provided a nice contrast to what was happening in my personal life at that point in time.

I was thirty-one years old and had been living in the Seattle area for ten years and had been in two serious relationships during that time. Relationships that took prime years of my life and didn't result in marriage. I had close male friends tell me that I should settle down. That being in the clubs in my thirties wasn't "a good look." I would reflect on those comments and think about how I was getting older and so was my mom. I thought about the pain I felt in my heart that I never had the opportunity to meet my grandparents and how I would never want that for my own children. Settling down started to sound like the next logical step for me. I didn't want to live life alone anymore. I didn't want to miss the opportunity to have my mother meet my children and vice versa. I didn't want to waste my time in dead-end relationships. For the first time in my life, the thought that "my clock was ticking" entered my mind.

At that time, I was dating a very successful man. He owned a thriving sports agency and represented the most elite of athletes. He was well connected and respected. He was reserved and not at all boastful. He never name dropped or told stories of any of his clients unless I specifically asked. Even then, he didn't divulge too much or any specific details. He didn't brag about what he owned or what he could buy, but he was never shy about stating comfort was key for him. He always stayed in the penthouse of any hotel and traveled first class. We went out to dinner at the finest restaurants and were always treated as VIPs. When it came to "us," he didn't make over the top overtures or empty promises. He would tell me what made me different in his life.

He didn't date or go out, his lifestyle didn't really allow for it. He traveled extensively for his work. His clients were very demanding, and he was often problem solving. In addition, given his profession, he had experienced women trying to "set him up." He didn't invite people to his house because he valued his privacy, and his home was his only sanctuary. For him, it was a huge deal to take me to see the house he was building on Lake Washington. He made it a point to say I was the "Queen of Firsts" in his life the first time I visited his house.

He claimed to do a lot that was out of character for him when it came to me. Like inviting me to dinner with one of his clients, a well-known NBA player. He told me I helped him relax and that was important to him because his work was so demanding and stressful. In all honesty, I never felt good enough for him, and the slow and reserved way he was courting me didn't make me feel confident that we were in something real. A huge contrast to Devin, who declared his interest, desire, and intentions to build something with me. I ultimately chose flash over substance; the biggest mistake of my life.

To say that hindsight is 20/20 is an understatement! What I initially interpreted as overtures in courting, I clearly now see as grooming for control and abuse. The man who had been so excited that I had called him began Phase II of his courtship. It was time to take me from feeling like a queen on a pedestal who had deemed him worthy of my attention to lucky to have attracted him. It was time for him to show me what he could have in his life. The adoring daily E-Cards had stopped. And it was now time to send emails with the intent to gaslight and undermine.

Devin......@wellsfargo.com
"See if you can find which one is my ex... lol."

I remember feeling shocked when I received this email. Shocked that a girl who looked like this would: A) live in Eugene; and B) date Devin. I have no doubt that he anticipated my questions, and sure enough, his answers were so ready and on point. He explained that he broke up with her. Why? Because she had no ambition in life. All she cared about was working out. All she aspired to was working at the gym, where she worked out. To me that explained why she was in a bikini and in what appeared to be some type of bikini or body competition. All she did was work out and work at the gym. His message to me was: "Yes, she is beautiful and has a banging body, but she isn't like you. She isn't smart; she has no career; and she isn't ambitious."

You are a better fit for me because you're like me, someone who wants the best in life and will work hard to get it. In addition, he was so secure within himself that he didn't mind that his girlfriend was parading around in almost nothing in random bars. I thought, *Wow, I don't know too many men who would go for that. He must be really secure within himself and what he has to offer.* Plus, who would lie about that? The girlfriend, the career, bikini competitions?

Not only was this email insidious in its nature, but it was also a complete lie. This woman was not his ex-girlfriend. She never lived in Eugene. She had never met him. Unfortunately for me, I didn't come to know this until I was already living with him and pregnant with his child. Not only was everything he told me about this woman a lie, but ninety-nine percent of what he stated about his real ex-girlfriend and their relationship was a lie. He lied about when, how, and why they broke up and where she was now.

Over time, the lies around his ex-girlfriend slowly started to fall apart. I called him out every time that he told me a "story" about his ex-girlfriend during our courtship that contradicted anything he said once we were in a relationship and living together. I despise liars, and I found myself catching him in a variety of discrepancies. The new lies and now gaslighting came in forms of revisionist history. It was not him who told me about his life experiences, situations, and people on his own, it was I who had prodded.

It was my prodding that resulted in him telling "half-truths" because I couldn't handle the real truth. By asking for clarification, that opened the door to more lies, or to an argument that would lead to him saying "I didn't tell you the truth because I knew you were insecure" and promptly storming out of the house. It became a signature move. Argument, call me insecure, followed by storming out of the house without saying where he was going.

Devin always has a story to tell. I would come to learn he has a set of stories to win people over. He tells them the same way, with the pauses and inflections in the same place. EVERY... SINGLE... TIME! For Devin, storytelling or sharing is an act of intention to always elicit empathy, understanding, and a sense of connection. A way to have people drop their guard and not pay close attention to the details.

The story of his marriage and who his ex-wife is would prove to be a masterpiece of a lie. It was a lie to groom and manipulate me into: A) disliking her so that I would never want a relationship with her; B) reacting in a way to prove that I was nothing like her; and C) undermining my own sense of self, self-esteem, and confidence.

Epilogue

Much like the, "See if you can find which one is my ex" email, he began his grooming by first putting his ex-wife, Corine, on a pedestal. He shared a couple of pictures. She was on stage, wearing a long shimmering dress and a huge crown on her head. In the next picture, there he was, in a suit standing by her side. She was a beauty pageant queen and Oregon royalty. Her family was well to do. She had been a star cheerleader for the Portland Trailblazers.

It was only when I asked why they divorced that he began to chip away at the pedestal he constructed. He said she hadn't been loyal and attributed it to her being like most White women. Easy and always looking to ride a Black star athlete's coattail. And that was who he was when he met her, a star athlete with a promising future in the NFL. He added that the only reason he married her was because she trapped him with a pregnancy and her family had demanded it.

He had been raised in the church, and his family name meant something to him. He told me he wanted to do the right thing for his child, and so he married her. At the time, again, I thought, *Why would he lie about that?* What man wants to admit they were cheated on? And he stayed because of his love and concern for his daughter. He was married to a woman who lacked integrity. A woman who only cared about her own happiness. A woman who was so superficial that she would enter beauty pageants that would take time away from her husband and child. She couldn't be trusted to raise their daughter. He feared that if he divorced her and pursued the life he really wanted, she would raise their daughter to be like her. There was no one he loved more than his daughter Haley, and so he "sacrificed" his own happiness to make sure she had a chance in life. Who lies about that?

This short first conversation about his ex-wife would later be expanded upon with much more detail. I would be subjected to hours of stories about Corine's infidelities. I came to really dislike her. Over time, I began to have a nagging thought take hold in my head. What kind of man puts up with that? It was a no-win question for me. It was either her hold on him was so complete and he still loved her, or he was the weakest and most spineless man I had ever met. Staying only for Haley could not explain the complete and utter disrespect that this woman had shown toward her marriage and family. I could not believe that any man worth his salt would tolerate what he claims to have tolerated.

According to Devin, Corine had cheated on him on a regular basis and with just about every man around. When his career in the NFL didn't pan out, she began sleeping with professional athletes. He told me about her sleeping with half the Portland Trailblazers and specifically called out Clay _____. He told a story of Clay and half the team driving up to his house in a convoy of Range Rovers all over some drama with Corine. She had been fired from the cheer team because she couldn't stop herself from sleeping with the players and they were fighting in the locker room over her. She had slept with his boss and several of his coworkers, his friends, guys from the gym.

To hear him tell it, she couldn't keep her legs closed to anyone. Devin spoke of how he hated her. He blamed her for his failure to have a successful career in the NFL. He would have gone so much further in his career and life if he had a loyal woman by his side. Corine had ruined his prospects at becoming a police officer. When he finally decided to divorce her, it was because he came to believe that she would set him up. He noticed she had been going to the gym a lot more than usual. She was going early and sometimes in the evening and staying later than usual.

He began to suspect she might be cheating again and using the gym as an excuse. Of course, he was right, and he caught her by showing up at the gym and seeing her work out with the man he claimed she would later marry. When he confronted her and

EPILOGUE

told her he wanted a divorce, she attacked him. In defending himself he pushed her down. She called the police and claimed he had attacked her. That was the last straw for him. She was willing to have him thrown in jail to protect her image of Oregon royalty, of her respectability, and that of her family, willing to lie.

Devin told me the story of his day in court. How he had feared Corine may win because of what had happened in the OJ Simpson trial. Corine and her family were out to portray him as a dangerous Black man, and she was a distressed White woman. Devin claims to have spectacularly defended himself by tripping her up and her lying family in court. He proved her dad had not witnessed the "assault" as he claimed. He said the judge threw out the domestic violence charge, but they didn't stop there. During the proceedings, they tried to have Haley lie in court, but it didn't work. Haley stood up for him; she told the court that "Daddy never hit Mommy" and that she wanted to be with him and not her. He couldn't trust her. After the divorce, during visitations, he always had someone with him and Haley because Corine couldn't be trusted.

And then there were the post-divorce stories. According to Devin, Corine ended up marrying the man she had cheated with at the gym. A man who seemed to want everything he wanted, and she helped bring to life all of his dreams. She helped him become a police officer, like he had wanted to be. They bought a house that was exactly as he had described his dream house. A house with a rounded driveway, blah blah blah… I came to loathe Corine based on the stories Devin told about her. They made me angry. I believed she had ruined a "good man." I believed she had hampered his dreams.

I see now that he intended to hammer those stories into my psyche for a very specific reason. There would come a time in which I would have to "prove" that I was not like Corine. I would have to prove through my actions, not just my words, that I could be trusted. Joint bank account and control of the household finances, check. That I wasn't a cheater. Passwords to my Facebook, my email, and access to my cell phone, check. That I wasn't insecure because his exes had been beautiful women and because he wasn't a cheater. Allow him to go hang out with his friends all night without doubting, check. I wasn't like Corine.

The first time I met her was the same day I met Devin's daughter Haley. It was on one of my trips to Eugene. But before I even met Corine, based on all the lies Devin told me about her, I felt like I understood exactly what type of woman I would be meeting. That day, Haley had spent the afternoon with us. Haley was and continues to be a lovely, friendly, and intelligent young woman. Their relationship came across as loving and fun. Devin had a nickname for Haley that became something of an inside joke because she was no longer "short." We made the best of it.

In Eugene, there isn't much to do. But looking back, I see that Devin never took his "mask" off in the courtship phase. And like the true sociopath that he is, Devin took this opportunity to make comments in front of Haley about her mother, the divorce, and the "trumped up" domestic violence and court hearings. I believe he did this as a tactic that was meant for me to interpret as a "confirmation" of his story. Confirmation provided by his own daughter of all that had transpired.

At the time he made the comments, we were in the car and Haley was sitting behind me, so I didn't see the expression on her face or her body language. I recall Haley not confirming or denying anything her father said, she simply said nothing. I do clearly recall thinking how horrible this must be for her. To have to listen to her father make derogatory comments about her mother to the new woman in his life. Regardless of whether the comments were true or not, Haley was between a rock and a hard place. Either confirming her mother or calling her father a liar would be less than noble. It is a feeling that I never vocalized to Devin because I wasn't a parent at that time, and although it felt wrong to me, I didn't believe I had enough context or history to comment. For all I knew, this was "normal" for them based on everything he had told me about his relationship with Corine.

As that day came to an end, we dropped Haley off at her mother and stepfather's house. It was dark, and our interaction with Corine was quick and cordial. A quick introduction just outside her door. Corine was friendly and seemed approachable. Nothing like the attention seeking or "thirsty" type that he painted her out to be. I remember walking back to the car bewildered by Devin's demeanor. After all that he claimed to have experienced with Corine, his words, body language, and general attitude toward her didn't add up. Especially after the comments he had just made about her earlier that day in front of Haley.

It would be a thought and feeling of "something is off" that I would push aside, as I had done with other "off" stories and interactions. I wouldn't voice my opinions about the oddness of his interactions with her until I was too deep in my own situation with Devin to easily get out. The much too late conversation would happen only after Corine and Haley came to visit when we were living in Georgia. It would be a cry for help to Devin's mother that would finally put words to the many feelings I had pushed aside.

On Tuesday, February 5, 2008, 9:57 AM, Erika_____ <_____@yahoo.com> wrote:
Hi, Mom,
I'm emailing you because Devin can't seem to keep his anger in check enough to not get violent with me. He got violent last night, and it happened in a way that could have hurt Kaitlyn as well. I tried to call the police, but he

Epilogue

stopped me and threatened to kill me on top of that if I did. I don't know what I can do to make things better? His mindset is that I don't have the right to speak my mind or say anything that he doesn't agree with or that upsets him. And because of that, I deserved him hitting me because I provoked him.

He is refusing to take responsibility for his choice to become violent when we don't agree or have an argument. I have asked him to talk to someone and he agreed to but has failed to do so. He refuses to consider that he is still angry, bitter, and full of resentment about what happened with his ex-wife. He says it's all me, it's all my fault, and that leaves me having to pay the price of his anger for being cheated on and his anger for being accused of something he claims to be innocent of.

I have found emails he sends to other women on the internet on several occasions, and when I ask what they are all about, he turns it into me accusing him. His idea of accusing him is me not believing the explanation he gives me. He calls me names and tells me he doesn't care if I believe him or not because I'm being insecure.

I know me telling you about this will probably only make things worse and cause a final break up between us, but I'm not going to continue to be afraid and ashamed of what's been going on, because it stops here one way or another.

I don't want to have to call the police, but I will if that's the only choice he leaves me. I want us to be two people who can agree to disagree and leave it at that without the violence. I don't know what to do, and I refuse to continue taking all the blame for everything that's wrong. It's not just me, and I don't deserve this treatment no matter how much he tries to justify it.

Please talk to him. I'm trying to salvage what's left of our relationship. And I know I'm not going to salvage it by letting him continue to abuse me. He has to be held accountable. I want Kaitlyn to have two loving parents. I want us to be loving toward each other, but it's getting harder to forgive and it's getting hard to not fight back. I know you might not get this email right away.

I would have called, but Devin took my cell phone, and I don't have your phone number memorized. I'm so sorry that I have to tell you these things, but I'm not going to keep this a dirty secret anymore, and it has to stop before it ruins all our lives.

Please help and give me some guidance and advice for my part as well as his. I cc'd Devin because I'm not trying to be sneaky like he accuses me of being. I'm putting it all on the table with you being someone I trust to be levelheaded and able to provide us with wisdom and good advice.

Erika

On Tuesday, February 5, 2008, 10:15 AM, _____ <_____@yahoo.com> wrote:

Thank you, baby, for allowing me to know just what is going on. I too am very concerned about these things that I hear. DEVIN, if you are aware of this email, please call me. He CAN NOT continue to mistreat you, because as you said, and as I well know, HURT IS NOT LOVE! I do need to speak to him. In fact, I'm going to stop now and call him. Try to hang on, because there is a child involved (and as you said, which is true, children need both parents). I'm not understanding him, you are in his corner and supporting what he does, what more does he want? He needs to stop!

Love you, Mom

On Tuesday, February 5, 2008, 5:11 PM, Erika_____ <_____@yahoo.com> wrote:

Thank you for understanding and your kind words. I don't know what to do. I've tried it all. I've gone from thinking that if I just don't say anything he will stop the verbal abuse on his own. When that didn't work, I fought back physically, and I am no match for him. I tried reasoning with him. Asked and asked him to stop the name calling and blaming me for everything that is wrong. And now I say exactly what's on my mind, and when he starts insulting me; it gets hard to watch my words when he has no consideration for my feelings. And now he feels that I deserve to get hit when he decides so.

I gave him my word that I wouldn't put my hands on him again in anger or while arguing, and I have kept it, even though he hasn't on three separate occasions now. Twice while I was breastfeeding Kaitlyn. And what's most hurtful is that he is one hundred percent capable of keeping a cool temper and choosing his words carefully. I witnessed it for myself in this house while Haley and Corine were here. He was careful not to insult Corine even though she sat here and lied about him in front of me and Haley. Not only claiming to not be the type of person to cheat on her husband EVER but also saying she hasn't received child

Epilogue

support in a year. Not only did she go out of her way to lie but she did it for the purpose of making Devin look bad in front of Haley… But always careful not to admit that she put Devin through the same thing with lies. And all the while, Devin kept his composure.

So, that tells me that he is capable of showing restraint, composure, and consideration. He can claim he did it for Haley, and I'm sure part of him did. But I can't help but feel like he did it more out of fear. As a woman who lied about putting him in jail for something he said he didn't deserve. What extreme would she go to if he did disrespect her and make her feel threatened? I think that's what he fears most and that's the main reason he kept his composure with her.

I have but to believe that the only thing keeping him under control is not just his love for Haley but fear of overstepping very clear boundaries set by Corine by sending him to jail without regard to the truth. And here I am putting up with it, and I wouldn't have to lie. I've protected him so far because I have a very clear understanding of the consequences of bringing the law into fights where he ends up hitting and threatening my life. I don't take that lightly, especially since he keeps doing it. Part of me has protected him because I used to get physical with him when the verbal abuse got to be too much. But I'm not going to pay for that forever.

I have tried to reason with him, but he has broken every promise he's ever made to me in regard to the disrespect and the violence. His apologies are almost meaningless.

If we're going to make it, he needs to give me what he went out of his way to give Corine. Respect for boundaries

Epilogue

and the consideration to show restraint when things get difficult in a disagreement or just a simple conversation. I have done so at times when I could have easily gone off the deep end on him. We need the help of someone who can help us sort out all the negative feelings that we've put in each other's hearts. Someone to help us heal from what we've gone through, and counseling not just for Devin but for me as well so that I don't become angry and bitter too.

As a mother now, I can't act the way I used to when I was angry at him, and I don't. But I won't back down when it comes to speaking my mind. That piece of advice Tim gave to the both of us; he told me to say what I had to say and not be afraid, and I'm not. I am capable of doing it without calling him names, but he can't do that for me or for Kaitlyn's sake.

If he can't do that, then I hope he will at least let me leave with Kaitlyn without having to bring the courts into this. Because I won't stay and put myself or Kaitlyn in harm's way anymore. I hope this helps you understand where I'm coming from and that no matter what happens I want what's best for Kaitlyn and for Devin and for me as well.

Thank you for caring.

Much love,
Erika

On Wednesday, February 6, 2008, 4:12 PM, _____ <_____@yahoo.com> wrote:

Epilogue

As a mother (of Devin) and being married for thirty-four years to a man who was also 'out of control' sometimes, I can understand that often a woman has to endure so much, MOST OFTEN, their heart, and their mind. They put up with so much and then they finally realize (after putting up with so much) ENOUGH IS ENOUGH!!! I don't want ANY woman to have heartaches, crying, or any trouble because of a man. LOVE DOES NOT HURT!

I'm PRAYING that you guys hurry and come here, even if you have to sell some of your stuff to get here. I pray that all goes well, and this is just a test. LOVE DOES TAKE YOU THROUGH A TEST. I'm praying that you guys can work this out. I'm keeping you close to my heart. Be encouraged, and hurry home. Kiss my baby, and I LOVE YOU, ALL OF YOU. My heart hurts when I hear of you guys not agreeing.

Mom

_____ <_____@yahoo.com> wrote:
I am praying SO MUCH for the BOTH of you! Please TRY to be adults, if not for yourself, for the BABY. IF you LOVE SOMETHING, YOU will always FIND a way to have PEACE. OFTEN, when couples are together, and there's MONEY, FUN, etc., ALL IS WELL... BUT, when JOBS ARE GONE; when MONEY IS FUNNY; when BILLS ARE ROLLING IN ONE BEHIND ANOTHER; then FIGHTING, ARGUING, NAME CALLING, HATING all start. WHY??? Was MONEY, FUN, etc. the REAL reason you're together, OR was it really LOVE? I can only pray that you guys can reason together... as I'll say, I'm praying. I'm NOT taking sides, nor giving either of you any type of opinion, I'm just

Epilogue

praying. And I PRAY that GOD gives you guys DIRECTION. Love, Ma

Erika_____ <_____@yahoo.com> wrote:
I've been praying too. And hopefully Devin and I can learn to talk. We've been fighting through good and bad times. The only difference is when it's fine financially he doesn't blame me for everything. It's one of the few times he acknowledges that the way he treats me is not right. He likes to spend money doing things he likes to do, like go to the games and buy stuff we don't really need. The little bit of money he gives me, I end up having to give back to pay bills etc.

I know I can aggravate him, and that's the only thing I can use against him and all the nasty things he says to me. But at the end, I'm always the one with the short end of the stick. My life here is so warped. I have no one to talk to, nowhere to go and get away when I feel anxious or depressed. And when Devin can't help me, he takes it personally and says I just have a bad attitude when it's nothing against him.

I know our problems are sometimes just our personalities, which are magnified by being out here alone and having money problems. I don't like to tell people my problems, and I've been ashamed of what's been happening, so it's been even more difficult to have an outlet for my frustrations. And I'm sure it's something Devin goes through too. I know we're both better than what we've been and love one another more than what we've shown. And that along with Kaitlyn is what keeps me hanging on, even when I feel like giving up.

Epilogue

I want to change how we talk to one another. I want to change the way we argue, and I want us to learn to walk away from dumb arguments that don't mean anything. I don't know how to do it consistently, and I feel he doesn't really try. I'm just going to keep praying for guidance and for the ability to be happy for what I have that's good in my life.

Thanks for taking the time, and you're right, this is not about sides. I guess I just need an outlet, and you make me feel loved and safe to tell you.

Love,
Erika

On Saturday, February 9, 2008, 7:57 AM, _____ <_____@yahoo.com> wrote:

Thank you for loving and caring enough about ME to trust me. That's what RELATIONSHIP and FAMILY is all about, TRUSTING! What you said is SO TRUE, and I KNOW that when you feel 'trapped' in a situation and can't find anyone to 'talk' to it's hard! And what's even harder is finding someone you can TRUST to talk to. Folks will listen and then tell everybody your business, even when you and your mate have 'forgiven each other and gone on.' Folks will continue to talk about what you have said, that's why it's IMPORTANT to find one person ONLY to talk to. Personalities, character, and sometimes goals are issues that every person has to adjust to, especially in relationships. Is it easy? No. Can you be successful in accomplishing these issues and working them out? Yes. As

Epilogue

I said, it's not easy, but you can do it. I read where you said, you and Devin CAN do it. That's a good start. First, knowing there's a problem, second, working on the problem, and finally being able to solve the problem. It's a process! But, with GOD, LOVE, TRUST, and my beautiful grandbaby on your side, I believe that you two can make it. Keep PRAYING, keep believing GOD, and KNOW that I AM always available to listen (and continue to love you); pray for you, and NO ONE else will hear the story unless they hear it from you two. Keep praying and hopefully I will see you guys in a few weeks. Start packing (don't forget to SELL the stuff you don't really need, that's extra money for you now), and I will call as soon as I hear from my boss. He called late last night, and they were working on your application then. Did you guys receive anything in email? Take care, hurry home, Love Ma

I look back at this email thread and I DO NOT RECOGNIZE the woman writing those emails. I cringe and I feel shame all over again. I was so stupid. I was so blind. My entire life, my perspective, my reasoning, and my actions were based on complete fabrications. My disdain and dislike for Corine was a creation of Devin's lies. I think back and wonder why I didn't question the situation differently, and all I can come up with is, "who lies about that?" My answer, "a sociopath!"

I did often find myself asking, "How did I go from being on a pedestal, admired, pursued, and courted with generosity and consideration to being in a vicious cycle of mental, emotional, verbal, and physical abuse?" By the time I wrote this letter, I had thought and had verbalized that the person I believed I had fallen in love with did not and had not EVER EXISTED. The man who had called me religiously every day. The man who swore I was everything he had ever wanted and looked for in a woman. The man who promised me the world with his hard work and ambition was a LIE. Devin had played me. He had played on my desire to have my mother be a grandmother to my children. He had played on my desire to not have to face the world alone anymore. He had played me. I actually played myself. The thought was so horrific, I could only entertain it for a few seconds. I had sold this man to my family and my friends as "the one."

Looking back, I realize I had to sell him because they could all see that he wasn't who I was meant to be with. They knew me as someone who was smart and knew what I wanted, and if I was saying he was the one, they had no reason to fight me on it even though they questioned it. "Are you sure?" was my friend's question as our relationship evolved. It was the question asked after Devin proposed and I said yes. It was the question asked when Devin asked me to move to Georgia and I said yes. It was the question asked when he offered me his car so that I wouldn't have to buy or lease a new car. I had never been irrational or careless with my life or my well-being. It was this side of me that found herself in denial and in a rage about living in Georgia with a complete liar. As all liars know, it gets harder and harder to keep track of all the lies.

After Devin and I began living together, we would find ourselves in conversations about his past. Stories that he had already told me on more than one occasion, but I would catch a slightly different version. The timing wasn't as before, whatever current lie he was telling didn't match up with the past one. When I would question him about it, his initial response was that he had told me the earlier version to "spare" my feelings or because "I was insecure and wouldn't have been able to handle the truth" or because I "had asked." All these responses angered me. As far as I was concerned, he was questioning what I believed to be reality, and that ticked me off.

In turn, he became angry at being questioned and called out on the inconsistencies of his stories. These inconsistencies soon went from a difference of opinion bickering into an onslaught of insults and name calling. The truth of him begging me to marry him and move to Georgia became I was riding his coattail to escape Seattle where I had screwed everyone and had no other prospects. Suddenly, the story was that he never wanted me to move to Georgia. The story now was that I was a lazy slut who was living off his success like Corine. I was a gold digger, and he was the most successful man I had ever dated. I was just jealous and insecure trying to take him down. The lie of him wanting to build something with me in the finance world became the truth of him spending hours playing video games. Nowhere to be found was the man who volunteered, who loved to keep busy "grinding and hustling" for success.

The things I did catch him doing to "grind and hustle" included going on Craigslist to solicit women into meeting him or sending pictures. Sending messages on Myspace to models and celebrities because he was trying to break into the personal security business for escorts, or because of his music label, or pending "movie deal," and not because he was a grimy lowlife trying to meet prostitutes or because he was fishing for responses from celebrities that he could brag about. And, of course, he didn't tell me about all of these efforts because I was so "jealous and insecure."

Being the woman that I am, I took great offense to his barrage of insults and attempts to have me question my memory and my reality. If I had known the term "gaslighting" back then, I would have realized that it was exactly what I was experiencing.

Epilogue

The first-time things became physical between us, I had already endured emotional, verbal, and mental abuse. The name calling, blatant history re-writes, as if I had not lived what I had lived through. I wasn't used to someone trying to have me question my sanity or reality. That day, we found ourselves disagreeing about yet another inconsistency in one of his stories about his ex-girlfriend. He was angry and kept calling me nasty names. He would come within an inch of my face and repeated, "c—t, c—t, c—t." I could feel the anger rise as I looked into his eyes, as he hissed and hurled this slur. His eyes and demeanor were arrogant, plainly saying, "what the f— are you going to do about it?" I finally snapped and slapped him across the face. His initial response was to put his hand around my throat. I immediately kicked him, and he backed off.

As I composed myself, he began to walk toward me again, and I kicked him again in the gut with one leg and in the leg with the other. Before I knew it, he had picked me up by the shirt as I punched at him. In no time, I found myself on my back on the floor. He had one hand on my throat and one cocked in a fist. I could see in his eyes, he was nowhere to be found. There was only a blackness that I had never seen in my life before, in anyone. There was no light behind his pupils. Just a black and empty stare and the rage in his face. I froze. I calmed myself down and braced for what I believed would be a direct fist to my face. I don't know if it was me not fighting back that brought him back, but he went limp and let me go. It was as if he could only fight if I was fighting him, and when I stopped, he stopped.

He got off his knees and said I was just like Corine, trying to get him "caught up." I got up and told him it was over. That I wanted to leave. He said nothing and went upstairs. I sat on the couch, shocked, shaking, and angry because I realized that my leaving completely depended on him being willing to let me go.

About thirty minutes later, he came back downstairs and threw a piece of paper at me and said, "here's your flight information." When I opened the folded piece of paper that he had thrown at me, it simply read, "f— you, c—t."

The time I lived in Georgia was the hardest and loneliest time of my life. I hate thinking about my time there. Everything and nothing happened there. It was a rollercoaster of emotions and experiences. Stomach churning pain and humiliation, side by side with fleeting moments of hope and something sometimes resembling happiness. The distance had me isolated from my family and friends, but so did the shame. The distance was both good and bad. Good that it enabled me to hide what was going on and bad that I had nowhere to run.

On the phone, I couldn't bring myself to speak about the horror that was my life in Georgia to my family. How could I talk about the many nights I endured being deprived of sleep with hours upon hours of being verbally berated and threatened? How could I speak the words out loud that I found myself feeling I had no choice but to have sex with Devin for the sake of not having an argument escalate into another sleepless night, or worse, a physical assault. How could I bring up to my family that I was being hit and threatened during my pregnancy? The stress I was experiencing could be overwhelming at times. With every argument, I could feel my blood pressure rise, which was compounded by feelings of helplessness and loneliness. There was no one I could run to and no one there to save me. There was no place for me to escape.

A reality that became all too clear the one and only time Devin and I physically fought in public. It was early on during one of our "good" weeks. We had been getting along and decided we needed a date night out. We got all dressed up and headed to downtown Atlanta. We ended up at a club that had a rooftop deck as well as

EPILOGUE

several floors, each playing different types of music. We started at the rooftop deck, as it was a beautiful night. It was my first time stepping out in Atlanta since arriving. It didn't take long for me to notice that Devin was an open ogler, something he had never done before. He had no problem staring at other women and made little effort to hide it. I'm not a jealous person. I understand that we all have eyes, and they are meant to see. I personally had experienced the jealousy of men in the past while out in social settings and tried to not be a wandering eye type when I was with someone. I expected that in return, especially when I was rebuffing the advances of men every time Devin went to the bar to get us a drink.

Unfortunately, that wasn't the case. As the night progressed, he didn't stop. I began to feel insulted and disrespected and decided that if he can do it, then so can I. As we were standing around near one of the dance floors, I found myself looking around the room. I noticed a man looking at me and instead of continuing my gaze away, I stopped and made eye contact. Devin noticed but didn't say anything. Not long afterward, Devin decided he was over being out and was ready to go home. I didn't think it was an issue, as Devin didn't say anything about it and nothing in his demeanor made me think he had a problem.

It wasn't until we were in the car and driving out of the parking lot that he went off about how I had disrespected him. He accused me of being an "untrustworthy b—tch" and called me "Corine's twin." He began to raise his voice more and more with every insult. The whole argument made me angry, and I pointed out that he was being a hypocrite given that he had no problem ogling other women in front of me all night. He asked me point blank if I had made eye contact on purpose and I said yes but only to prove a point.

Epilogue

Before I could make my point, he backhanded me across the face as he was driving. The sting and embarrassment of being slapped in the face elicited only one thing, to fight back. I began to punch him in the face and head as he was driving, calling him a "f—ing motherf—r," as I did. I yelled at him "who the f—k do you think you are to hit me in the face!" I was relentless in my attack as pure fury ran through my veins, and I had no concern whatsoever for my safety or that we were in public. Devin continued to drive, and with his free hand he grabbed me by the hair and pulled my head down. He pulled so hard that I wasn't able to continue to hit him. I don't know what got into me, but I decided to pull my leg up far enough to pull my heel off. I took my shoe off and began to hit him with it, using the heel as a weapon. I swung enough times to make contact, and on my last swing, I managed to stab him in the head with it. I had struck him so hard that the heel of my shoe became stuck in his head.

It was at this point that he stopped the car in the middle of the street in downtown Atlanta. It was late at night and there weren't many cars on the road. He told me to "get out" of his car. I refused and he began to drive when a man walked up to the car on my side and said "Yo! Man, I saw what she did to you, man!" Devin was in a complete rage as he made his way onto the interstate leading "home." My adrenaline was subsiding as his anger increased. Fear began to settle in. I was going back to "his" house. I had nowhere to go but with him. He cussed at me the entire way home. For extra fun, he rolled my window down so that I would endure the cold air at seventy-plus miles an hour on the interstate, hitting me in the head, daring me to fight back.

He steadily worked himself into a frenzy with insults that I didn't respond to. It seemed to make him even more angry that I had calmed down and wasn't saying anything. I was too busy thinking of all the horrible ways that this night could possibly end.

Epilogue

He decided to get off the freeway at some random exit. For anyone who has been to Georgia, they know it is not uncommon to be on a one-lane lonely dark road with no houses or buildings for miles once you get off the interstate. And that is exactly the kind of road we were on.

He drove about half a mile before he pulled over. It was a one lane road in each direction with a ditch alongside it and nothing but trees on both sides. I began to really believe that I may just die by the side of the road. It dawned on me just how alone I was and how no one could save me or come to help me in time, or at all. All my family and friends were thousands of miles away. They had no idea that this could even happen. From the time Devin exited the freeway, he was threatening to kill me and leave me in a ditch, and I believed him.

He got out of the car, walked around, opened my door, and yelled at me to "get out!" He tried to drag me out of the car, but I resisted. Insulting and threatening me the entire time, he was trying to yank me out of the car. I said nothing, I feared that if I fought back, it would only fuel his anger and I would lose my life on this dark and lonely road. I don't know what made him stop, but he did and got back in the car, then went right back to insulting me. By the time we arrived at our exit, I was exhausted. I was dreading what would happen next.

For Devin, it seemed that he couldn't quite figure out how else to insult, threaten or humiliate me. I imagine that even for him, there is only so much satisfaction you can get from calling someone nasty names. As he turned on the road leading to the house, pulled over, and told me to get out! This time I did. I knew where I was. I knew I could walk to a nearby gas station and at the very least call the police. I got out and started to walk away. I thought Devin would drive off, but he didn't. Instead, he got out of the car and as I was walking away yelled insults at me. I kept walking; I didn't care. I was glad to be out of the car and getting away from him.

Devin got back in his car and seemed to drive away. It was not even five seconds before he turned back around, drove alongside me, and told me to get back in the car. I said nothing and continued walking. He stopped the car, got out, and physically began to pull me toward the car. In that split moment, I thought it would be better if I did get back in the car and made it back to the house, at least there I could make a run for a neighbor's house. That was my plan; I would run and seek refuge at one of the neighbor's houses.

If there was one thing I had come to understand about Devin, it's that he is all about his image, and I knew that if I made it to a neighbor's house, he wouldn't escalate the scene. I don't know if he sensed that, but it seemed that he was ready for me to make a run for it. As soon as he parked the car in the driveway, I opened the door and made a run for the neighbor's house screaming, "Help me!" I didn't make it. Before I knew it, he had caught up to me. He picked me up as I continued to scream, "Help me!" until he put his hand over my mouth. He dragged me into the house. At that point, I was resigned to surviving whatever was in store for me the rest of the night.

As soon as we made it into the house, he began to call me "Corine's twin." He accused me of trying to play the victim by running to the neighbors for help. I was trying to have him "catch a case." He blamed the entire night on me and was quickly angered when he noticed the blood all over his shirt. Devin called threatened to kill me if I ever put my hands on him again. However, even though he was angry that I had attempted to make a run for the neighbor's house, it became clear to me that he was in no mood to continue. I was also exhausted and didn't have the energy to be angry about his gall to try to play the victim.

Epilogue

I honestly can't remember how specifically we got past that night. All I can say is that I know I made excuses such as "maybe he would not have reacted that way if I had not argued, debated or questioned him." Or if I had not tried to "prove a point" or have the "last word." On top of all that, I was in <u>denial</u>. This was not happening to me. This was not supposed to happen to someone like me. I only ever dated good guys who treated me well. I had the good sense and good judgment to weed out others. Only weak women dated men who mistreated them, and I was not weak. I stood up for myself and I fought back! And how was I going to tell my family that I had made a mistake uprooting my life and moving all the way to Georgia? How could I face my friends?

I was afraid everyone might judge and look down on me. I was so ashamed of the thought that I had been so wrong. I couldn't be wrong. There was no way I could be this wrong. This was just a rough adjustment for the both of us. We had both done a bad job of communicating, listening, and being kind and considerate toward one another, that was all. The Devin I fell for was real, he had to be real! All I knew was that I was having all these conversations with myself. I had no one to talk honestly to about my life with Devin in Georgia.

It was during this time that my thought process and perspective began to be corrupted, poisoned, and distorted. For Devin's part, his excuses included that I made him feel "less than" or that he felt he was "letting me down" because he was not quite fulfilling all that he wanted and believed he was capable of. There were so many apologies from him that it got to the point that the line between the "evil" Devin and the "good" Devin was blurred. I didn't know which one was real. It was this doubt and being pregnant that made me stay. I had nothing but idiotic hope that we could get back on track.

Epilogue

The seventeen months I lived in Georgia were completely life altering. In that time, I went from being a self-sufficient, independent woman to an abused, trapped mother who was completely dependent on the grace and mercy of an abusive, lying, cheating male.

The recession hit us hard financially. Our income was commission based and as the mortgage industry began to collapse, so did all the work we had in the pipeline. The mortgage and HOA payments got behind, utilities and cell phones bills got behind and finally cut off. Bank accounts became overdrawn and credit cards were maxed out. I found myself, for the first time in my life applying for public assistance. As if all that wasn't bad enough, it was all happening as I found out I was pregnant. At thirty-one years old, despite finding myself in a miserable situation with a piece of crap of a male, I could not bring myself to terminate the pregnancy. I had terminated two pregnancies in my twenties and something in me couldn't do it again. I made the decision to have my child knowing that I would likely end up being a single mother.

Devin initially was excited about the pregnancy. We happened to be on good terms when we found out, but as usual, it was no big deal for him to rewrite history. During an argument, our child became "the trap" because, apparently, he still fancied himself a catch. He demanded I have an abortion at week sixteen, knowing that was no longer an option. By week twenty-eight, I found myself hospitalized. There wasn't enough amniotic fluid around the baby. I would have to be on bed rest until we knew what was causing it or the fluid levels increased back to normal. As far as I was concerned, there was likely a rupture in the amniotic sack from being pushed down by Devin more than once. I was certain that the stress caused by the abuse contributed greatly to the complications.

Epilogue

My doctor suspected as much as well. During one visit, he informed me that I would need to see a specialist because of the low amniotic fluid. Later, he asked to speak to me alone, away from Devin. He asked me directly if I was being physically abused. I said no. I couldn't bring myself to admit it, to say it out loud. I was sure the shame that I felt showed on my face, but I stayed steadfast in my denial. Despite all we experienced with the pregnancy, the day our daughter was born, Devin accused me of trying to pass off another man's child as his. Apparently, our daughter wasn't dark enough. Her hair wasn't curly enough. All of a sudden, the math didn't add up. As I would come to understand, there is no low, low enough for Devin to stoop.

Mentally, I had become someone who had soured on happiness and the idea that people are generally good. By the time we moved to Los Angeles to live with his mother, I found myself something like a zombie. I was resigned to the living nightmare I was in. During my time in Georgia, I only called the police once. As an excuse to be gone all night, Devin accused me of flirting with his nephew and slapped me across the face as I held our daughter in my arms. I had asked too many questions in front of his visiting nephew. They stormed out of the house, and he didn't return until early the next morning.

When his nephew left the next day, we argued again. I told him I didn't want to expose my daughter to the abuse I was enduring. I told Devin I was going to call my family to come get me. He threatened to kill me if I left with our child. At that moment, it became clear to me that he was threatening our daughter as well. I told him he couldn't force me to stay. I picked up the phone and dialed 911. When the operator answered and asked what was my emergency, I told her that I wanted to leave with my daughter but that my fiancée would not let us leave. When

Epilogue

the police arrived, I told them that I want to leave the state with my daughter but Devin won't let me leave.

When the police officer asked me why I wanted to leave, I spoke of the physical abuse for the first time. I told him about Devin slapping me across the face as I held our daughter and that it wasn't the first time. And right on cue, the police officer, with judgement in his voice, asked why I had just not left or called the police. I explained I had been threatened, that I had the car keys taken from me, along with my wallet. Devin chimed in to call me a liar, that I did have friends there. All of a sudden, his friends were my friends.

Devin went on to say we argued over me seeing something on his phone and "you know how women get" became the narrative. The police officer told me I had no right to leave with our daughter. That I would have to obtain permission from a judge. He said Devin had the same parental rights that I did. He went on to suggest that the baby and I leave the house for the night. He asked if I had somewhere that I could go. I said, "No, I don't have any friends here in Georgia." Again, Devin chimed in to call me a liar and that I knew I could go stay at his friend Tim's house. While the police officer was there, Devin called Tim and asked him if I could spend the night at his house with our daughter. He explained that I had called the police and just needed to cool off. Tim agreed and the police waited until he came.

That night was like any other night that Devin decided he wanted to abuse me all night. He called incessantly. When I didn't answer he would call Tim's phone. The whole time calling me names and accusing me of trying to set him up. His friend Tim appeared to be in shock. He told me he never knew Devin to be this way, but then again, he hadn't really seen or been around him in about twenty years. Tim tried to play mediator and to reason with Devin, but to no avail. I explained to Tim that this was

EPILOGUE

something I was experiencing on a regular basis. He seemed disturbed by what he was witnessing but I didn't trust it. As far as I was concerned, he was putting on an act.

I wouldn't get the police involved again until I finally had a real opportunity to leave.

By the time I arrived in California, I found myself unable to laugh around him. It was such a contradiction to be able to laugh around the person who brought so much misery into my life. I became distrustful of everyone Devin introduced me to. As far as I was concerned there was always an angle, a con, an ulterior motive for every action, every conversation, and every introduction. Sadly, I was nowhere near imagining just how fowl of a human being Devin was.

It was even more sad for his mother, brother, and sister to find out how fowl their own blood really was toward me and them. For Devin, my demeanor was the perfect cover for him to keep me isolated even when I was surrounded by his family. I was a "stuck up brat" who thought she was "too good" for them. That was the narrative to his family when they apparently asked him why I was so quiet. The story became "she doesn't like you guys" and at the same time, his story to me was "no one in my family likes you." I had heard the "my friends can't stand you" narrative in Georgia, so I wasn't shocked to hear the family sentiment. The reality was that I could care less! I knew I had no friends amongst his family. It wasn't long before I realized how they dealt with one another. We would run into a cousin and Devin would talk mess about other family members to them...

The physical abuse I had experienced in Georgia stopped during my time in California. In exchange, the mental and emotional abuse ramped up. The simple act of getting to work became a weapon. "Screw you ...B...! Walk to work," was what Devin said to me one morning after an argument. "I'm not giving you a ride in my car." I walked to work. It was obvious to my coworkers I had walked because I was late and they didn't see the car drop me off. And just like the manipulator Devin is, he decided to stop by later that morning to drop off a cup of coffee for me. The image of a loving, considerate, and thoughtful man had to be maintained, especially since I worked for the school district where his mother had been employed for twenty-five years and my boss happened to be one of her oldest and dearest friends.

When I finally returned to work fulltime with the school district, I was the primary breadwinner. It was my income that paid the mortgage and paid for the car that was only "ours" when "we" had to pay the monthly note, otherwise it was his car. Out of all the time I lived in California, the only time I found myself hopeful was after the last physical altercation Devin and I had. This altercation was different. This time there were witnesses, and this time there was physical proof. The night of the altercation we fought about an email I found in which a woman went into explicit detail about their sexual encounter. As I read the email, I was both disgusted and hopeful. I was disgusted because it was yet another thing pointing toward him being a man of no morals.

There had been other emails, a college friend accusing him of raping his wife. Emails on Facebooks between him and female "high school friends" wanting to reconnect. Proof of accounts with Devin's personal information to access sketchy dating websites like Adult Friend Finder. All of which he had some ridiculous excuse that I could neither prove nor disprove and made me question whether I was going crazy. But, as I mentioned, I was also hopeful because I believed I finally had proof that I needed to break up with Devin once and for all. It was my ticket out, and I was like a dog with a bone.

EPILOGUE

For months now, I had been trying to convince Devin for us to go our separate ways. I would point out how he could be free to enjoy the LA life as a single man. I promised I would never deny him access to our daughter. I tried to paint a picture of great co-parenting possibilities, but all my pleas fell on deaf ears and always ended in death threats to me and my family. He repeatedly told me I wasn't going anywhere with our daughter, especially because it was me who had "wasted his time" with my fake love.

There was no reasoning with him. He wasn't a rational actor. Every time we had that conversation, I was appalled by his ability to blatantly lie to himself and to me. As if I had not just witnessed for myself what a piece of ... human being he was. He had the gall to paint himself as the victim, as the one who had been duped into the relationship. That night, I was fed up, and I had resigned myself to not backing down even if it meant taking a beating. My time in Los Angeles had led me to the conclusion that the only way I was going to get out of this relationship was after a major physical assault that I may not survive.

We argued, and I didn't back down. He became enraged. He lunged at me, and I managed to barely escape his grasp but found myself backed up to our daughter's crib. He lunged at me again and tried to grab my hair. Instead, his fingernails scraped down the side of my face. I felt a sharp sting followed by a wetness rolling down my face. By now, his sister had heard the commotion and walked into the room just as he had lunged at me and scratched my face. She grabbed Devin and tried to hold him back. He was cursing and calling me names the entire time. I ran to the bathroom, and I saw my face. There were red marks and blood streaking from my forehead, over my eyelids, and down to my lip. As I looked closer, I could see that he had scratched the skin off my face. I became enraged and came out the bathroom ready to attack, I yelled something like "you scarred my face you fat b...!"

EPILOGUE

During the time I was in the bathroom, his sister had pushed him out of the room and locked the door. Devin was out in the hallway cussing and yelling profanities. I yelled back "I am calling the police!" I asked for my phone and couldn't find it, so I asked his sister to call the police. I yelled back in response to his insults, "Screw you, I'm done, I'm calling the police, and I'm pressing charges!"

This whole time, his sister was making every effort to calm both of us down. She kept telling her brother to calm down, shut up, and leave the house. His sister is a nurse, and it was her instinct to want to take care of my wounds. She asked me to calm down; she said that she needed to treat me. She said we could talk about it afterward, and if I still wanted her to call the police, she would. It was clear to me that she was in "protect my brother" mode. It also began to dawn on me again that I was all alone in this mess. If I called the police, I would have his entire Los Angeles family to face. And his most loyal and ardent supporter was his sister, and she was under the same roof.

I didn't call the police that night and finally achieve my escape, but a few months later, there was no one to stop me, and I had his sister and brother's support. It turns out that Devin is not just a despicable partner, he is also the worst kind of son and brother as well. He accused his sister of being a freeloader… He actively encouraged his brother-in-law to… He slept with his brother's… He hid money from me… And was accused of sleeping with various high school girls. By the time I left, the house was on the brink of foreclosure even though Devin withdrew money from our account every month to pay the mortgage.

To make a long story short, I successfully left the state of California with my daughter, filed a criminal complaint, and pressed charges. Devin was arrested on his return flight from Oregon after a week of football camp. He had no idea I had left,

Epilogue

and when he found himself in jail, he called his family and told one of his female cousins to "go see her" and get her to "drop the charges." If I refused, he alluded to being okay with them putting their hands on me. He called former Oregon co-workers and football players and coaches begging them to bail him out. He was unsuccessful.

And when I was summoned at court, I heard him plead guilty to assault resulting in bodily injury and making terrorist threats. The judge also granted a ten-year criminal no contact order because of his prior history of physical abuse toward his first wife Corine Lewis.

Like most sociopaths, Devin had what I can only describe as a "memento" envelope. In it was a pristine copy of the court documents from his Oregon criminal case, including the details of the charges and a summary report of the injuries suffered by Corine at his hands. August 18th, 2009 was the day he was found guilty and sentenced to one year in prison with five years of probation afterward. That was the last time I ever saw Devin, and sadly it was also our daughter's birthday.

Since then, I have moved on and bettered my life and that of my daughter's. I have also tried to keep my daughter in touch with Corine's daughter Haley. During my time with Devin, Haley visited us twice, once when we were in Georgia, before I knew I was pregnant with Kaitlyn, and once when we were in California and Kaitlyn was a little over a year old. Since we have been in Washington, we have traveled to see her in Oregon, once just the two of us, once with their grandmother Pearl, and the last time with my husband. Each time, Kaitlyn has bonded with her sister Haley in a new way, and each time I have been impressed and touched by Haley's desire to connect with her "Sissy." It is a joy to see the ease with which they pick up and just be with one another. And I am forever impressed with the young lady that Haley has been striving to be every time I see her, especially because I have an idea of what she has been through when it comes to her father.

Over the years, Kaitlyn struggled to reconcile in her heart and mind who her father is and what he represents. Fortunately, my husband has shown her what a real father is and how a real father loves. In the process, he has earned her love and respect. She has accepted him as her father and released Devin and herself from the pain that he represented in her life.

Today, I am grateful for my daughter and focus on the blessings that got us here and not on what we went through. I am grateful that I got a second chance to get it right in love and family."

Respectfully,
Erika Ramos

Acknowledgments

I am proud to be an Oregonian. I am equally proud of having been affiliated with the University of Oregon and the athletic department for more than fifteen years. I want to thank every staff member I had the privilege of working with during my tenure. To the late Dave Frohnmayer, our beloved University President, it was an honor to know you. To the fabulous athletic directors and associate athletic directors who supported our cheerleading program, I am eternally grateful for your time and dedication. I believe we had the best cheerleading program in the PAC-10 and PAC-12 hands down. This accomplishment was undoubtedly in part because of the backing we received from the head coaches from both Men's and Women's sports programs. To the Daisy Ducks, Oregon Club, and The Order of the O, we would have been nothing without you. Lastly, to Phil and Penny Knight, please allow me to extend my gratitude for everything you have done for the Oregon cheerleaders. We looked great and performed at the highest level because of your generosity. I love the University of Oregon and everything the institution stands for. I say out loud and proud "GO DUCKS!"

Thank you to all of the cheerleaders and mascots I've had the privilege of performing and competing with at Willamette High School 1985-1989. My heartfelt thank you to Marshall, Ronda, and Shawn Waterman for your unconditional love and support throughout my life. I also want thank Cheryl Hains and the Tanning Hut crew for your love and friendship, and Mike Maulding for being hands down the best coach I've ever had! You have been invaluable to all of your cheerleaders at U of O!!!

ACKNOWLEDGMENTS

Thank you to my Blazer dancer sisters for the best cheerleading experience of my life!! I love each of you tremendously! Thank you to each and every cheerleader and mascot I've ever coached at University of Oregon. Words cannot describe the love, respect, and adoration I have for all of you.

To Todd Bezatis, Matt Newton, and Ed Emberlin, I owe you the biggest debt of gratitude. Oregon cheerleading would not have been the same without you by my side.

Michael Westbrook, you are the Ambassador of my Quan! I love you!

To My Love Ryan Jeffries THANK YOU! You have been my rock from day one. I appreciate you, King.

To Rob Ward, Daryl Reed, Johnny Taylor, Shane Kessler, James Harper, Michael Helms, and Latin Berry, THANK YOU from the bottom of my heart. Your love and support have always been unwavering. Melvin, you already know! You are my real one for eternity!

To the entire Chicago Crew, thank you for welcoming me into the family! Your love and support have been invaluable. Bennett Johnson III, you have become my pillar of strength.

Mom and Dad, you've been the best examples of love possible. Thank you for giving me the best life I could have ever dreamed for. There are no two people on this earth I have more respect for than you. I love you, and I've got the key! Big Brother, I love you to the moon and back! You are and will always be my hero. To my sister-in-law Joy, I love you so much!

Brenda and Erica Winger, thank you for being a constant in my life. You have supported me from day one. To say I love you both is an understatement!

To my Colombian dearest friend Jordan, I'm so thankful you married into the family and came into my life. You are the best!

ACKNOWLEDGMENTS

To the "Boss" Dee Dee Brant and the Mrs. Oregon "Haz Beens," oh how I love you! Keep smiling, beautiful Queens!

Julie and TK, you are my day ones! I love being an honorary Kaanapu! Thank you for everything you are in my life.

To my SkyWest Crews, you are the best! Thank you, Lawrence Dixon, for encouraging and supporting me to write this book. You have been an invaluable friend and colleague. I appreciate you!

Becca Mora, my soul sister! I cannot thank you enough for loving me through the best and hardest of times. You have been such a huge influence in my life. Thank you for your contribution in this book and your unconditional love.

Erika Ramos, you exemplify strength, beauty, and grace. I am so proud to call you family. Thank you for encouraging me and contributing to the book.

Keith Allen, I appreciate your wisdom and strength. You are such an important part of my life. Thank you for everything.

Andiel Brown, you light up my world! Thank you for the countless hours of singing, dancing, listening, and praying. You are an invaluable part of my family!

Leesa Wilder AKA Jasmine! Thank you, girlfriend, for more than a decade of friendship, partnership, love, and laughs! Love you to the moon and back!

Shawna Peterson, we did it! Love you, girlfriend!

Michelle Bush, you are so loved, adored, and appreciated! Thank you for thirty plus years of friendship. I love you!

Mama Pearl and Glenda, thank you for keeping me as part of your family. You are loved and appreciated unconditionally.

To Jessica Elena, my blonde beauty, I love you! Thank you for the support and extended family in Switzerland!

Acknowledgments

A special thank you to Curtis Irving and David Driskill for teaching me the ropes and standing firmly by my side through it all. My deepest love and gratitude.

Thank you, Sarah Hookland, for always making me feel so beautiful! You have become such an instrumental person in my life. I'm looking forward to all of our adventures ahead!

Mark McMillian "Mighty Mouse," you have been such an inspiration to me. Thank you for taking a chance on me as your co-host and giving me the opportunities of a lifetime! FOE!

Derrick and Eileen Deadwiler, Joshua and Talia Stroud, Karissa and Steven Stavros, Joslyn Jenkins, and the entire Jenkins family, I am honored to know you. I am truly grateful to have you in my life. My love, respect, and admiration for you is unconditional.

Jeremy Bright, Danna Ghonaim, Rachael Gojko, and Sarah Hookland, thank you for the wonderful book cover, makeup expertise, and beautiful hairstyling. You didn't have much to work with, but your work was incredible.

Damion Hall, thank you for fifteen plus years of unconditional love, support, and encouragement! You are such an important part of my life. I love and appreciate you beyond measure.

And finally, I want to thank my friend and editor Oscar Turner, who helped me process some of the life lessons. Oscar has undergone his own transformation. He started his career in banking, providing loans for corporate clients. He then served as a corporate executive for the Quaker Oats Company, CompuServe, and Paramount Pictures. Oscar also served as Chief Operating Officer for Tyler Perry Studios before starting his own production company, Gallery Road Productions, He is currently developing a James Bond style espionage series which is absolutely incredible. When I told him about my journey, Oscar was so encouraging. Little did he know that I was going to put him to work.

Appendix

Resources

The following organizations represent trusted sources that victims of sexual assault and domestic abuse can readily access.

RAINN ("Rape, Abuse, & Incest National Network") is the nation's largest anti-sexual violence organization. RAINN operates the National Sexual Assault Hotline (800-656-HOPE). If you are in danger or need immediate assistance, call for help! For more information: Sexual Assault www.rainn.org

The National Domestic Violence Hotline operates twenty-four hours, seven days a week, 365 days a year. The hotline provides essential tools and support to help survivors of domestic violence. For immediate assistance call the National Domestic Violence Hotline: 1-800-799-SAFE (7233)
TTY 1-800-787-3224
Chat Live
Text "START" to 88788
For more information see: Domestic Violence
www.thehotline.org

JDoe is an anonymous, encrypted platform for reporting sexual assault and sexual misconduct.
Contact JDoe Email: ryan@jdoe.io
Address: 2223 Avenida De La Playa
Or for more information on how to report Sexual Misconduct:
www.jdoe.io

Appendix

End Rape On Campus (EROC) works to end campus sexual violence through direct support for survivors and their communities; prevention through education and policy reform at the campus, local, state, and federal levels. For additional information see:
www.endrapeoncampus.org

The National Suicide Prevention Lifeline works to help prevent suicide. The lifeline provides 24/7 free and confidential support for people in distress.
National Suicide Prevention Lifeline: 800-273-TALK (8255)
Suicide Prevention www.suicidepreventionlifeline.org

The National Human Trafficking Hotline: 1-888-373-7888
SMS: 233733 (Text "HELP" or "INFO")
Hours: Twenty-four hours, seven days a week
Languages: English, Spanish, and two hundred more languages
For additional information see: www.humantraffickinghotline.org

The Human Rights Campaign has spent forty years creating one of the most powerful movements for equality in the country. Their goal is to ensure that all LGBTQ+ people are treated as full and equal citizens across the country and around the world. For additional information see: LGBTQIA www.hrc.org

Glossary

Active Measures: A Russian form of political warfare that includes disinformation, propaganda, deception, sabotage, destabilization, and violence. Such actions are sometimes used by angry, destructive partners.

Blame Shifting: Occurs when an abuser refuses to take responsibility for their actions and attempts to lay blame on others, sometimes in a conspiratorial fashion. Blame shifting can result in highly toxic and violent behavior where the abuser feels justified in their anger and conduct.

The CL Way: A set of principles designed to help fortify, encourage, inspire, and transform women and other victims into the best versions of themselves.

Cognitive Dissonance: Occurs when there is a psychological disconnect between experiencing traumatic violence and wanting to remain in an abusive relationship. The symptoms include complete denial, rationalizing and justifying the abuser's behavior, self-blame, or minimizing the abuse in order to project a more positive view of the relationship.

Consent: An active, uncoerced agreement to engage in sexual activity by persons of legal age and sufficient capacity.

Displacement: Represents a form of mental substitution or misdirected anger. For example, when a partner comes home and curses his neighbor, berates his partner, and kicks the dog in response to problems at work.

Glossary

Disinformation: False information used to intentionally mislead.

Domestic Violence: Violence against a partner or spouse, either heterosexual or same-sex relationships. In its broadest sense, domestic violence can also involve violence against children, parents, grandparents, and other family members.

Gaslighting: The act of trying to manipulate a partner into questioning their own sanity through lies, propaganda, denial of truth, blame shifting, displacement, and other psychological means.

Grey Rocking: A technique used to interact with manipulative, abusive, narcissistic, and toxic people by limiting the level of engagement, refusing to provide fuel for their fodder, and becoming as boring as a grey rock.

Grooming: Occurs when an abuser steps into the role of both benefactor and mind controller. As benefactor, the abuser will move heaven and earth in order to achieve a level of trust including providing gifts, bribes, affection, advice, social status, emotional support, and more. In the role of mind-controller, the abuser attempts to exert extreme dominance and control over their partner's thoughts, values, goals, and views. In extreme cases, the duality can be the precursor to a "trauma bond," which makes it difficult for the victim to leave.

Intimate Partner Violence: Is a pattern of assault and coercive behavior that includes violence, psychological abuse, sexual assault, progressive isolation, stalking, deprivation, intimidation, and reproductive coercion. It is typically perpetrated by someone

GLOSSARY

in an intimate or dating relationship and is aimed at establishing control.

JDoe: A survivor or witness of sexual assault that files an anonymous report.

Love Bombing: The practice of lavishing someone with praise, attention, affection, gifts, and other perks as methods of influence and manipulation.

Manipulation: The act of persuading a partner in a skillful or unscrupulous manner in order to exercise control, influence, and power.

MICE: A mnemonic for money, ideology, coercion, and ego. Spy agencies use bribery, ideology, coercion, and ego stroking to entice foreign nationals and double agents to betray their country and values.

Narcissist: A partner who exhibits an excessive interest in and admiration of themselves without regard to the impact on others. The symptoms can be boastfulness, exaggeration of achievements, lack of empathy, fragile self-esteem, rage, exaggerated mood swings, and violence when criticized.

Overcomer: One who overcomes extensive pain or obstacles to achieve a goal or regain control over their circumstances, especially in cases of rape, sexual violence, and domestic abuse.

Power: The ability to direct, control, or significantly influence the behavior of a partner as a result of resources, coercion, status, kids, or other means.

Glossary

Projection: Occurs when a partner assigns their values and behaviors to another in a given situation. For example, if a partner is cheating with a business colleague, they may accuse the other partner of the same.

Propaganda: Acts of intimidation, the use of false or misleading information, or the introduction of fear tactics, doubt, terror, and uncertainty in order to weaken a partner's morale and mental wellbeing without physical force.

Psychological Warfare: Actions and techniques used to reduce a partner's morale, mental wellbeing, self-confidence, and self-esteem. Key techniques include disinformation, gaslighting, propaganda, threats, coercion, fear tactics, terror, fake news, intimidation, and violence.

Rape: Forcing another to have sexual intercourse against their will; sexual intercourse with a minor or incapacitated person; or the penetration of any one of several sexual organs without consent. This applies to longstanding partners, wives, girlfriends, boyfriends, husbands, and others.

Reconnaissance: Information gathering in support of preparing a plan or an attack.

Red Flag: Emotional risk factors that may signal the potential for mental abuse and violence.

Repression: Subduing a partner by force or mental abuse, or the suppression of one's own thoughts and actions in order to avoid conflict.

GLOSSARY

Self Esteem: Self-respect and confidence in one's self-worth and abilities.

Sexual Assault: Intentionally touching a person in a sexual manner or with sexual intent without their consent. This can also apply to actions involving intimate partners, wives, girlfriends, boyfriends, husbands, and others.

Sexual Coercion: Threatening or pressuring someone into sex against their will through financial, emotional, or other non-physical means of force.

Sexual Harassment: Unwanted verbal or physical behavior of a sexual nature performed with the intent of creating discomfort. It often entails repeated, continuous, and sustained behavior over a period of time.

Special Forces Units: Elite, specially trained and equipped military teams designed to conduct specific operations and achieve specific objectives.

Spotter: One who assists another in times of distress or helps others to achieve a level of performance that would otherwise be unachievable.

Sociopath: A person with a severe personality disorder who acts with extreme antisocial behavior and without regard to others or conscience.

Stockholm Syndrome: Occurs when a victim bonds and identifies with their captor or abuser. The term originated in the 1970s when four people were taken hostage during a bank robbery in Stockholm. After being released, the hostages defended their captors and refused to testify against them.

Survivor: One who survives a near-death, highly stressful, extreme, or difficult predicament against improbable odds.

Trauma Bonding: A strong emotional bond formed between a partner and their abuser in response to a <u>recurring</u> cycle of violence and abuse, offset by periods of peace, love, kindness, and affection. The partner experiencing abuse can develop deep attachment to the abuser, which can deepen through recurring cycles of abuse and rewards. Trauma bonding is different from Stockholm Syndrome in that trauma bonding is one-directional, meaning only the victim forms a true emotional attachment. A trauma bond can be a dangerous state for the victim, resulting in low self-esteem, negative self-image, self-blame, depression, bipolar disorder, mania, suicide, addiction, and generational abuse. To maintain a trauma bond typically requires four elements: a significant power imbalance, either real or perceived; a recurring cycle of abuse and rewards; social isolation; and perceived credible death threats or the fear of significant retribution.

The Unvirtuous Cycle: Relationships that follow an escalating pattern of violence and mental abuse described as: grooming and courtship, trial by fire, danger and denial, reality and surrealism, and fight or flight,

Victim: A person murdered, dead by suicide, undergoing mental or physical trauma as a result of sexual violence, domestic abuse, or chronic social stigma on social media and elsewhere.

Glossary

War Crime: A violation of the international laws of war such as targeted killing of civilians, torture, taking of hostages, destruction of civilian property, genocide, ethnic cleansing, rape, and sexual violence.

Whataboutism: A technique of responding to an accusation by leveling an unrelated accusation in order to create a false equivalency.

About The Author

Corine Lewis is a leading advocate in the fight against sexual abuse and violence against women. Having gone through more than a decade of physical and psychological trauma, Corine's powerful new memoir represents a chilling account of living life in the public eye while masking the pain of rape and domestic violence. Through hard work, determination, perseverance, and faith.

Corine's journey has become a story of resilience and resurrection. She has recaptured her power and speaks out in a powerful way to encourage and empower other women everywhere. As a young girl, Corine pursued her passion for cheerleading, achieving excellence at a state, national, and international level. She was a four-year member of the Willamette High School state championship team; the first freshman to make the nationally elite University of Oregon cheerleading squad; a four-year member of the Portland Trailblazer dancers; and the coach and choreographer of the 2005 USA National Cheerleading Stunt Championship team. During her time with the Blazers, Corine performed during the 1992 NBA Championship Series against the Chicago Bulls and for the 1992 USA Olympic Basketball Team - "The Dream Team." Corine had a distinguished fifteen-year career as a cheerleading coach and choreographer at the University of Oregon, where she led hundreds of cheerleaders in numerous bowl appearances, including the Rose Bowl, Cotton Bowl, Las Vegas Bowl, Aloha Bowl, Sun Bowl, Holiday Bowl, and Fiesta Bowl. Corine also served as the coach of the 2009 USA National Hip Hop Dance

About the Author

champions and has conducted cheerleading camps throughout the US, Europe, and Canada.

In 1996, Corine was crowned Mrs. Oregon International and later starred in the Comcast Sports eleven-week reality series *The Making of an Oregon Cheerleader*. Corine served as a co-host of the talk radio sports show "Hard Hittin' Radio" and as an on-field reporter for the televised Blue Grey All-American Bowl.

Corine shook the internet when her picture was tweeted out by an Arizona Cardinals player during the 2015 National Championship game between the University of Oregon and Ohio State. The tweet went viral and was viewed by more than a million people. In her new book, **SMILE, Chin Up**! Corine tells a sometimes difficult account of what it's like to be raped and undergo nearly ten years of domestic violence. Here, Corine describes a set of warning signs that she calls the "Red Flags & Risk Factors" and a set of empowerment principles entitled the "CL Way."

Corine enjoys travel and meeting people. She's a regular at the gym and gives new meaning to the term "survival of the fittest." She is a mother of two and has been informally counseling victims of sexual assault and domestic violence for more than ten years. In advance of the book release, Corine plans to launch a podcast to serve as a platform of hope, inspiration, encouragement, and women's empowerment, helping victims all around the world tell their stories.

In Memoriam:
My friend Lisa Flormoe was such a beautiful person.
She was taken away from us far too early.

More from the Author

SMILECHINUP.COM

References

References, Notes and Citations

1. Private Desmond Doss – page 10. **Citations**: 2016 Film Hacksaw Ridge and Wikipedia page on Desmond Doss.

2. Flashback – Diane Downs – page 25. **Citations:** Wikipedia page on Diane Downs.

3. Band Free – All right now – p37. **Citations:** Lyrics to song All Right Now. Wikipedia page on Rock Band Free.

4. Lisa Flormore – page 45. **Citations:** The Oregonian 1/9/2019. "50 years again for convicted killer Todd Davilla in 1991 stabbing." Article entitled "Todd Davilla."

5. Todd Davilla – page 46. **Citations:** The Oregonian 1/9/2019. "50 years again for convicted killer Todd Davilla in 1991 stabbing." Article entitled "Todd Davilla."

6. A Current Affair – Maury Povich – page 47. **Citations:** January 1991 report by Maury Povich on "A Current Affair."

7. Clint Eastwood – the Unforgiven – page 61. **Citations**: Wikipedia article "1993 in the United States."

8. Steven Spielberg – Jurassic Park – page 61. **Citations:** Wikipedia article "1993 in the United States."

9. Aldrich Ames – page 65.
https://www.brainyquote.com/authors/frederick-douglass-quotes.

References

10. MICE – page 65. **Citations:** "The Recruiter: Spying and the lost art of American Intelligence" by Douglas London.

11. Jackie Kennedy Onassis – page 68. **Citations**: Wikipedia article "Jacqueline Kennedy."

12. Trial of the century – page 70. **Citations**: Biography.com article "O.J. Simpson's Trial for Murder."

13. Ex-wife of O.J. Simpson – page 70. **Citations:** Biography.com article "O.J. Simpson's Trial for Murder."

14. The History Channel – page 74. **Citations:** Wikipedia article "History Channel."

15. Endless Love by Lionel Richie and Diana Ross – page 101. **Citations:** "Endless Love" song by Lionel Richie and Dianna Ross."

16. The lady doth protest too much – page 105. **Citations**: The play "Hamlet" by William Shakespeare.

17. Frederick Douglas "Show me how injustice a man will allow, and I will show you exactly how much injustice a man will endure – page 111. **Citations**: Frederick Douglass Quotes: https://www.brainyquote.com/authors/frederick-douglass-quotes. See article entitled "Submission."

18. Trauma Bond – page 111. **Citations**: Wikipedia article "Traumatic Bonding."

19. Stockholm Syndrome – page 111. **Citations**: Wikipedia article "Traumatic Bonding."

References

20. Timothy McVeigh – page 112. **Citations**: History.com "Timothy McVeigh."

21. Eugene's Register Guard – page 123. **Citations**: None! Probably not necessary.

22. Titanic won 11 Oscars – page 125. **Citations**: Wikipedia article "Key events in1998." See article "1998."

23. Anti-trust lawsuit against Microsoft, Bill Gates vs Justice Department – page 125: **Citations**: techlawjournal.com article "Janet Reno statement." See article titled "Antitrust suit against Microsoft."

24. Gotham's Reckoning – page 131. **Citations**: 2012 Movie: "The Dark Knight Rises - Gotham's Reckoning."

25. Showtime at the Apollo – page -140. **Citations**: Syndicated variety show beginning 1987.

26. "In awe of you." Page 146 City: by Hill songs. **Citations:** Song "In awe of you" by Hill Songs

27. Elian Gonzalez and Janet Reno – page 159. **Citations:** Wikipedia article "Elián González."

28. Katrina – page 165. **Citations:** Wikipedia article "Hurricane Katrina."

29. No Country for old men – page169. **Citations:** Wikipedia article "No Country for Old Men."

30. Nino Brown – page 169. **Citations:** Fictional character in the 1991 movie "New Jack City."

References

31. Bernie Madoff – page 213. **Citations:** Reuters March 13, 2009. See article "Madoff pleads guilty."

32. Larry Nassar – page 255. **Citations:** CNN January 2018. See article "Larry Nassar Sentenced."

33. Lewis Gordon quote – page 276. **Citations:** Lewis Gordon quotes. See https://www.azquotes.com/author/44347-Lewis_Gordon

34. The Wedding Crashers – page 303. **Citations:** 2005 movie "Wedding Crashers."

35. Russel's pit viper – 319. **Citations:** NY Post 10/15/21. See article "Indian man gets life sentence for killing wife with cobra."

36. Trauma bond – page 320. **Citations:** Wikipedia article "Traumatic Bonding."

37. Vanessa Guillen – page 328. **Citations:** Wikipedia article "Killing of Vanessa Guillén." See article "Vanessa Guillén."

38. Lloyd Austin – page 329. **Citations**: U.S. Department of Defense. See articles "Independent Review"; "Independent Review Commission on Sexual Assault in the Military "; and "Senior Leaders Focused on Restoring Trust as DOD Makes Sexual Assault Reforms."

39. Harvey Weinstein – page 330. **Citations:** New York Times June 15, 2021. See article "Harvey Weinstein's Stunning Downfall."

40. Harvey Weinstein – page 331. **Citations:** New York Times June 15, 2021. See article "Harvey Weinstein's Stunning Downfall."

References

41. Madeline Albright – page 332. **Citations:** "Madeleine K. Albright > Quotes." See article "Special place in hell."

42. Harvey Weinstein – page 333. **Citations:** New York Times June 15, 2021. See article "Harvey Weinstein's Stunning Downfall."

43. Andrew Cunanan – page – 335. **Citations:** Wikipedia article "Andrew Cunanan."

44. Andrew Cunanan – page – 336. **Citations:** Wikipedia article "Andrew Cunanan."

45. Gabby Petito - page – 337. **Citations:** CNN 3/11/2022. See article "Gabby Petito's parents sue Brian Laundrie's parents. Gabby Petito's mother files wrongful death lawsuit (CNN 5/7/22). See articles "Gabby Petito" and "Gabby Petito's mother."

46. Gabby Petito - page – 338. **Citations:** CNN 3/11/2022. See article "Gabby Petito's parents sue Brian Laundrie's parents. Gabby Petito's mother files wrongful death lawsuit (CNN 5/7/22). See articles "Gabby Petito" and "Gabby Petito's mother."

47. Kip Kinkel – page- 338. **Citations:** Wikipedia article "Kipland Kinkel."

48. Kip Kinkel – page- 339. **Citations:** Wikipedia article "Kipland Kinkel."

49. Hacksaw Ridge – page 342. **Citations**: 2016 Film Hacksaw Ridge and Wikipedia page on Desmond Doss.

References

50. Desmond Doss – page 342. **Citations**: 2016 Film Hacksaw Ridge and Wikipedia page on Desmond Doss.

51. Hacksaw Ridge – page 343. **Citations**: 2016 Film Hacksaw Ridge and Wikipedia page on Desmond Doss.

52. Desmond Doss – page 343. **Citations**: 2016 Film Hacksaw Ridge and Wikipedia page on Desmond Doss.

53. Desmond Doss – page 344. **Citations**: 2016 Film Hacksaw Ridge and Wikipedia page on Desmond Doss.

54. Audrie and Daisy – page 349. **Citations:** "Audrie and Daisy" 2016 Netflix documentary.

55. The Huffington Post named Daisy one of the 13 most fearless teens – page 350. **Citations:** https://www.huffingtonpost.co.uk. See article "13 most fearless teens."

56. Active Measures – page 359. **Citations:** Wikipedia article "Active Measures."

57. Cognitive dissonance – page 359. **Citations:** Wikipedia article "Traumatic Bonding."

58. Displacement – page 359. **Citations:** https://www.psychologytoday.com/us/basics/displacement See article "Displacement."

59. Gaslighting – page 360. Citations: https://www.merriam-webster.com/dictionary/gaslighting. See article "Gaslighting."

References

60. Grey Rocking – page 360. Citations: https://www.medicalnewstoday.com/articles/grey-rock. See article "Grey Rocking."

61. Grooming – page 360. Citations: https://www.rainn.org/news/grooming-know-warning-signs. See article "Grooming Know the Warning Signs."

62. Ref: Love Bombing – page 361. Citations: https://health.clevelandclinic.org/love-bombing. See "What Is Love Bombing."

63. MICE – page 361. **Citations:** "The Recruiter: Spying and the lost art of American Intelligence" by Douglas London.

64. Narcissist – page 361. **Citations:** https://www.mayoclinic.org/diseases-conditions/narcissistic-personality-disorder. See article "Narcissistic personality disorder."

65. Projection – page 362. **Citations:** https://www.psychologytoday.com/us/basics/projection. See article "Projection."

66. Psychological warfare – page 362. **Citations:** Wikipedia article "Psychological Warfare."

67. Repression – page 363. **Citations:** https://www.verywellhealth.com/repression-7775455. See article "Repression."

68. Sociopath – page 364. **Citations:** https://www.healthline.com/health/mental-health/sociopath. See article "What is a sociopath."

REFERENCES

69. Stockholm Syndrome – page 364. **Citations:** Wikipedia article "Traumatic Bonding."

70. Trauma Bonding – page 364. **Citations:** Wikipedia article "Traumatic Bonding.

Index

8

80th Academy Award, 191

A

A Current Affair, 54
ABC Kids, 111
absurdities, 326
abuse prevention, 376
abusers, 127
accomplice, 228
accountability, 179
Accountability, 179
accusations, 326
Active 20-30 International, 15
active measures, 227
advocate, 156
age, 353
Airbnb, 295
Alabama, 325
Albero Salizar, 32
Aldrich Ames, 75
Allison Park Christian Center, 130
Alyssa Milano, 369
American Flag, 316
American Title Group, 119, 189
amifications, 357
Andiel Brown, 358
Andrea Lowell, 272
Andrew Cunanan, 372
Another One Bites the Dust, 34
Anthony Newman, 123
Arco Arena, 83
Arena Football League, 82
Aria Resort and Casino, 233
Arizona Cardinals, 249, 272
arrested, 139
Asia, 304
Assistant DA, 152
Audrie & Daisy, 387
Autzen Stadium, 98, 252
awareness, 376

B

Band of Brothers, 381
Barstool Sports, 272
battered wives, 108
battered women, 320
Battle of Okinawa, ix
battle of the bands, 41
Baywatch, 73
beguiled, 223
Bengals, 325
Bethesda Lutheran, 165
betrayal, 122
Beverly Hills High School, 181
Bill Gates, 143
Bill Musgrave, 196

Billy Bob Thornton, 26
bionic woman, 329
blame shifting, 227
Blazer Dancers, 57
Blazer Stunt Team, 66
body shaming, 388
booking agency, 103
boundaries, 352
Boyz N The Hood, 73
Brain Laundrie, 375
brainwashed, 124
Brian Mcknight, 240
brutality, 326
Byron Evans, 211

C

C- Section, 75
Caesars Palace, 372
calipers, 176
Camp 29, 394
Camp Easter Seal, 245
Canadian Football League, 289
Canadians, 28
cancer, 282
Carol Burnett, 31
Cascade Middle School, 26, 241
casting couch, 368
celebrity, 357
Centralia "Tigers.", 25
Centralia High School, 25
Champions Night Club, 115
Chandler, 239
Charbonneau, Oregon, 51

Charles Barley, 66
Charlie's Angels, 52
cheating, 77
Check Back, 387
Chiweenie puppy, 330
Chicago Bulls, 65
Chuck E. Cheese, 251
CIA, 75
City of Roses, 65
Civil War, 41
Clint Eastwood's, 71
Clyde Drexler, 66
Coach Bill Bowerman, 33
Coach Rich Brooks, 86
CoCo, 166
Coldwell Banker, 129
Comcast Sports, 191
complacency, 356
confusion, 93, 321
Consentsis, 359
conspiracies, 326
content, 4
control, 77, 81, 123, 150, 151, 179, 205, 227, 228, 229, 259, 326, 344, 351, 354, 402, 408, 413, 415, 446, 447
Control, 124
controlling, 77
corollary, 362
Corpus Christi, Texas, 87
Cosmopolitan, 372
courage, 49, 108
COVID-19, 307
Craigslist, 420

INDEX

crime., 54, 55, 151, 377
criminal trial, 130
Curtis Irving, 189
cyber bullying, 388

D

Daisy Coleman, 387
Dallas Cowboys, 41, 305
Damion Hall, 233
Dan Henson, 99
Danger and Denial, 353
Darnell Dockett, 272
David Driskill, 189
DeeDee Brant, 99
delusional, 215
denial, 228
Department of Justice, 143
dependency, 77
dependent, 226
Deral Boykin, 199
Desmond Doss, 382
Desmond Doss Rule, 361
despair, 356
desperation, 326
Destination Weddings, 265
Diana Ross, 115
Diane Downs, 28
disillusioned, 23, 156, 353
Disney World Magic Kingdom, 173
disparaging, 146
displacement, 353, 446
District Attorney's Office, 152
DJ Playtime, 335

document the abuse, 354
domestic abuse, ix, 127, 178, 358, 361, 362, 373, 380, 394, 443, 447, 450
domestic violence, 15, 16, 17, 29, 55, 82, 89, 108, 118, 152, 157, 159, 192, 230, 282, 325, 345, 346, 357, 362, 376, 386, 407, 408, 443, 446, 453, 454
Dr. Blake Sampson, 281
Driven by Safety, 387
Ducks, 32, 36, 37, 41, 45, 86, 172, 187, 271, 358, 437

E

Efudex treatment, 281
Elián González, 181
Emanuel Hospital, 75
embarrassment, 49
Emperor of Japan, 302
empowerment., 388
encouragement, 49
Endless Love, 115
entrapment, 222
epidemic, 358
Ericka Lassiter, 237
ESPN, 191
ESPN Las Vegas, 394
Eugene's Register-Guard, 140
Euro, 295
Europe's Elite, 285
European Nationals, 298
evolved, 313

INDEX

excuses, 228

F

Facebook, 191, 271
family and football, 26
fear, 49
Fight or Flight, 354
first amendment, 151
First Lady of the United States, 79
Flamingo, 372
Footloose, 25
Ford SUV, 201
Forgiveness, 344
Fort Hood in Texas, 365
Forty-Niners, 249
foundation, 323
fraternizing, 60
Fredrick Douglass, 125
free, 4
Free, 42
Friday Night Lights, 26

G

Gabby Petito, 375
Garibaldi's, 33
gaslight, 129, 227
generational curses, 330
George Foreman, 83
Georgia Tech, 196
Germaine's Luau, 280
Gladiators Cheerleaders Basel squad, 298
Gloria Allred, 369
Gold's Gym, 81

Google maps, 65
Google translator, 295
Gospel Choirs & Ensembles, 358
Governor Kate Brown, 54
GPS, 65
Grillin McMillian, 394
groomed, 123
grooming, 77
Grooming and Courtship, 351
grooming phase, 222
grooming process, 222
gun, 83
GUY, 233
Guys and Dolls, 31

H

Hacksaw Ridge, 380
Hallmark movie, 296
Hard Hittin' Radio, 211, 305
Hard Hittin' Radio Foundation, 236
Harley Quinn, 33
Harvey Weinstein, 367
hate crimes, 388
Hawaii, 319
Hayward Field, 32
Heins Ward, 199
History Channel, 85
Hollywood production, 46
Hollywood Reporter, 355
Honolulu International airport, 279
hopped, 321

INDEX

hostage, 325
Houston Texans, 190
Huffington Post, 388
Hula Bowl All-Stars, 35
Hula-Bowl in Honolulu, 123
Hult Center for Performing Arts, 115

I

Independence Bowl, 41
indoctrination, 124
inner circle, 141
insecure, 326
insecurity, 77
Instagram, 271
instincts, 222, 352
interdependent, 226
intimidation, 353
intuition, 222
Iowa State memorabilia, 138
iPhone, 345
iron, 151
Isolating, 228
isolation, 77, 321, 446, 450

J

Jackie Kennedy Onassis, 79
Janet Fryback, 250
Janet Jackson, 100
Janet Reno, 143, 181
Japanese National Championships, 302
Japanese Olympic Team, 302
Jerome Bettis, 199

Jerry Whaley, 35
Jim Fassel, 261
John Belushi's Animal House, 32
Johnny "Flash" Taylor, 71
Johnny Oceans Diner, 246
Joshua Stroud, 340
Jubilee World Outreach, 165, 167
Judge Judy, 116
Judge Judy show, 116
Judy Garland, 368
Julia Roberts, 89
Julie Kaanapu, 171
Junior Spivey, 237
Jurassic Park, 71

K

Kakegawa, 302
Kasey Brooks, 37
Katrina, 187
Keith Jenkins, 166
Keith Lewis, 249
Kentucky Derby, 107
Kipland Kinkel, 376
Kiss, 28
Kowloon's, 202
Kroger's, 188
KVAL TV, 100
Kwamie Lassiter, 237

L

Laker Girls, 41
Lakers, 61, 62

Index

Lane Community College, 48
Lane County Courthouse, 152
Larry Bird, 66
Larry Nassar, 285
Las Vegas Locomotives, 261
Lassiter, 237
LBTL, 250
legislation, 362
Life Beyond the League, 237
Lionel Ritchie, 115
Lisa Flormoe, 52, 55, 166
Lloyd Austin, 366
Logic, 250
Los Angeles Rams, 123
love bombing, 123
Love Field in Dallas, 309
Lumberman football team, 32

M

MAC, 266
Mac Court, 45
Mack truck, 181
Madden 2000, 183
Madeline Albright, 368
Magic Johnson, 66
Magnolia Hotel, 306
Maki Nakayama, 302
Malabon Elementary, 34
manipulation, 93, 156, 216, 222, 227, 230, 321, 447
Mark McMillian, 211
Marriott, 71
Mary Decker Slaney, 32
Maurie Povich, 54
May 1983, 28
mayhem, 357
McDonalds, 87
Me Too Movement, 48
media, 357
mental health professionals, 156
mental institution, 112
Mercedes Benz, 195
MeToo, 369, 370
MeToo Movement, 369
MICE, 75, 87, 277, 447
Michael Jordan, 65, 66
Michael Westbrook, 237
Mieke Oort, 208
Mike Maulding, 38
Miranda Priestly, 104
misdirected anger, 353, 445
misdirection, 216
Miss America, 99
Miss Hawaiian Tropics, 103
Miss Oregon America Pageant, 103
Miss Universe pageants, 99
Miss USA, 99
MLB player, 236
Mongoose, 33
Morgan Farris, 26
Morris Day and the Time, 27
Mother's Day, 87
Mötley Crüe, 28
Moulin Rouge, 41

INDEX

Mrs. Kansas, 107
Mrs. Oregon, 105
Mrs. Oregon International, 54
Mrs. West Eugene, 100
Multnomah County Deputy Sheriff, 331
My Cousin Vinny, 152
My Space, 185
Myspace, 420

N

Napa Valley, 334
narcissist, 117
narcissistic sociopaths, 326
National Football League., 261
national statistics, 207
naysayers, 148
NBA, 23, 57, 59, 62, 65, 82, 112, 303, 402, 453
NBA commentators, 62
NBA Portland Trailblazers, 57
NCAA, 136
necrosis, 357
New York Giants, 58
New York Times, 355
NFL, 123
NFL draft, 39
NFL Draft party, 131
NFL Europe, 289
Nicole Brown Simpson, 81
night terrors, 169
nightmare, 49

NIKE, 176
Nike Corporation, 33
NIKE Town, 32
National Domestic Violence, 327, 443
No Country for Old Men, 191
non-contact policy, 60
NRG Stadium, 187

O

O.J Simpson, 81
O'Hare Airport, 287
obrdrive, 322
obsession, 77, 205
obstacles, 253
Off the Field Wives Association, 240
offenders, 362
OJ Simpson, 407
Olympic trails, 33
Oompa Loompa, 237
Oregon Club, 203
Oregon Fight Song, 302
Oregon Rally Squad, 36
Oregon State Bar, 207
OSAA, 172
Outside the League, 199, 233

P

P3, 285
P3 Company, 194
PAC 10, 345
Pac-10 tournament, 47
Pac10 tournament, 45
Pacific 10 Conference, 41

Pandora's Box, 185
Paramount Pictures, 440
Patrick Ewing, 66
patterns, 356
Peaches and Herb, 116
permission, 4
pernicious tactic, 227
personal safety, 376
petition, 60
Phil Knight, 33
policy makers, 357
political, 357
Pop Warner Cheerleading Squad, 32
Portland Coliseum, 61, 66
Portland Trailblazer, 54
power, 179
Powers Auditorium, 168
predator's instinct, 155
Predators, 223
Prince, 27
Prince and Princess of Wales, 28
Princess of Wales, 27
Private Desmond Doss, ix
projection, 153
protection, 347
psychological warfare, 93
PTSD, 144
Pure Pro Productions, 285
purpose, 4
Pussycat Dolls, 41

Q

Quaker Oats Company, 440

R

rage, 77
Raiders, 401
Rams, 325
raped, 108
Reality and Surrealism, 353
Rebecca Schaeffer, 207
red flag, 203
red flags, 123
Red Flags, 225
Red October, 130
Register Guard, 28
restraining order, 321
retribution, 327
Revenge Porn, 277
Rich Brooks, 38
Rip City, 65
Rodney Stearns, 322, 327, 387
Romeo Bandison, 286
Rose Bowl, 86, 173
rotectiveness, 351
Rubicon, 79, 80, 353
Ryan Jeffries, 212, 438

S

Sacramento Attack, 82
Sacred Heart Hospital, 90
SafeBAE, 388
Sam Boyd Stadium, 262
San Francisco Forty Niners, 211
San Francisco Forty-Niners, 27

INDEX

Saving Private Ryan, 381
schizophrenia, 112
Schooner's, 200
Scottie Pippen, 66
Selena, 87
self-confidence, 227
self-doubt, 268
self-esteem, 227
self-hate, 268
self-loathing, 268
self-shame, 169
sexual assault, 22, 55, 160, 178, 192, 282, 285, 345, 357, 362, 365, 366, 367, 369, 375, 379, 387, 388, 394, 443, 446, 447, 454
sexual coercion, 365
sexual harassment, 178
sexual misconduct, 76
sexual offender, 146
sexually assaulted, 108
shame, 112
Shane Kessler, 98
Sheila E, 26
Shelley Kurtz, 99
Shirley Temple, 368
Shreveport, Louisiana, 41
Sissach, 293, 295
Skateworld, 260
skin cancer, 281
smoke and mirrors, 216
smokescreen, 326
social media, 388
sociopaths, 117
Solid Gold Dancers, 31
Sonny and Cher, 116
Sound of Music, 290
Southern Oregon State College, 26
spinal fusion surgery, 329
Spivey's, 237
Sports Illustrated, 191
Springfield High School, 250
stalking, 207
stalking victimization, 207
Steve Prefontaine, 32
Steven Spielberg, 71, 381
Stockholm Syndrome, 125
Subway, 149
suicide, 366
summer camps, 35
Summer Solstice Festival, 396
Super Bowl, 58, 59, 240, 325, 327
Super Bowl XXV, 58
Swiss All-Girl National Team, 293

T

Tabitha Spivey, 237
tailbone, 88, 89, 235
Tanning Hut, 52
Tao Asian Bistro, 234
Tarana Burke, 369
Teens Modeling and Talent Agency, 111
Teri Newman, 123
terrorists, 127
the Aguilera rule, 385

Index

The American Dolls, 307
The Bachelor, 309
The Beach Boys, 35
The Buffalo Bills, 58
The Cooler, 252
The Devil Wears Prada, 104
The Dream Team, 65
The Gram, 388
The Hurt Locker, 211
The Impossible, 188
The Kwamie Lassiter Foundation, 306
The Making of an Oregon Cheerleader, 191
The Mrs. Oregon International Pageant, 97
The Playboy Morning Show, 272
The Prairie Schooner, 200
The Producer, 277
The Restaurant Sternen, 296
The Sidebar, 251
The Trial of the Century, 82
the unvirtuous cycle, 156
The Unvirtuous Cycle, 347
The Voice, 396
The Wizard of Oz, 31
therapeutic, 324
threatening, 151
Threats, 353
three Amigos, 136, 138, 139
TikTok, 375
Timothy McVeigh, 127
titanium rods, 329
Title 9, 360
Todd Davilla, 55
Tom Hanks, 381
Torii Hunter, 236
Torre Blake, 285
tournaments, 256
Track City U.S.A, 32
Trailblazers, 61, 66, 67, 82, 405, 406
trapped, 325, 353, 405, 417, 428
trauma, 23, 49, 55, 58, 89, 111, 114, 147, 152, 159, 160, 163, 168, 169, 185, 197, 214, 225, 228, 247, 260, 277, 282, 312, 320, 321, 332, 356, 375, 395, 446, 450, 453
trauma bond, 125
traumatized, 321
Trial by Fire, 352
trust, 351
Tucson, Arizona, 45
Tupac Shakur., 252
Twitter, 271
Tyler Perry Studios, 440

U

Uber, 279
UCA, 51
UCA All-Star team, 172
UCLA, 73
uncertainty, 49
Unforgiven, 71
United Airlines, 288
United Football League, 261

INDEX

United States Army, 381
United States Military, 365
Universal Cheerleaders
  Association, 51, 172, 301
University of Colorado, 286
University of Houston, 187
University of Oregon, 15,
  32, 37, 38, 39, 41, 48, 51,
  54, 85, 94, 98, 105, 111,
  123, 135, 163, 172, 173,
  181, 187, 191, 194, 200,
  211, 241, 246, 249, 302,
  303, 358, 372, 379, 393,
  401, 437, 438, 453, 454
University of Oregon
  Ducks, 32
University's Casanova
  Center, 136
USA Basketball Academy,
  303
USC, 45, 57

V

value, 4
Vancouver, 28
Venetian Hotel, 234
verbal abuse, 77
verbally abusive, 82
VERSACE, 372
victim shaming, 368
victimization, 228
victims' rights, 323
Vienna, 289
Vienna, Austria, 286
violation, 178

violence, 156
Voice America Sports, 305

W

Waco, Texas, 127
Walter Cronkite, 43
wandering eye, 124
Washington Post, 355
Washington Redskins, 303
waterfalls, 46
WHS, 27, 28, 32, 34, 103, 112,
  145, 150, 172, 173, 241
Wild Horse Pass Hotel and
  Casino, 211, 236
Will Smith, 34
Willamette High School, 26, 85
Willamette Marching Band, 28
wiss Franc, 294
womanizing, 146
Women's Space, 16
Women's Space, 152
works, 4
World Cheerleading
  Championships, 301
World Expo 86, 26

Y

Y2K, 181
You Got Served, 42

Z

Zurich, 295

If you enjoyed this book, please post a review on the platform where you purchased, SMILE, *Chin Up*! Or, please Scan the QR Code to post a review on Amazon.

Thank you!

www.ingramcontent.com/pod-product-compliance
Lightning Source LLC
Chambersburg PA
CBHW070042080526
44586CB00013B/882